A Black
Woman's West

A Black Woman's West

The Life of Rose B. Gordon

MICHAEL K. JOHNSON

MONTANA HISTORICAL SOCIETY PRESS
Helena

Front cover photograph: Rose B. Gordon and friend, ca. 1905. Emmanuel Taylor Gordon Collection, PAc 82-19 F06, MHS Photograph Archives. Frontispiece: Rose B. Gordon in 1927. 951-716, MHS Photograph Archives

Cover and book design by Diane Gleba Hall
Typeset in Arno Pro

Printed in the United States

Distributed by Farcountry Press, 2750 Broadwater Avenue, Helena, MT 59602
(800) 821-3874, farcountrypress.com

ISBN 978-1-94052-797-0 (paperback; alkaline paper)
ISBN 978-1-94052-701-7 (ebook)

Library of Congress Cataloging-in-Publication Data
NAMES: Johnson, Michael K. (Michael Kyle), 1963– author.
TITLE: A black woman's west : the life of Rose B. Gordon / Michael K. Johnson.
OTHER TITLES: Life of Rose B. Gordon | Meagher County news.
DESCRIPTION: Helena, MT : Montana Historical Society Press, [2022] | Includes bibliographical references and index. | Summary: "This biography tells the remarkable life story of Rose B. Gordon, an African American resident of White Sulphur Springs, Montana. Born in 1883, Gordon established her economic independence as a restaurant owner and massage therapist. She also authored a regular column in the local newspaper, the Meagher Country News. Her story offers unique insights into the Black experience in the rural West in the first half of the twentieth century"—Provided by publisher.
IDENTIFIERS: LCCN 2022001008 (print) | LCCN 2022001009 (ebook) | ISBN 9781940527970 (paperback) | ISBN 9781940527017 (ebook)
SUBJECTS: LCSH: Gordon, Rose B. (Rose Beatrice), 1883-1968. | African American women—Montana—Biography. | Restaurateurs—Montana—White Sulphur Springs—Biography. | Physiotherapists—Montana—White Sulphur Springs—Biography. | Gordon, Taylor, 1893–1971—Family. | Meagher County (Mont.)—Race relations. | Frontier and pioneer life—Montana—White Sulphur Springs. | White Sulphur Springs (Mont.)—Biography.
CLASSIFICATION: LCC F739.W44 J64 2022 (print) | LCC F739.W44 (ebook) | DDC 305.89960786092 [B]—dc23/eng/20220125
LC RECORD available at https://lccn.loc.gov/2022001008
LC EBOOK RECORD available at https://lccn.loc.gov/2022001009

Contents

Contents

Illustrations follow page 96

Acknowledgments

Of the archival sources referenced here, the most important collection is the Emmanuel Taylor Gordon Family Papers, 1882–1980, MC 150, located at the Montana Historical Society Archives in Helena, Montana. Most of the quotations from letters, unpublished manuscripts, and so forth, come from sources within this collection.

Thanks to the *Meagher County News* for permission to reprint selections from Rose B. Gordon's newspaper contributions.

Because I have been writing about the Gordon family for a number of years, bits and pieces of the biography draw from previously published work. *A Black Woman's West* presents in revised and expanded form some of the Gordon family history and White Sulphur Springs history that is sketched out in *Can't Stand Still: Taylor Gordon and the Harlem Renaissance* (University Press of Mississippi, 2019). Some discussion of African American participation in White Sulphur Springs's performance culture was included as part of a larger overview of African American performers in the American West in a chapter from *Hoo-Doo Cowboys and Bronze Buckaroos: Conceptions of the African American West* (University Press of Mississippi, 2014). Likewise, my earliest discussion of Rose Gordon's newspaper writing first appeared as a partial chapter in *Hoo-Doo Cowboys and Bronze Buckaroos*.

I would also like to thank a number of people who helped me out along the way, particularly the editorial staff at the Montana Historical Society

Press—Diana Di Stefano, Jeff Bartos, and Laura Ferguson—and special thanks to Cody Dodge Ewert, who copyedited the manuscript. Thanks as well to Molly Holz for her encouragement in the early stages of the project, MHS Press book designer Diane Gleba Hall, and indexer Amanda Katz. Special thanks also to Sheryl McGuire of the Meagher County Historical Association for her assistance with photographs and identifications. Earlier versions of some of the chapters here were presented on panels at Western Literature Association and American Literature Association conferences, and I want to thank fellow presenters for their comments and conversations about the Rose Gordon project, especially Eric Gardner, Gioia Woods, Victoria Lamont, and Hollis Robbins.

Thanks as well to the staff at the Montana Historical Society Museum and Archives for their helpfulness, especially Kirby Lambert, Rodric Coslet, Jody Foley, Karen Bjork, Rich Aarstad, Molly Kruckenberg, and Jeff Malcomson. Thanks also to the many friends and colleagues in Montana who have supported my work on the Gordon family in various ways over the years: Lee Rostad, Paul Wylie, Patty Dean, O. Alan Weltzien, Susan Kollin, Eric Warren, Ashley Warren, Precious McKenzie, Shadrey Sands, and Nancy Cook. Also, special thanks to Sarah Otley at Mantor Library at the University of Maine-Farmington for tracking down interlibrary loan items, especially all those back issues of Montana newspapers on microfilm.

Finally I'd like to express my appreciation to the donors who helped support publication of this book. In particular, I'd like to acknowledge the Charles Redd Center for Western History at Brigham Young University. The center generously supported my research through a Faculty Research Award in 2006 and again with a publications grant in 2022.

A Black
Woman's West

Introduction

Rose Beatrice Gordon (1883–1968) was a remarkable individual: a pioneer whose lifelong residence in Montana began when the state was still a territory; a hardy Westerner who hunted and fished until the age of seventy-five, registering two elk kills during her final hunting season; and a businesswoman who managed a successful career as one of the few African American residents of White Sulphur Springs, Montana.

Rose was a well-known and much admired figure in her community—and, like her mother, a woman of enduring strength and determination. Named Rosa Anne by her parents at birth, she changed her name to Rose Beatrice as a child, an early sign of her independence of mind. As a teenager and young woman, she gave public recitations as a member of one of the town's literary organizations. A pianist and singer, she often shared her musical talents at public events. With her mother, Anna Gordon, she operated a restaurant in White Sulphur Springs for several decades. She also volunteered throughout her life as a healthcare worker, and, after World War II, closed the restaurant to devote herself to a career as a massage therapist. At one point, she even declared as a candidate for mayor. She also became a regular contributor to the *Meagher County News*, the local newspaper, offering letters about current events, columns on county history, and memorial tributes to community members.

Born in the Barker mining district in central Montana Territory in 1883, Rose was the second of five surviving children born to John Francis and Mary Anna Goodall Gordon. Her parents met in Cairo, Illinois, and married in 1879. Offered a job as a chef by a gold-mining company, John left Illinois to join one of the company's operations in Fort Benton, Montana Territory. Anna and their first son, Robert, who was born in Cairo in 1881, soon followed. After some time spent moving between camps—including a silver mining operation where Rose was born—the family settled in White Sulphur Springs, where John Francis Gordon Jr. was born in 1885, followed by brothers George Washington Gordon in 1888 and Emmanuel Taylor "Mannie" Gordon in 1893. A sixth child, Arthur, died in infancy.

I was introduced to the Gordon family through Taylor Gordon's 1929 autobiography *Born to Be*.[1] Taylor left White Sulphur Springs in 1910, working on and off as a chauffeur, a Pullman porter, and then as the personal porter on circus impresario John Ringling's private railway car. *Born to Be* describes Taylor's life growing up in White Sulphur Springs before turning to his adventures with John Ringling, his education at the Colored Music Settlement in New York City, and his vaudeville career. From 1919 to 1925, Taylor sang tenor in the group J. Rosamond Johnson and the Inimitable Five. He and pianist Johnson then formed a duo that specialized in performing spirituals. The pair enjoyed a period of fame in the late 1920s that culminated in Taylor's celebrity autobiography.

I did not learn much about Rose from *Born to Be*. While Taylor passed along the information about Rose's name change and mentioned how "Sis" would read to the family from the newspaper in the evenings, he had more to say about his brother George than his much older sister. Rather, I got to know Rose primarily through the Emmanuel Taylor Gordon Family Papers collection at the Montana Historical Society (MHS) Archives in Helena. Taylor was an important cultural figure in the 1920s, and his stories of growing up in White Sulphur Springs in *Born to Be* are an essential document of African American life in the West. Thus, it is not surprising that his papers were deemed significant enough to be collected by an archive. What was surprising to me was how much material in the collection was devoted to Rose.[2]

I first visited Helena in 2004 to talk with the archivists at MHS about putting together a tabletop exhibit on Taylor Gordon's life for display at the annual Western Literature Conference to be held that year in Big Sky. The conference's Montana location offered an ideal opportunity for literary scholars to learn about Taylor Gordon. At the time, I had only a vague idea of what was in the collection, so a staff member suggested that I start by requesting all the materials to get a sense of its scope.

I was not expecting what seemed like a parade of archivists to arrive pushing two wheeled carts loaded with cardboard boxes filled with materials from the Gordon family members' lives. Instead of being overjoyed by the collection's abundance, my first reaction was "Good lord, what am I getting myself into?" It would not be the last time I had that thought during the fifteen or so years I spent exploring the life histories of the Gordons.

One of the first items relating to Rose that I looked at was her 1958 big game license, with two of the elk tags removed, indicating that she killed and tagged two of the three elk permitted. Although this discovery shaped my early image of Rose, a more complicated figure began to emerge as I dug further, one who was best known in her town as a restaurant and café owner, a caterer, and a chef more renowned for her skills with a pan and skillet than a rod and rifle. Beyond her culinary abilities, Rose was appreciated in White Sulphur Springs for the greatness of her heart. Fellow community members valued the same attributes in Rose that she valued in them: possessing a genuine concern for others, being a good neighbor, and having a passion for local history. When White Sulphur Springs was hit hard by the 1918 influenza pandemic, Rose served as a volunteer nurse and took care of the sick. When I started writing this book in 2020 during the coronavirus pandemic, I knew exactly what Rose would be doing were she alive: helping vulnerable members of her community.

Although Rose did not become a celebrity like her brother Taylor, she was a remarkable figure in her own right. During a period when Black women in America were consistently denied a public role and voice, and when their primary economic role was as domestic servants, Rose both established her economic independence and made a place for herself in the public sphere of White Sulphur Springs.[3] Although she began training in 1905 for a career as a practical nurse, she ultimately became proprietor of a restaurant that served clientele under several names—including the Gordon Delicatessen, Gordon Restaurant and Notion Store, and Rose's Café—and at various locations in the small town for over thirty years.

She never completely gave up on nursing, and, as she had during the 1918 influenza pandemic, she volunteered to care for others on numerous occasions. She also offered massage and physical therapy services in addition to operating the restaurant. In the 1940s, frustrated by the difficulties that wartime price controls and rationing posed, she closed the restaurant permanently and enrolled in a Swedish massage course. For the last twenty or so years of her life, she embarked on a successful career as a physiotherapist. In addition to these accomplishments, Rose served as an officer in business and religious organizations, attended state and national physiotherapist conventions, and held various positions in the White Sulphur Springs branch of the Episcopal Churchwomen. She also established herself as an important community voice, in part through regular newspaper columns and letters to the editor. Over time, she became known to locals as the village historian of White Sulphur Springs.

I was struck by finding Rose's hunting license in the Gordon archives, but I was even more interested to discover that she was also a writer. When I came across a scrapbook containing an article that she published in the *Meagher County News* titled "My Mother Was a Slave," I began to understand Rose's significance as both an African American and Western writer. My primary field of study over the past twenty years has been the African American West, which is what led me to Taylor Gordon's autobiography initially, so I knew how rare it was to find a story like "My Mother Was a Slave." Published in 1955 as an as-told-to biography of Anna Gordon within the larger framework of an autobiography of Rose, "My Mother Was a Slave" is the only published first-person narrative of nineteenth-century African American migration to Montana.[4] "My Mother Was a Slave" is a distinctive literary document—a story of slavery, emancipation, and migration, as well as the Gordon family's settlement and growth in Montana Territory.

As historian Quintard Taylor argues in *In Search of the Racial Frontier*, African Americans have been present at every stage of westward expansion. Even though historical writing over the past few decades has paid increasing attention to the African American experience in the West, we "still know woefully little about large areas of the African American past" in the region.[5] African American women in particular have "suffered near-invisibility in western history," according to historian Glenda Riley.[6] Rose Gordon, I thought, was a writer and a Montanan who could help make that history more visible.

The story of the Gordon family's ability to thrive in what would seemingly be unfriendly territory for African Americans—a predominantly white, rural Montana town—illuminates a relatively unknown segment of the history of the American West: Black life in rural areas. Because of Taylor's celebrity status in the 1920s, we have an extensive archive related to Rose's life and career that otherwise might have been lost. While by most measures Rose lived a remarkable life, she was not widely known outside her hometown. As an ordinary person who left an extensive archival collection, Rose offers a unique opportunity to explore the ordinary and extraordinary experiences of a Black woman and her family in Montana.

One aspect of Rose Gordon's story that makes it a significant contribution to our understanding of the African American West is that she described her experiences in her own words. At some point in the 1930s, Rose started working on a book manuscript titled "Gone are the Days," a combination of memoir and Montana history with White Sulphur Springs as its focus.[7] Although never published, it informed the shorter articles she began writing for the *Meagher County News* in the 1940s. She contributed hundreds of items to the same newspaper until her death in 1968. Her specialty was the memorial tribute, short and informal pieces written in acknowledgment of the contributions that the recently deceased had made to the community. Some of Rose's articles ran only a few sentences long, while others took up several newspaper columns, including "My Mother Was a Slave," her tribute to Anna Gordon.

Rose's writing offers us a glimpse of her interiority, or how she saw herself. Her descriptions of interactions with fellow community members also reveal how she saw herself in relation to others. As a massage therapist and part-time nurse, Rose quite literally touched the lives of hundreds of individuals in her community. As a restaurant owner, she fed thousands more, offering advice, wisdom, humor, and encouragement along with her trademark chicken dinners. As early as 1904, an item in the *Meagher Republican* observed, "Miss Gordon enjoys the friendship of many people in this community who recognize in her a young lady of exceptional ability to whom credit is due for what educational and social advantages she has attained."[8] On the occasion of her death in 1968, the same newspaper, now called the *Meagher County News*, announced that although "Miss Gordon was an Episcopalian," funeral services were to be held in the St. Bartholomew Catholic Church because it was "the only church large enough to accommodate the number of persons expected at her funeral."[9] The epitaph on Rose's tombstone, located in the Mayn Cemetery on the outskirts of White Sulphur Springs, reads "Our Rose." Indeed, every indication suggests that Rose belonged to and was treasured by this predominantly white community throughout her lifetime.

Rose's published and unpublished writings provide the backbone for this biography, supplying information and stories about her life and the lives of her family members. As Rose's articles are difficult to access, hidden in back issues of White Sulphur Springs newspapers, I have included a selection of her newspaper articles in the appendix to provide a sense of the range of her writing from the 1940s through the 1960s.

Although her primary method of recording local history—through written recollections, notes, letters, tributes, and penned observations—was unconventional and generated the sort of material not generally accorded the status of literature, I argue here for the significance of Rose's accomplishments as a writer. She ultimately invented her own literary genre, the memorial tribute, which perfectly accommodated her blend of interests and cleverly ensured that her writing would appeal to the citizens of White Sulphur Springs, whose friends and family were often the subjects of those pieces. She found an ideal balance between her own desires as a writer and her audience's interests as readers. Additionally, the newspaper format allowed her a wide degree of flexibility in terms of topic and form. She used that flexibility to comment on both national and local issues. Ultimately, Rose's greatest accomplishment as a writer is that she constructed a voice that was both distinctively Western and African American, a balance that enabled her to appeal to her community and to express her own unique experience as a Black woman in the West.

This biography covers Rose's life from birth to death, but I place particular emphasis on the time of her childhood through young adulthood, 1885 to 1910. Since my interest here is in Rose as a writer, this period is important because it is the central focus of her output. Furthermore, this emphasis enables an extended exploration and documentation of the

African American community in White Sulphur Springs and Meagher County before it started to fade. Long before she began contributing to the *Meagher County News*, Rose was a public figure in White Sulphur Springs as a performer, speaker, and business owner. Her efforts to craft the voice and public persona that emerged in her mid-twentieth-century newspaper writing was already taking place in the 1890s when she first stepped onto the stage to sing, recite, and debate as a member of the Monday Evening Club, a local literary society. The earlier sections of this biography reveal how the public self that Rose cultivated as a performer—and the contradictions inherent in that persona—influenced the development of her voice as a writer who often addressed distinctly Western themes in her writing.

The story of Rose's life also would not be complete without considering her famous brother, Taylor. Rose maintained a strong connection to her youngest brother, even though most of their lives were spent apart. The focus here, however, is Rose. While I documented the entirety of Taylor's life and career in *Can't Stand Still: Taylor Gordon and the Harlem Renaissance*, here I focus on his childhood in Montana and the parts of his history that illuminate Rose's story.[10] As his career faded in the 1930s, Taylor increasingly suffered from mental illness, resulting in periods of institutionalization in the 1940s and 1950s. Rose, who still lived in White Sulphur Springs during this period, tried to help Taylor even though the distance between Montana and New York complicated those efforts. In the last part of her life, Rose Gordon performed a remarkable balancing act that included building a new career as a physiotherapist, becoming a dedicated contributor to the *Meagher County News*, caring for her aging brothers in Montana, and working tirelessly to get Taylor Gordon released from a New York mental institution, after which he returned to White Sulphur Springs and lived with Rose. She did it all with characteristic good humor and empathy.

Although the Gordon family's residence in White Sulphur Springs has been demolished, the building on Main Street that once housed Rose's restaurant is currently the home of Red Ants Pants, a women's workwear company. I've also been told that the massage table Rose bought in the 1940s for her therapy business is still in use by another masseuse somewhere in town. A portrait of Taylor Gordon painted by New York artist Bob Chanler is still on display at the Castle Museum, as is Taylor's stylish shaving mirror with its rattlesnake hide back. The Gordons, it seems, are still part of the town's material existence. And they are still very much part of the town's living memory.

While visiting White Sulphur Springs on a frigid October day, I stayed at the Spa Hot Springs Motel, where I had my first up-close experience with the town's famed hot springs. The Spa Motel pipes the mineral water into two heated swimming pools. Carrying my bags, I followed the narrow walkway between the pools, steam billowing from them in the cold air. The mixture of freezing temperatures, warm moist air, and the faint but distinctive smell of sulfur was oddly enjoyable. I detected the same smell in the parking lot behind the hotel, from where I could see—beyond the barbed-wire fence that separated the parking lot from a field—steam rising in the cold air, revealing a wide expanse of land where the hot water rose to the surface. Near the edge of the lot, meanwhile, the vapor condensed and froze on weeds and grasses at the edge of a shallow ditch filled with the warm water from the springs. White Sulphur Springs feels a little otherworldly to me, both as a present-day place that I know primarily from reading about its past and even more so as a landscape of hot water, ice, steam, and sulfur.

I had traveled to White Sulphur Springs to give a talk on Taylor Gordon's life and career and, more generally, the Gordon family's relationship to the town. Afterward, about thirty or so attendees approached me with stories to share about the Gordons. Several mentioned having been present when Taylor sang at a wedding in the 1960s. He had been seated in the church balcony, and most congregants didn't know he was there until they heard his voice ringing out. Even in his seventies, Taylor had a flair for dramatic performance. Yet most of the stories people shared that day were about Rose. They were mainly small, intimate stories, undramatic but detailed and quietly moving. I was struck by how vividly she lived on in people's remembrances fifty years after her death, and by how strongly the memories of her kindness and goodwill toward others still resonated among those who had been touched by her presence, many of whom only knew her when they were children. This is her story.

CHAPTER 1

The Gordon Family in the Late Nineteenth Century

"In the year of 1881," Rose Gordon wrote in 1955, "a brown-skinned colored woman who bore the name of Mrs. Annie Gordon stood at the boat landing at Cairo, Illinois, where the Ohio flows into the mighty Mississippi. Tears rolled down her cheeks and were falling on her baby boy whom she held in her arms." This young, formerly enslaved woman was on her way upriver to Montana Territory, carrying her son, Robert. Her friends had gathered to bid her farewell. Her baggage and trunks had been loaded on a river steamer called the *Katie*. First, she sailed on the Mississippi River to St. Louis. There, she boarded a second steamboat and began her journey up the Missouri River to Fort Benton, where she planned to join her husband, John.[1] Eventually, Anna and John settled in White Sulphur Springs, a small but rapidly growing town that served nearby ranches and mining operations and that was developing a reputation as a resort destination. Situated in the Smith River valley in central Montana, the local newspapers proclaimed that White Sulphur Springs was "wide awake and progressive."[2] It also turned out to be a place where an African American man with an expanding family could earn a good living as a chef at a hotel that served the visitors who came to enjoy the hot springs.

Born into slavery in 1853, Anna grew up on a plantation near Lexington, Kentucky.[3] In a retrospective essay titled "My Mother Was a Slave," Rose writes that her mother told her that the Poindexters, the family that bought her as a small child, "were distillers and race horse people."[4] During the Civil War, nine-year-old Anna's primary duty was to stay with her mistress's horse, which was hidden in the woods for fear the Union army would confiscate it. After nightfall, Anna "would return to the plantation, and then her mistress would ride in the dark with a black blanket that almost covered the white horse."[5]

The 1870 census includes the household of forty-one-year-old Alexander and thirty-five-year-old Harriet Goodloe (probably a misspelling of Goodlow), an African American couple in Licking River, Boyle County, Kentucky. Six other members of the Goodloe family, likely the couple's children, lived there as well and ranged in age from three-year-old Nancy to the oldest, Mary Anna.[6] It seems possible this was the future Mary Anna Gordon. Sometime between 1870 and 1879, Anna left the Goodloe family. She met her husband-to-be, John Francis Gordon, in Cairo, Illinois, where they married in 1879. The 1880 census records twenty-five-year-old Anna still living in Cairo, Illinois, and working as a servant in the household of an African American farmer named Wright, while it indicates that John F. Gordon—age twenty-nine, born in Kentucky—was living in Fort Benton, Chouteau County, Montana Territory, and was employed as a cook.[7] Trained in culinary sciences, it is likely he worked and lodged at the Hotel Overland. By 1881, he had moved on to a silver mining camp in the Barker mining district in a deep canyon in the Little Belt Mountains of central Montana Territory, where he held a similar job. It appears that John departed for Montana Territory before the birth of their first son, leaving Anna with the Wright family until he was established.

Although she must have been glad to receive word from John to join him in Fort Benton, Anna cried as she boarded the *Katie*—not only in sadness at leaving her friends and "her beautiful Kentucky home" but also in apprehension for the future ahead of her in unknown territory. Rose later explained that her mother "told me she was glad it took a long time to come up the river as it gave her time to think things over."[8] Periods of weeping punctuated her three-month journey as she suffered from the ordeals of travel, taking care of infant Robert by herself, and being alone and friendless. Seeing her distress, an African American stewardess confronted her and asked, "Child, what are you crying about?" After Anna's sobbing attempt to explain her sadness, the stewardess told her bluntly, "You are going to tough country and you must nerve up."[9]

This quintessentially Western advice served as a tonic for Anna, as did her continuing friendship with the stewardess, whom Anna credited for preparing her to "brave the great difficulties" that later "confronted her in the wild west." The stewardess also helped in more practical ways, giving her work aboard the ship as a waitress. The job kept her occupied, and she began to enjoy life on board, admiring the beautiful linen and silverware used to set the table and the occasional views of bison drinking in the river or wandering across the prairie. She also saw for the first time the Indigenous peoples whose homelands bordered the Missouri River, as they sometimes gathered on the shore when the boat docked at a landing.[10]

With infant Robert in her arms, Anna disembarked in Fort Benton, where John was waiting for them. Anna found herself for the first time in what might have seemed like a dime novel version of the Wild West. As Joseph Kinsey Howard later described it, Fort Benton, Montana Territory, was a "rough river town," where "as late as 1882 visitors were warned, 'Walk in the middle of the street and mind your own business; this is a tough town!'"[11] In addition to accommodating river traffic and serving as the primary trade hub in the territory, Fort Benton was patronized by cowboys from nearby ranches and was "frequently 'shot up' by cowboys in for a carouse." Howard noted that the town was infamous for its gambling and drinking establishments, adding, "Fort Benton's sidewalks were at times so thickly carpeted with discarded playing cards that it was difficult to see the wooden planking."[12]

Fort Benton, established in 1846 as a fur trading post, was one of the first places in Montana Territory to have a substantial African American population. Historian Barbara Carol Behan notes the reasons African Americans were drawn to this rough trade town on the Missouri: "Since the early 18th century, enslaved African Americans had worked as steamboat laborers and servants in the southern states," and traffic on the Missouri River brought Blacks to Fort Benton in the 1850s and 1860s, even though "using enslaved workers on river boats became problematic" as those boats entered free territories. After the Civil War, however, increased freighting by river continued to bring Black laborers to Fort Benton, which "had one of the highest concentrations of African American residents in Montana" in the years following emancipation. By the time the Gordons arrived, Fort Benton's Black population had increased from twenty individuals to "over fifty African American men, women, and children," numbers roughly in keeping with the overall population increase of African Americans in Montana Territory from 183 in 1870 to 346 in 1880.[13]

From Fort Benton, Anna, John, and Robert made their way by stagecoach to Barker, some eighty miles to the south. This trip provided further evidence of the "tough country" they had entered. A severe storm swept in during their travels, frightening the horses to such a degree that they lost the trail and drove around in a circle until deciding to camp on the prairie for the night. Anna recalled taking her turn "watching for Indians while some of the other passengers slept." Despite her fears, no raiding parties came in the night, and the stage continued on to Barker.[14]

At the northern edge of what is now the Helena-Lewis and Clark National Forest in the Little Belt Mountains, Barker was pretty much at "the end of the earth," or so it seemed to Anna, even after having witnessed Fort Benton's remoteness. John had rented "a neat little cabin" for the family to live in, but this lodging seemed particularly bleak to Anna, who had appreciated the linens and silverware aboard the steamboat.

At Barker, Anna met and interacted with some of the "Indians" who lived in the area, likely the Métis descendants of the fur trade era.[15] She was startled when, the day after her arrival, an "Indian woman" stopped by their cabin. Rose, writing later, recorded her mother's initial surprise: "Someone knocked at the door. Pappa went to the door. It was an Indian woman. . . . The Indian woman said something. Mamma did not know what it was." At a loss as to how to receive her guest, Anna resorted to domestic diplomacy and served coffee and cake. Whatever the many social and cultural differences between the women, they became friends, and Anna's "tea parties" with Indigenous women became regular events. In fact, these friendships grew to the point that Anna was attended solely by an Indigenous or Métis midwife when Rose was born in 1883.[16]

Prospector Joseph Meek, one of several African American residents of Meagher County in the late nineteenth century, had discovered silver in the Barker District. Meek and his wife, Rose remembered, became "great friends of our family."[17] Although the silver mines in the area were thriving when John Gordon first arrived, they soon "played out, as all mining camps did in Montana." The company that owned the mine that employed John, as Taylor later explained, "sold out and moved the headquarters back to Chicago."[18] Although the company wanted John to return with them to Chicago, he and Anna had fallen in love with Montana and decided to stay. It would not be farfetched to surmise that the Gordons would have encountered Meek during their time in Barker, which may have attracted them to settle in White Sulphur Springs in Meagher County, where the Meeks also settled. Once there, the Gordon family expanded to include three more sons: John Francis Jr., born in 1885, George Washington in 1888, and Emmanuel Taylor in 1893. In this town of some six hundred inhabitants, the Gordon children would come of age.[19]

White Sulphur Springs got its start in 1866, when James Brewer, "one of the hardy pioneers of the great northwest" and one of Montana's early gold prospectors, happened upon the mineral hot springs that would provide a name for the town that grew around them. Originally called Brewer's White Sulphur Springs, the town's name was shortened by the post office in 1875. The town owed much of its prosperity to the hot springs, as their alleged healing powers drew regular seasonal visitors to "take the water."[20] "There is not the shadow of a doubt about White Sulphur Springs being the healthiest town in the state," the *Rocky Mountain Husbandman* reported in 1899. The newspaper credited the town's good health to "the healing medical waters that pour forth from the earth in the midst of the town" and "impregnate the atmosphere of the locality with medicated fumes."[21] Visitors could soak in the hot springs, breathe in the "medicated fumes," and even drink the mineral-rich water. At one point, water from the springs was bottled and sold across the country.[22]

By 1871, the first herds of cattle and sheep arrived in Meagher County.[23] While the mining industry was a big draw to the newly established county, ranching provided a more stable basis for its long-term economy. In 1880, White Sulphur Springs became the seat of Meagher County, contributing to the town's further growth and development. When in session, the Meagher County Courthouse brought a lively group of visitors to the town, including reporters, lawyers, jurors, and, of course, lawbreakers on trial. Newspapers from throughout the state covered the William Gay (1896) and Henry Metzger (1905) murder trials and executions by hanging. The First National Bank, the oldest bank in Montana, was established in the town in 1883.[24]

Taylor Gordon memorably described White Sulphur Springs as "one of those Western Towns built between two high hills in a valley surrounded by mountains. The highest peak, that forms the shelter on the west, is listed geographically as Mount Edith; Old Baldy, the natives call it, because of its snow cap year round."[25] The town's setting in the Smith River valley offered local ranchers ideal conditions for raising cattle and sheep, and the surrounding mountains provided good hunting and plenty of potential for prospecting and mining.

From 1885 to 1910—the twenty-five-year period that roughly encompasses the Gordon family's arrival, Rose's passage from child to adult, and Taylor's early life from birth to late teens—White Sulphur Springs was a vibrant and growing community populated by interesting characters. For a number of years, the fortunes and population of White Sulphur Springs fluctuated with the boom and bust of the mining industry. By 1890, according to census reports, Meagher County had a growing population of 4,668. A mining boom had sparked that growth, especially in the Castle District. Downturns in the national economy hurt the area, however, as when the Panic of 1893 cratered silver prices and made mining the Castle District impractical. The larger-than-life James Brewer owned a livery stable and operated stage routes between White Sulphur and other towns.[26] Dr. William Parberry arrived, purchased the hot springs from Brewer for $1,000, and platted the townsite.[27] Jonas Higgins, another distinctive figure, built the Higgins House, a hotel, so that it jutted into Main Street, where it disrupted the flow of traffic for eighty years, primarily to spite Parberry. Meanwhile, in 1892, B. R. Sherman, a wealthy and powerful ranch and livery stable owner, built a whimsical stone "castle" that still dominates the town's skyline.[28] His son, "Cattle King" C. H. Sherman, ran cattle in the valley and took a young Taylor "Mannie" Gordon under his wing. Around the same time, the beautiful and talented Eleanor Armstrong came to While Sulphur Springs as a teacher. She left as a celebrity songwriter and as the leader of an "all-woman orchestra." Her daughters, Ruth and Grayce Brewer, were child musical prodigies whose piano and dance performances on the town stage launched them to national stardom. Then there was Tom Meixsell, who celebrated one New Year by firing bullets from his pistol into the ceiling of the town's auditorium. According to Rose, "He really shot the old year out and the new year in."[29]

Rose recalled seeing long trains of oxen-drawn wagons pass through town on their way to nearby communities, each one filled with freight from the steamboats in Fort Benton. White Sulphur Springs was a convenient stopping point for stages and freighters that served central Montana Territory, and the hot springs and their curative powers attracted a steady stream of visitors from all walks of life. Rose remembered in particular the day that Calamity Jane visited town:

> I must tell you about the thrill we children had the day they
> told us that Calamity Jane was coming in on the six-horse
> stagecoach. She was a legend to us. The day came and we
> saw her. She was rugged looking woman and weather beaten.
> When she smiled at us you could see so much kindness in her
> face. She wore dark clothes and a black cap that came down
> to her neck. It was very cold. We went to bed that night very
> happy. We had had the pleasure of seeing Calamity Jane.[30]

Circus impresarios John and Richard Ringling, who later employed Rose's brother Taylor, also came to White Sulphur and eventually purchased a ranch in Meagher County.

During Rose's childhood, White Sulphur Springs offered a surprisingly multicultural environment, including among its residents white immigrants from European countries, a substantial Chinese population, and African Americans. The *Meagher County News* published on its "Local News" page a variety of business advertisements that provide evidence of this cultural mix. For example, in 1890, the newspaper featured prominently placed ads for a blacksmith shop operated by the African American Irwin Smith and his white business partner John Nanno, a German immigrant; the Charley Chinn Laundry; and a restaurant operated by Kung Faun and

Kung Kam that offered "Meals at All Hours, Day and Night." Although Chinese-owned businesses cultivated the patronage of the town's white citizens, who also enjoyed the elaborate and expensive fireworks displays celebrating the Chinese New Year, Chinese immigrants themselves remained socially segregated in White Sulphur.

While advertisements in the local newspapers suggest a fairly equitable business environment, at least in the late nineteenth century, there was strong anti-Chinese sentiment in Montana generally and evidence of similar sentiment in Meagher County as well.[31] Like the Chinese, Montana's American Indian population, including Flathead, Shoshoni, Blackfeet, Crow, and Assiniboine, were also notably separate from the settler population, although the newspapers occasionally reported groups of Indians passing through and thus appearing as part of the backdrop of frontier life. From 1851 through 1890, Montana saw a concerted effort toward removal of Indians from their traditional territories and onto reservation lands, while the landless Métis, Chippewas, and Crees were pushed from place to place. The effects of that process can be glimpsed in the relative absence of reference to Indigenous and Métis peoples in the town's newspapers and in Rose's own writing.[32]

Upon moving to White Sulphur Springs, the Gordon family integrated themselves into the town's economy and social life. John Gordon was "tall and straight with large eyes and pearly teeth that made his smooth black skin seem much darker than he really was."[33] While he claimed Zulu ancestry, his father had migrated to England as a young man, where he was employed as a servant by a Scottish family who brought him along to America. John was likely born around 1851. Records list his place of birth at various times and places, including Kentucky, Tennessee, Illinois, and even the old Northwest Territories. As Taylor would note, "Somehow, after the Civil War, Grandfather and Father landed in Ohio." At that point, John trained to be a chef at Wilberforce University.[34] He was also a skilled musician, playing the horn and eventually performing as a member of the White Sulphur Springs town band. He passed his musical talent down to his children, particularly Robert, who matched his father's skills with a horn. But it was his abilities as a chef that supported his family. "I still remember," Rose wrote, "the good food he used to cook for Mamma."[35]

Christmas dinner in the Gordon household was a particular treat: "Papa would come home and cook. . . . We would have turkey, duck, and chicken, and all the trimmings."[36] As Rose later described, "I have no words in my vocabulary that would express the Joy that reigned in our home at Christmas Time."[37]

John Gordon served as Higgins House's first chef. Jonas Higgins had built the hotel in 1884 to capitalize on the town's status as a resort destination and later added a dining room. After enjoying dinner, guests staying at Higgins House were encouraged to take the water. As one newspaper item noted, "Bath tickets may be had at the office, and it is just a pleasant walk from the hotel to the springs over a good plank pavement."[38] The *Rocky Mountain Husbandman* offered high praise for John's work: "The new chef at the Springs hotel continues to please the regular and fastidious borders, and transient customers pronounce the tables set at this house the best in the territory."[39] He proved to be a popular addition to the hotel staff and provided continuity after J. C. Hussey purchased the hotel. As the *Husbandman* raved, "The culinary department is presided over by a *chef le cuisine* of splendid reputation."[40] John's training in continental cuisine served him well here, as a typical menu included items such as *Saumon Sauce au buerra decrevisse, Faisans de Boheme au jus,* and *Petits-poise a la francaise.* Even though some of the diners may have been "men used only to frontier life," as puzzled by the finger bowls as the French-language menu, John's cooking, perhaps despite the civilized pretensions of the Higgins House style, quickly won them over.[41]

John's position at Higgins House paid well enough that the Gordons purchased a house soon after their arrival. The deed for "Lot Number 7" in block twenty-nine registers the sale of the property from R. S. Price to John Gordon on September 19, 1885, for the sum of $350.[42] The house was certainly modest. Taylor described it as "a little three-room shack" with "two gables, two doors, four windows and cloth ceiling." It also featured a back porch made of two-by-fours where Taylor and George liked to sit "just enjoying ourselves" and a front room "where we all gathered at night with Sis reading the news" and Robert playing music.[43] At least one of the Gordons—whether Anna, Robert, or Rose—resided in the house until Rose's death in 1968. Taylor then lived in the house until his death in 1971. Whatever else their father provided for them, the family home established an enduring stability that lasted nearly a century. The property was important enough that Taylor referred to it in the opening sentence of his memoir: "The first thing I can remember is my home."[44] For Rose and Taylor, the house their father purchased was the foundation of their identities. In their writing, each paid homage to this place associated with their first notions of self.

Growing up in White Sulphur Springs was a formative experience that both Rose and Taylor recalled fondly, their memories touched with nostalgia and a sense of loss. For both, documenting the history of that time and place became a central activity in their later years. Rose's distinctive voice as a writer emerged in part from her fascination with the frontier town of her youth, and White Sulphur Springs's pioneer era became a subject she returned to repeatedly in her letters and in her columns for the *Meagher County News*. Scattered over thirty years of letters and columns, Rose's newspaper writing provides a vivid picture of the town's heyday. The town's vibrant print and performance culture certainly aided the Gordon children's development. Rose recalled fondly the mentors who brought her into that culture, particularly her piano teacher, Eleanor Brewer, and R. N. Sutherlin, a family friend who edited one of White Sulphur's newspapers.

For a small community, White Sulphur Springs was somewhat unusual in having two independent newspapers. Edited by brothers William H. and Robert N. Sutherlin, who came to Montana from Missouri during the gold rush, the *Rocky Mountain Husbandman* became Montana's primary agricultural and stock growing newspaper after its start in 1875. The *Husbandman*'s reach far exceeded that of a usual small-town newspaper, as it was distributed statewide. The self-proclaimed "pioneer agricultural newspaper of the great Northwestern territories," the *Husbandman*, according to one historian, published "without interruption for nearly seven decades" despite several moves in location and made "a lasting impact, not only on journalism, but on the agricultural economy and history of Montana."[45] Editor Robert Sutherlin, a farmer himself, was so enthusiastic about the *Husbandman*'s agricultural mission and the importance of farming to Montana that he once suggested that "there was no better way to pass the long winter evenings than to have the man of the household read agricultural reports aloud with his family gathered around him."[46]

Despite having no "experience in typography or journalism," Sutherlin typeset and printed the paper himself, went from farm to farm selling subscriptions in the earliest days of publication, and set the editorial content.[47] After its start in 1875 in Diamond City, a panned-out gold placer mining town in the Big Belt Mountains and the former Meagher County seat, the publication moved when White Sulphur Springs became the new county seat. From a financially precarious starting point of three hundred subscriptions and no paid advertising, Sutherlin built the subscription base to eight hundred by the fall of 1876, and "by 1879 the subscription list had grown to over thirteen hundred, and the capacity of the original printing press had been reached."[48] By 1880, "the *Husbandman* was well on the road to success. Financially sound, widely read, located in a promising new town, it held out promise for a new and growing country."[49] The newspaper also contributed to the growth of White Sulphur Springs through its advocacy—most apparent in the newspaper's role in relocating the Meagher County seat to the town.

Sutherlin befriended the Gordons not long after the family arrived in town, serving as a mentor for Robert and Rose in particular. He brought Robert and Rose onto the stage for the first time and saw that they were included in the town's public life in a variety of ways. Although Sutherlin, who eventually would be regarded as a pioneering journalist and one of the major figures in Montana newspaper history, had long passed on by the time Rose began flourishing as a newspaper writer in the 1940s and 1950s, she could hardly have had a better role model and mentor.[50]

Sutherlin's newspaper was not without a challenger in White Sulphur Springs, where a second newspaper began publishing in 1889. The *Meagher County News* began under the editorship of Alexander Rhone and continued to be operated by a series of editors who thoroughly enjoyed their rivalry with the Sutherlins. C. E. Wight took over the *Meagher County News* in 1897, but the paper ceased publication shortly thereafter. In 1900, attorney Max Waterman briefly revived the paper under the name the *Meagher Republican* to promote his candidacy on the Republican ticket for county attorney, but he shut it down after he won the election. The

Republican was reborn in 1902, again under Waterman's editorship, this time with printing facilities that exceeded the capacity of the *Rocky Mountain Husbandman* and benefited financially from Waterman directing city and county printing needs to the press. Ultimately, the loss of business forced Sutherlin's *Husbandman* to relocate to Great Falls in 1904. The battling, sniping, and name calling—Rhone referred to Sutherlin only as "the Gimlet"—that volleyed back and forth between the competing papers for the fifteen years or so that they coexisted in the same town certainly suggests the general liveliness of political discourse in turn-of-the-century White Sulphur Springs.[51]

Despite the political differences and economic rivalry between the newspapers, the editors shared a common vision. In its initial issue in 1904, the reborn *Meagher Republican* described itself as a "wide-awake newspaper devoted to the interests of the taxpayers and residents of Meagher County" and proclaimed itself to be "fearless and progressive in its editorial department" as well as attentive to "embracing every village in the county."[52] The *Husbandman*, throughout its run in White Sulphur Springs, used the same language to describe both its own and the town's distinctive character and philosophy. "We have a live town," the *Husbandman* once declared, where "people are wide awake and progressive" with an "unwavering confidence in the town, in its future."[53] From the editors' points of view, White Sulphur Springs was poised to take the lead in securing Montana's prosperous future.

During White Sulphur Springs's boom years, the town lacked one major feature: a link to the railroad. In 1892, the *Husbandman* asserted, "We are not of the class of journals [that indulge in] building railroads on paper from any point of the compass without any semblance of a prospect for a road." Having established that the *Husbandman* was not a purveyor of false hopes, the editors proclaimed, "We are happy to state that we are authorized to announce that a railroad will be built the coming summer from Helena to White Sulphur Springs and Castle."[54] Optimistic assessments of the railroad's imminent arrival appeared throughout the year, but these expectations proved to be premature by nearly two decades.

Editor Sutherlin was not the only local resident who expected the imminent arrival of the railway. In one of her reminiscences, published under the title "Rose Gordon's Recollection," Rose profiled "grand old timer" Powell Black, who had a law practice in town. Rose described a visit Black made to see his uncle, Preston H. Leslie, a former territorial governor, in Helena in 1891. Leslie "talked him into turning his ticket in for Seattle, which was a little town at the time and never was going to amount to anything, and practice law in White Sulphur Springs, Montana, which was going to be one of the largest towns in Montana, as the Northern Pacific railroad was going to build through White Sulphur Springs right away. He waited 20 years for the railroad which did not come."[55] For Rose, the late arrival of the railroad was not necessarily cause for lamentation, as it may have been for Black; it was just another colorful part of the town's history.

White Sulphur Springs kept busy while waiting for the railroad to arrive, and, in 1892, foundations were laid for two structures that became cultural landmarks for the Gordon children and the townspeople. The *Husbandman* reported that "B. R. Sherman broke dirt for his palatial residence on Knob Hill last week." The paper noted that, according to the architectural plan, "it will be two stories with a basement and contain seventeen rooms and about ten closets," and, most spectacularly of all, "it will be constructed of stone."[56] The *Husbandman* followed the building's construction, observing in late July 1892 that "Sherman's new stone residence now begins to rear itself above the ground, and the massive blocks of blue sandstone makes an imposing appearance."[57] The resulting structure was eventually named the "Castle." As its walls went up, excavation began on another building, which became known as the Auditorium, a large brick structure that housed performances, dances, masquerades, and other town events.

Both the Castle and the Auditorium played important roles in the education and development of the Gordon children. In addition, the Gordons established an important friendship with the Sherman family, several members of which became lifelong correspondents with Taylor and Rose. During his childhood and adolescence, Taylor spent as much time at the Castle as he did in his own home, and in the 1960s, he was instrumental in restoring the building after it had fallen into disrepair. The Auditorium exposed the Gordon children to the sort of professional performances that would have been unavailable in most towns the size of White Sulphur. It put the town on the circuit of Butte's Sutton Opera House and drew professional touring performance groups, including African American performers. It also served as a venue for local performances, and it was on its stage that Rose participated most directly in White Sulphur Springs's public life in her youth.

For Rose, the structures of her childhood were not just landmarks but "old friends," places with unique histories and distinct characters. Her writing often referenced the early settlers of White Sulphur Springs as the "grand old timers," and buildings such as the Castle, the Auditorium, the Mammoth Red Barn, the Higgins House, and Richard Ringling's Creamery were as much "grand old timers" as the pioneers who built them and whose names they sometimes carried. The Higgins House had drawn the Gordons to White Sulphur. As the place where her father had worked, the Higgins House was not only an "old friend" but one of the Gordon family's first benefactors. Before Higgins House, which later operated as the Phipps Hotel and finally the Sherman Hotel, was demolished in 1963, the community held a farewell party for the building. Although Rose observed in her letter to the newspaper on the occasion that the attendees "enjoyed a pleasant evening," she also compared the event to "losing an old friend."[58]

White Sulphur Springs, its setting, its streets, businesses, buildings, and its people—especially its newspapers and the progressive philosophy they shared—were all of crucial importance to Rose and her siblings. Rose recalled how her identity and personality first took shape in this context: "As a child I carried a lantern about at night doing little tasks. Dear mother and I would go to church at night coming home by lantern light, so on down the years I learned to love every nook and corner of the town, every alley and alley cat, knew their breed and color." She also came to know every dog in town, and "my canine friends were of many kinds and breeds. . . . They were all my friends and helped to make the little town loveable and unforgettable."[59] In the Gordon siblings' later life, the early days of this "loveable and unforgettable" little town remained at the forefront of their thoughts. Rose and Taylor acknowledged again and again in their writings that they were who they were as people—and as the writers they became—because of their early experiences in this frontier town. Rose and Taylor each made turn-of-the-century White Sulphur Springs one of the central topics of their writing. *Born to Be* is a celebrity autobiography, but the first quarter of Taylor's memoir is a love letter to the White Sulphur Springs of his childhood. For Rose, meanwhile, White Sulphur Springs became the central topic of her life as a writer.

CHAPTER 2

Meagher County's African American Community

"Never once when I was a child," Rose Gordon asserted in "Gone are the Days," "was I treated as if I were any color except white."[1] Her younger brother felt differently. "I knew I was black and different in appearance from most of the kids I played with," wrote Taylor Gordon in *Born to Be*, "but my being so never changed the values of the game we might be playing. I got a chance to pitch or bat at the time my merits won for me either of the positions."[2] It is certainly possible that the Gordon siblings experienced childhoods relatively free of overt racism. John Francis Gordon's standing in the community as a family man and dependable wage earner may have garnered him and his family respectable status, a hedge against the pervasive prejudice that existed, and still exists, in America. Likewise, Anna Gordon, well-practiced in negotiating unequal social relations after growing up under slavery, may have been effective at protecting her children from the blatant prejudice and discrimination that Blacks experienced elsewhere.

Despite their assertions to the contrary, Taylor and Rose covertly revealed evidence of the prejudice that they claimed did not exist among what Rose called the "grand old timers" of White Sulphur Springs. Taylor's various childhood nicknames (Snowball, Zip, Blacky) suggest that the town's residents clearly marked differences in "appearance." As he pointed out, however, "They called Jimmy Keen 'Blacky' too, and really the only thing black about him was his hair."[3] Yet no white child in White Sulphur seems to have been nicknamed "Sambo," a stereotypical term for African Americans popular in the late nineteenth century, as was his brother John Francis Jr. In their writing, Rose and Taylor re-created the White Sulphur of their childhood in ways that demonstrated their multiple purposes. Perhaps the key phrase in Rose's comment was "never once when I was a child," suggesting a different story about her adult life. For Taylor, White Sulphur Springs served as a contrast to the more visible prejudice he encountered elsewhere. Taylor explicitly, and Rose implicitly, used the town's past to highlight the prejudices of its present.

There is more than a grain of truth, however, to the vision of turn-of-the-century White Sulphur Springs that appears in their writing. The presence of the town's small but significant Black population in the late nineteenth century indicates that, like the Gordons, other African Americans found the growing community, and to some degree Montana Territory in general, largely hospitable.

⁂

Between 1870 and 1910, the Black population in the mountain and western coastal states increased significantly, although it dropped sharply by 1920.[4] The 1870 census reveals that Montana already had a Black population of 183 out of a tabulated territorial population of just more than 20,000 residents, excluding Native Americans.[5] The demographics of this earliest group of Black pioneers "mirrored that of the territory's white population" of the period: single men living alone in areas "tied to transportation or mining."[6] Although only twenty-nine African American women were listed in the 1870 census (18 percent of the total African American population in territorial Montana), that number increased significantly, from twenty-nine to seventy-two by 1880. In Montana, historian Quintard Taylor notes, the African American population continued to rise, from 346 in 1880 to 1,490 in 1890 to 1,523 in 1900, in part because of births in the territory rather than immigration.[7] Of the African American children listed in the 1880 census, for example, almost two-thirds "were born in Montana, suggesting a certain level of persistence among the families."[8]

The destruction of most of the 1890 U.S. Census records by fire left a huge gap in the recorded history of Montana's Black community. We do know that statewide, according to Behan's research, "the African American population was about 1,490—approximately four times the 1880 figure."[9] Statewide, the Black population peaked at over 2,000 in 1910, with Helena claiming the largest number of African American residents.[10] As the state's Black population grew, so did Helena's, expanding from 71 in 1870 to 420 in 1910, 3.4 percent of Helena's total population of 12,515.[11] Subsequent census reports, however, reveal a steady decline in Helena's Black population—to 131 in 1930, 88 in 1950, and 45 in 1970—mirroring a statewide exodus throughout the twentieth century.[12] The growth and decline of the Helena community was reflective more generally of the fluctuations statewide.

By 1950, Rose and her brother Robert were the only two African Americans living in all of Meagher County. During the Gordon children's youth, however, White Sulphur Springs and the surrounding towns had a significant number of African American citizens who were fairly well integrated into the economic and social life of Meagher County between the late 1870s and 1910. The 1880 census lists around a dozen African Americans living in Meagher County, including Belt City residents Millie Ringold, her boarder Frank Marion, and her neighbor Joseph Meek. Irvin and Carrie Smith and their boarder, Andrew Heart, lived in White Sulphur Springs, as did Alex Maxfield, a twenty-two-year-old farmhand who worked for and lodged with the William Parberry family. By 1900, Meagher County recorded an African American population of thirty (six of whom were the Gordons), a number that remained stable at least through the 1910 census.[13] Local newspapers from 1885 to 1895 frequently mentioned Meagher County's African American residents, many of whom were not listed in the county census records. Individuals such as Ernest Penny, Wash Madison, and Robert Langhorne may have moved into White Sulphur after 1880 and left or died before the 1900 census; thus their presence exists only in the newspaper. Indeed, the newspaper record indicates that the county's Black population might have peaked above what the 1900 and 1910 census reported.

Articles in the *Indianapolis Freeman*, a weekly newspaper for Black audiences nationwide, suggest some of the reasons that Montana was a draw for Black migrants. In an article titled "A Servant Girl's Paradise," the *Freeman* declared, "Servants wages are 100 percent higher in Montana than in New York. The cooks on the railway dining [car] receive $60 a month. In private families $30 is the lowest wage offered, and some are paid as much as $100." A brief notice from 1890 informed the *Freeman's* readers, "If you of the south can't live in peace, save your small earnings and go west, to Washington, Oregon or Montana. Your services are in demand out there at 'white men's' wages and treatment, at that."[14] Likewise, African Americans participated in ranching and cattle drives as both cowboys and cooks, but "neither territorial census lists any black cowboys," perhaps because the "censuses were taken when cattle workers were on the range."[15] T. G. Steward, a chaplain stationed at Fort Missoula, wrote in a letter to the *Freeman*, "I should take Montana to be a good place for colored people, as there seems to be no special prejudice against them and wages are good."[16]

The *Freeman* frequently published celebratory articles about Black soldiers stationed at several military forts in Montana, in particular the Twenty-Fourth Infantry and its award-winning band, as well as reports and letters from African American servicemen. Brief reports detailing everyday life in the forts appeared with some frequency in the paper. From Fort Custer, near Hardin, came a note in 1895 that "Sergeant Robert J. Noal arrived last week from Hot Springs Ark.," and "Sergeant Letcher and party returned last week from a fishing trip."[17] In an earlier report from Fort Custer, an article described a dance and supper involving the African American Tenth Cavalry and the Twenty-Fifth Infantry. "The hop was grand and the music first-class," the article reported. Following the dance, thirty-three couples marched to the "dining room where a handsome spread awaited them."[18] These articles portrayed a vibrant African American community within Montana's military post population, which included both men and women.

For John Francis Gordon and several other Black workers who settled in central Montana Territory, the mining frontier was a draw. "The Montana goldfields," historian Michael Malone explains, "attracted a sizable number of African Americans, especially after the Civil War." More frequently, however, Black migrants "came as servants of white families, many more to work in the service economy as day laborers, and a fraction of them as miners and entrepreneurs."[19] Although Montana's African American population came from a variety of places, most, including the Gordons, migrated from southern states. Author-editor J. W. Smurr notes of the first wave of Black migration to Montana that two-thirds emigrated from southern states, "and of those four-fifths came from only four states: Missouri, Kentucky, West Virginia, and Virginia."[20] Historian Barbara Carol Behan compared the origins of Montana's Black population to that of whites arriving at the same time: "The 1870 Montana territorial census shows 41 percent of African Americans listing Missouri and Kentucky as their birth states—a higher proportion than in the white population." Behan notes that the "proximity to transportation up the Missouri River" for African Americans residing in Missouri and Kentucky was another factor in the high number of migrants coming from those states.[21]

One of the more fascinating characters to follow the river to central Montana Territory was Millie Ringold, admiringly described in the *Rocky Mountain Husbandman* as "the celebrated African prospector."[22] Born into slavery in Maryland, Ringold traveled to Fort Benton in 1879 as a servant of an army general and his family who were stationed at Fort Shaw.[23] When the general transferred back east, Ringold decided she liked Montana well enough to stay. Acquaintance Finch David, one of the many amateur historians whose accounts of early Montana the *Meagher County News* printed, explained Ringold's determination to survive in the territory: "She bought a pair of condemned army mules and [a] wagon. She went to Fort Benton and loaded up in grub and a barrel of whiskey, and headed for Yogo, then a boom town. She had $1800.00 when she got to Yogo."[24]

Rose Gordon also "had the pleasure of knowing Mary [*sic*] Ringold, pioneer of the sapphire mines," and relayed the story of Ringold finding "a sapphire in the craw of the turkey" she was dressing. The discovery led her to establish several mining claims in the Yogo area, although ultimately those claims did not pan out. Rose remembered Ringold fondly: "She was very musical. She played odd instruments, hand saws, mouth harps and dish pans."[25] Finch David similarly admired Ringold's musical talent, saying, "She could make better music in an empty five gallon can than most people could on a piano." Though Ringold didn't strike it rich, she acquired a wide community of friends whom she entertained by playing songs such as "Coming Through the Rye" and "Coal Oil Johnnie on a Bum-Bum Spree" on her odd collection of instruments.[26]

Civil War veteran Joseph Meek also traveled up the Missouri to Montana Territory, arriving in Fort Benton with his brother Charles around 1880.[27] Both brothers were born into slavery in Tennessee but subsequently joined the Union army at the outset of the Civil War. On May 12, 1863, Meek, under the name Joseph W. Meeks, joined Company E of the Fifty-Fourth Massachusetts Infantry, a segregated regiment of African American soldiers and white officers. A twenty-year-old single man and a shoemaker by profession, Meek was recruited out of Springfield, Ohio, and served with the unit until mustering out at the war's conclusion.[28] He would have taken part in the regiment's most famous action, the July 18, 1863, attack on Fort Wagner in South Carolina, which would later be dramatized in the 1989 film *Glory*. Rose Gordon recalled, "We loved to hear Mr. Meek tell Civil War stories."[29] According to Rose, Joseph Meek resided "in a little house north of town on a hill top for many years" with his wife. Laura Meek "nursed for many families in town" and "assisted Dr. Kumpe and Dr. McKay and together they brought many fine children in the world."[30]

Meek's brother, Charles, spent much of the war as an aide to General Ulysses S. Grant. In Montana Territory, Charles worked with his brother at the Barker Mine, but they subsequently split up. While Joseph settled in White Sulphur Springs, Charles worked as a porter in Great Falls, spent some time farming, and became an active member of the Republican Party. Charles's interest in mining inspired him to leave Montana during the Klondike gold rush in 1898. He later went on to mines in Idaho and Washington before finally moving back to Great Falls in 1909 after a mining accident left him severely injured.[31]

In addition to military posts and mining ventures, urban areas drew large numbers of Blacks to Montana. Helena, in particular, developed a dynamic African American community in the late nineteenth century. The capital city was large enough to support two Black-owned newspapers: *The Colored Citizen*, edited by J. P. Ball Jr., for a brief run in 1894, and the *Montana Plaindealer*, edited by Joseph B. Bass, from 1906 to 1911.[32] Black social life centered around the St. James African Methodist Episcopal Church, several fraternal lodges, and "an underside of gamblers, prostitutes, pimps, and hustlers who congregated in saloons along Clore Street."[33] The *Indianapolis Freeman* turned happenings in Helena's African American community into national news by reporting interesting and significant local events to its readership. In 1892, for instance, the paper duly noted A. F. Smith's candidacy for justice of the peace, acknowledging that he was "the first colored man who ever put up for such an office in the history of Montana." The same article lauded J. P. Ball, "one of Helena's best photographers," and George M. Lea, porter of "the finest hotel in Helena, called 'The Helena,'" where the "waiters are all colored."[34] As part of a tour of western cities printed in the *Freeman* in 1913, Booker T. Washington reported that in the Black communities of Butte and Helena, "one will meet some individuals who are as wide awake and progressive as can be found anywhere in the country," singling out Helena in particular for establishing a Negro Business League and in general for the "intelligence and culture" of the community.[35]

Even within the same town or area, different groups of African Americans could have varying experiences of prejudice. Montana historian William L. Lang observes a "relative lack of racial conflict in Helena," which he attributes to both "the moderate size of the black population, which never constituted a social or economic threat to whites" and "the absence of residential segregation."[36]

Virginia City, located just over one hundred miles southwest of White Sulphur Springs, shares in a similar history as a center of growth in the late nineteenth century that subsequently experienced an economic and population decline. This booming mining camp and territorial seat was home to a small African American community that eventually dispersed or died out. Laura Joanne Arata, in her study of that community and of African American resident Sarah Bickford, notes that Virginia City's Black residents seem to have been accepted in the 1870s and 1880s: "Though in sheer numbers they represented a tiny percentage of the total population of Virginia City—less than one percent—their visibility in business and other daily activities suggests that some of these individuals held relatively prominent positions within the community."[37] African Americans in Virginia City owned and operated barbershops, restaurants, and a general store; they worked as miners, day laborers, and teamsters.[38]

Virginia City's example, however, reveals contradictory attitudes about race. While white residents could be both respectful and tolerant of the community's own Black residents, they were simultaneously "derisive and demeaning" regarding African Americans in general, which surfaced in derogatory racial discourse in the town's newspaper. "The way Virginia City residents responded to matters of race," Arata writes, "seems both specific to a unique set of local factors and representative of a larger phenomenon—a certain plasticity of race that existed more broadly in the rural west."[39]

Although the phrase "a certain plasticity of race" also applies to the circumstances in White Sulphur Springs, there were key differences between the two towns: White Sulphur Springs's newspapers similarly printed items suggesting respect and tolerance for African American residents, but they rarely published material that was "derisive and demeaning" toward specific Black individuals. Stereotypical representations of Blackness nonetheless circulated in White Sulphur Springs, as evidenced by the popularity of minstrel shows. The newspapers sometimes drew on those stereotypes when publishing items about the town's Black citizens, but the kind of hostile descriptions of African Americans typical in other Western newspapers were absent.

Arata observes Virginia City's newspapers' "willingness to identify some residents by race while omitting such references to others," and argues that "it is surely meaningful that *certain* African American residents were *never* identified by race."[40] In some ways, the White Sulphur Springs newspapers frequently did distinguish African Americans by their race, usually by adding "colored" in parentheses after the individual's name.[41]

Well-known Meagher County residents such as the Gordons, Irvin Smith, and Joe Meek, however, often appeared without that parenthetical designation as well as with it, suggesting the town's African Americans were integrated in some respects but continued to exist as a racially distinct group.[42] Even when race was not indicated by the "colored" tag, the newspapers acknowledged the distinctiveness of the town's African American citizens in other ways. For example, on several occasions the newspapers describe Smith as a former slave. In these ways, local newspapers recognized the town's Black citizens as African American, acknowledging that their racial identity was part of who they were due to their historical experiences, and that those markers made them distinctive within the community.

Small-town newspapers also played a significant role in establishing a community's values and prejudices. In their investigation of early African American newspapers in the West, scholars Gayle Berardi and Thomas Segady concluded that newspapers of the late nineteenth and early twentieth centuries, by focusing primarily on local and regional news, "provided a basis for a sense of community in a population that consisted largely of individuals who had recently migrated to the area." The communities represented in the newspapers, however, "tended to be highly selective, reflecting racial and ethnic biases within the rapidly growing towns."[43] In general, Western newspapers repeated a familiar pattern when it came to news about African American citizens, emphasizing stories "reflecting negative characteristics."[44] Lang observes a similar pattern in the white Helena newspapers, which "found newsworthy only the notorious incidents in the black community; a violent crime by a black or a humorous anecdote demonstrating the purportedly low intelligence of Afro-Americans merited news space."[45] Notably, again, the White Sulphur Springs newspapers departed from this pattern. While newspapers elsewhere in the state and region helped create an unwelcoming or hostile environment for African Americans, the *Rocky Mountain Husbandman* and the *Meagher Republican* were at worst neutral in their documentation of the town's Black citizens and at best laudatory when presenting their accomplishments in print.

One of the earliest mentions of the Gordon family in the local newspapers is a notice in the *Rocky Mountain Husbandman* of the death of one of the children in 1891: "Mr. and Mrs. Gordon (colored) had the misfortune to lose their youngest child last week with whooping cough."[46] Although the announcement does not name the child, Taylor mentions in his autobiography that the child's name was Arthur, the fifth of the Gordon children. He was only a year old when he died.[47] The notice differs from any other account of a family tragedy published in the *Husbandman* only in the parenthetical addition of the word "colored" to the Gordons' names. As the *Husbandman* noted somberly some time later, "Mrs.

Gordon's little boy Francis fell from a horse last Saturday and was pretty badly hurt. Town Marshall Allen carried him to Dr. McKay and had his dislocated arm dressed before the boy's mother was informed of the accident. It is thought the arm is fractured at the elbow joint."[48] Noteworthy in this announcement is the immediate response of town officials as well as the paper's respectful references to "Mr. and Mrs. Gordon," as identifying African Americans by first name only was still a widespread practice in the United States well into the twentieth century. Although Anna Gordon was known by some residents of White Sulphur Springs by the racially marked nickname "Mammie" Gordon, the newspapers always referred to her as Mrs. Gordon, indicating their regard for her as an upstanding citizen of the community.

The editors of the town's newspapers believed White Sulphur Springs was poised to become one of Montana's leading cities. While other growing Montana towns no doubt possessed similar ambitions, White Sulphur is remarkable in its explicit inclusion—by providing a wide-ranging record of the activities of the town's African American citizens—of its African American residents as partners in that enterprise. By doing so, White Sulphur's newspapers helped create an environment amenable to African Americans and contributed to the stability of the African American population in Meagher County between 1880 and 1910.

Although Meagher County lacked a distinctive African American community in the form of institutions such as churches or fraternal lodges like those in the more populous cities of Helena and Great Falls, the evidence shows that the area's Black residents developed a sense of identity both as a specific group within the larger community and as contributing members of that larger, partially integrated society. The Gordon family became part of a Black community that took pride both in its specific cultural identity and in its participation in the town's growth, prosperity, and social activity. Part of the attraction of White Sulphur must have been this small group of fellow Black Westerners who were raising families and making lives for themselves in the post-emancipation United States.

Joseph Meek, whose prospecting activities were reported on regularly in the newspapers, was not the only prominent Black citizen to garner attention from local newspapers. Irvin Smith, an "enterprising" blacksmith, was also one of the town's pioneer settlers, whose smithy contributed to the town's growth and development.[49] Smith owned and operated his own forge from 1880 until at least 1900, contributing materially to the construction of the town.[50] Rose Gordon remembered him primarily for his contribution to the children's entertainment, describing in one of her "Centennial Notes" how Smith and George Keys "made large sleds for coasting which everyone enjoyed."[51] Smith's first blacksmith shop, operated with business partner John Woodson, was established by the time the *Husbandman* moved to town in 1883. The shop was one of the earliest supporters of the *Husbandman*, with its advertisement promising "all work warranted first-class and at Helena Prices" appearing in each weekly edition of the newspaper during the year 1883, an important and regular source of advertising income for the newly established paper. The *Husbandman* returned the favor by frequently reporting Smith's activities in its local news section.

Smith was successful, as occasional newspaper notices of his business transactions, his ranch, or his stock of horses evinces. He was active in party politics, attending at least one state Republican convention in Helena and joining with the African American cornet band, in which he played bass drum, to provide music at local rallies for Republican candidates for office. In addition, he was a talented storyteller, and the newspapers transcribed and printed his accounts of slavery.[52] He also managed and acted in a series of minstrel entertainments.

Perhaps the most remarkable news item relating to Smith appeared in the *Rocky Mountain Husbandman* on his sixty-fifth birthday in October 1897: "For fifty-one years he has stood by the flaming forge and pounded red-hot iron, and though well advanced in years his strong and sinewy arms still ply with wonderful force and the merry ring of his anvil as with dexterity he plies the hammer is music to the neighborhood. Mr. Smith was born in Kentucky in slavery times and went into the shop at the age of fourteen." This piece presents Smith as an integral part of the community, lauding him as a "veteran knight of the forge" who had "served more constant years than any other man in the state" as a blacksmith, offering a symbol of White Sulphur Springs's competitive edge when compared to other communities and appearing as an icon of manliness celebrated for his physical strength and character.[53] Smith's birthday provided the occasion for the *Husbandman* to print something of a rarity: a concise but fairly complete biography of one of Montana's African American citizens, a pioneer whose arrival in 1880 was well before statehood and one whose contributions at the forge were instrumental to the development of White Sulphur Springs.

In addition to the Meeks and the Smiths, the town's Black community counted several other men—such as Robert Thompson, Wash Madison, Caesar Fields, and Eli Shelby—among its members at the end of the nineteenth century.[54] The *Husbandman* described Thompson as "a well-respected citizen of this place."[55] Similarly, the paper lauded Wash Madison, the coachman at the Higgins House, as "a captal [*sic*] good fellow and good citizen."[56] Caesar Fields, an elderly African American man whose stories of his life during slavery chilled the young Rose Gordon, made a living doing errands and odd jobs. Five feet tall and walking with a cane, Fields was a favorite of the White Sulphur Springs children. According to Rose, every evening he would bring out a chair from his "little log cabin" to "watch the beautiful sunset" and soon be "surrounded by children from all over the neighborhood."[57] Fields had arrived in Montana from Missouri around 1882.[58] Although single men like him were in the majority in nineteenth-century Montana, it seems likely that some had wives and families whose presence may not have been documented, as newspapers more frequently referenced men.[59] Eli Shelby came to Montana Territory as a prospector in 1879, and by 1883 he had abandoned mining and moved to White Sulphur Springs, where he operated the Cottage Café. Shelby became acquainted with John Francis Gordon, and even after he moved to Great Falls, he kept in touch with the Gordon family, returning to visit on at least one occasion.[60]

African Americans Robert Langhorne, a talented musician and performer noted for his banjo playing, and blacksmith George Mason arrived in the late 1880s, not long after the Gordons.[61] Mason worked in Irvin Smith's shop before starting his own forge with Frank Scott. Of Mason's abilities, the *Meagher County News* reported, "He is one of the finest horse shoers in the state and can make anything from a horse-shoe nail up. His work speaks for itself."[62] Notably, the opening of Mason's shop meant that White Sulphur now had two forges owned and operated by African Americans.

John Wilson, a farmer and vegetable seller, arrived in the area in 1888, making frequent trips to White Sulphur Springs while living in Duck Creek.[63] The *Husbandman* praised his industry, the quality of his service, and his contribution to the community: "We are indebted to John Wilson, the enterprising gardener who has been visiting our town with so many loads of elegant vegetables for a sample of the tomatoes, squash and chicken grown by him. The tomatoes were large and ripe and the squash was very excellent."[64] The *Husbandman* rarely offered higher praise than "enterprising," aside from "wide awake," a term it reserved for the businessmen the editors most admired. A few weeks later, the paper published a response from Wilson: "A Card of Thanks" for the opportunity that the people of White Sulphur had offered him and "for their kindness and liberality in patronizing me in the way of buying vegetables." His journey west had been opposed by his friends, who believed he would find "that a colored man would be imposed upon in every respect," but he discovered instead that "the people of Montana have been full of kindness toward me, and I have never received better treatment anywhere."[65] Wilson painted a picture of life in Montana as distinct from the rest of the country in regard to racial matters.

Although Wilson's experience may have been an anomaly, it corresponded with those of other African Americans in Montana. As author Scott Meredith notes, "African Americans made a place for themselves in the state. If racial equality remained elusive, . . . there is also evidence that in Montana African Americans felt they had as much of a chance to make good here as in many other places."[66] Certainly, accounts in the local newspapers must be taken in context of the boosterism, hyperbole, and general mythmaking that characterized such outlets. Nonetheless, it seems clear that many African American pioneers found an opportunity in Montana to make a living, became contributing members of a community, and even experienced "kindness and liberality" from their white neighbors.[67] For the *Husbandman* and the *Meagher County News* and *Republican*, reporting about African Americans provided an opportunity to tell a story of a wide awake town able to bypass the prejudices that prevented other places from progressing, a town where Black citizens—who sometimes told their stories in their own words, which the papers duly printed—contributed to social and economic growth. The newspapers' practice of reporting positively on its African American citizens stands out against the more usual reportage in Montana newspapers and Western newspapers generally.

As White Sulphur's Black residents integrated themselves in the larger society, they cultivated close ties with one another, finding support and sustenance in a shared cultural identity. For instance, in 1893 the *Meagher County News* reported that the "colored people of the town held a very nice gathering at the residence of Ernest Penny last Saturday night. Refreshments were served and a general good time enjoyed."[68] Throughout the West, African American pioneers and settlers, who often represented a small minority of a settlement's residents, enjoyed the "good time" and the building of community identity. What is remarkable here is that the town's white-owned newspaper considered such a gathering to be as newsworthy as white residents' berry-picking parties and whist gatherings.

The Gordon family often played a central role in the Black community's social life. In one of her later letters, Rose recounted one of Millie Ringold's visits to town: "She came to White Sulphur Springs on the stage coach and asked where she could stop. They told her to go to Mrs. Gordon's house. She was here a week." The children clearly found their houseguest quite a draw: "We couldn't get home from school soon enough to visit Millie." Ringold seemed to enjoy her time with the Gordons, as Rose noted that she still had "the photograph of Millie Ringold given to my late brother George Gordon."[69] Anna Gordon took in boarders to help make ends meet, and it is not clear from Rose's account whether Ringold was directed to the Gordons' house because of segregated lodging elsewhere in town, or whether she was one of many visitors, Black or white, who were sent their way. Whatever the case, Ringold found a congenial environment at the Gordon home, and the incident is suggestive of the way the African American community in the town supported friends and strangers alike.

Perhaps the clearest indication of the way that African American citizens existed as a distinct group within White Sulphur is the visible Black music culture that formed part of the town's remarkable emphasis on performance. For all the members of the community, the ability to stage musical performances, revues, dramatic readings, literary recitations, and debates contributed to the town's self-image as a growing and progressive community in step with American cultural norms of the day. Sometimes African Americans shared the stage with white performers, playing duets together or performing as part of the same musical groups. Other times, African Americans performed solo or in all-Black ensembles such as an African American brass band. In 1889, the *Husbandman* reported on the band's debut: "The colored band made their first appearance on our streets Monday evening last. They marched in good order and halted at the prominent points on Main Street and played several tunes after which they visited the houses of the colored people of town."[70] The band provided Black residents a means for participation in the town's public life and an opportunity to do so in a way that expressed a sense of pride in their cultural identity while showcasing their musical skills.

From 1889 through 1893, White Sulphur Springs witnessed a flourishing of "colored" performance groups: the cornet band, a quartet that specialized in spirituals, and even a minstrel troupe. Of these groups, the cornet band garnered the most attention. The *Meagher County News* described the group in detail: "Bob Langhorn plays the cornet, Irwin Smith, the bass drum and Geo. Mason pounds the devil out of the snare."[71] With the town's blacksmiths hammering the drums, this particular band could make some noise. They played a variety of events, from church services to weddings. The band also provided overtures for the White Sulphur Springs Amateur Dramatic Company between performances of dramatic excerpts such as the balcony scene from *Romeo and Juliet*.[72] The cornet band developed a flair for the spectacular, making it a noticeable and in-demand feature of White Sulphur's cultural life. "The colored band have received their new uniforms from Philadelphia and will parade the streets," the *Meagher County News* proclaimed in April of 1892, "and that evening [will] give their interesting concert at O'Marr's hall. The chariot will be drawn by six Arabian war horses."[73]

The cornet band demonstrates one way that African Americans participated in public life in White Sulphur Springs, in this case through performative assertions of a racial distinctiveness. When groups such as the White Sulphur Springs Colored Quartette sang as part of a program inclusive of white and Black performers, they were distinguished by race in the newspaper and printed program. The material they performed, such as "Swanee River" and "Roll, Jordan, Roll," underscored that distinction, with the group drawing on two "colored" traditions: the minstrel tradition represented by Stephen Foster's "Swanee River" and the more authentic African American form of the spiritual exemplified by "Roll, Jordan, Roll." The town's African American citizens used these public performances to assert an identity that was, as the name of the quartet suggests, both part of the local public life and definitively "colored." Given these assertions of racial identity, the newspapers of White Sulphur Springs would have been hard-pressed to ignore the race of the citizens who frequently asserted their identity as Black.

In what could be interpreted as a more overt declaration of racial identity, the town's African American citizens put together an even more ambitious program later that same month, forming the Home Colored Minstrel Company and producing a full-length minstrel show complete with stock comedic characters, Tambo and Bones, along with comic skits and vocal and instrumental performances.[74] Originally, minstrel performers were white men in blackface. It was not until the end of the nineteenth century that companies of "colored" minstrels began competing with the white blackface groups. Minstrelsy, with its reliance on stereotypes of African American people, is certainly a form of participation in the public sphere that has its limitations. Nonetheless, by the end of the nineteenth century, Black performers used the nationwide interest in minstrelsy to build lucrative careers in a segregated entertainment industry.

The three members of the colored band, Robert Langhorne, George Mason, and Irvin Smith—the latter of whom appeared under the stage name M. Organ—played major roles in the minstrel production. Each man filled one of the three parts in the traditional minstrel overture: the interlocutor or emcee, and Bones and Tambo, the two "end men," whose banter was coordinated by the interlocutor—who played straight man to the comic end men. The company incorporated several children in the performance, including Maud and John Smith, daughter and son of Irwin Smith, and eleven-year-old Robert Gordon, who made his first entrance onto the public stage and earned his first mention in the town's newspapers.[75]

The concert was a huge success, drawing "the largest crowd of people we have seen assembled in one room at White Sulphur for a long time," according to the *Husbandman*, and earning enough money "to liquidate the expense of equipping the colored folks' cornet band."[76] The Home Colored Minstrel Company saw their performances as a contribution to the civic life of their community. The *Rocky Mountain Husbandman* published a letter from the company, addressed "To the People of White Sulphur Springs," thanking them for attending and explaining the purpose of the event: "Having incurred a considerable debt in equipping a cornet band with instruments, uniform and band wagon, which is a public enterprise, and designed as such, we thought it would not be out of place to ask the people of the town and valley to assist us by patronizing an entertainment gotten up among our people for the purpose of paying off our indebtedness."[77] The members of the company and the cornet band considered their performances a contribution by the Black citizens to the betterment of the town. They proposed another entertainment, the proceeds of which would be applied to building a new town hall and toward other enterprises "designed for the good of our town."[78] This remarkable letter confirms that White Sulphur Springs's African American citizens saw the town as "our town" and regarded themselves as partners in the enterprise of civic improvement.

While minstrelsy provided a means for African Americans to enter the public sphere, it limited that participation because whites often expected Black people to behave the way that minstrel characters acted on stage in real life. Although obviously fake, minstrelsy claimed to portray authentic Black life, or at least a version of it that had existed under slavery. In a brief item about Higgins House coachman Washington Madison, the *Husbandman* praised his "fun-making" and observed, "Wash is a typical colored man of antebellum days, is always polite and obliging, and can do the song and dance in a manner that would do credit to Billy Emerson and other celebrities."[79] Part of what made Wash Madison a "typical colored man of antebellum days," according to the paper, was that his behavior conformed to expectations established by minstrelsy with his supposed resemblance to a white blackface performer, the Irish-born Billy Emerson.[80] The simultaneous praise of the town's Black performers and stereotyping of a Black resident expose the complicated layers of racial relationships in White Sulphur Springs that could swing from respectful to condescending.

Not to be outdone, the white citizens of White Sulphur periodically formed their own blackface minstrel clubs. The *Rocky Mountain Husbandman* reported in the mid-1880s, "Our town just now seems to have the club mania" and listed among several musical clubs a minstrel group called the "Minstrel Company." The company's program for an upcoming performance included songs that evoked stereotypes of African Americans as being prone to violence, such as "Dar'l be Razors Flyin' fro' de air."[81] In contrast, the all-Black Home Colored Minstrel Company's program represented a departure from the more tendentious material associated with minstrelsy, at least in terms of the musical performance, which included spirituals—referred to as "Jubilee Songs"—as well as comic songs. The comic songs, however, did not emphasize the usual minstrel conventions of fractured dialect and references to razor fights, watermelons, chicken stealing, and the like. While using white America's avid interest in minstrel performance to gain access to the public sphere, African American performers in White Sulphur Springs offered a different version of minstrelsy, one that revised the more offensive aspects of white blackface minstrelsy and thus offered a more palatable corrective to stereotypes than other methods.[82]

Nonetheless, the presence of minstrelsy—even in the "corrected" form of the Home Colored Minstrels—suggests that in some racial matters White Sulphur Springs was similar to the rest of America. Blacks in White Sulphur Springs found it useful and perhaps necessary to don the mask of minstrelsy. Engaging in masking and racial role playing was a survival skill for African Americans negotiating the complex interracial politics of an unequal social system in which wealth was concentrated in white hands, one that had been established during slavery and honed and passed down during the era of Jim Crow segregation.

Asserting a Black identity through performance in White Sulphur Springs sometimes meant drawing on Black cultural traditions, but performative Blackness also required adapting to the expectations of white audiences. Wash Madison knew how to wear the mask, participating in "fun making" to negotiate the surrounding white world. The members of the Gordon family also displayed that same ability at various times, as revealed in their acceptance of racially marked nicknames or in their willingness to engage in similar behavior.

The Gordon family was not immune to the expectations that minstrelsy created. In a letter to the *Meagher County News*, Rose's former classmate Eva Roderick passed along a memory of Anna Gordon, whom she remembered fondly as having "fun making" skills similar to those of Madison. She recalled one time when "Mammy" Gordon "danced 'jolly miggles' as she called it . . . in the middle of the street, she was too large to move about on the little old sidewalks and for some time there was a shortage of crowd in the hall."[83] Whatever her reasons for dancing in the street, Anna understood the strategic necessity of being "obliging" or entertaining and helpful to her fellow citizens.

Rose, in a later tribute to one of her teachers in the lower grades, Walter E. Rowe, remembered that he kept a disciplined classroom— except for the time Rose disrupted it with her own dance performance. Rose recalled a day when "school was out and the girls were in the hall," one of whom implored, "'Oh, Rose, do the cake walk for us,'" referencing a dance made popular on the minstrel stage. Rose obliged, noting, "I was in the mood, doing the walk, when Professor Rowe appeared on the scene. He just looked. We were all frozen. He was very nice and did not scold us."[84] This incident seemingly tells a story quite different from Rose's assertion that not once as a child "was I treated as if I were any color except white." As her cake walk story reveals, Rose understood at an early age the advantages of performing to racial expectations. Her writing is sprinkled with bits of minstrel humor, indicating her ability and willingness to occasionally slip on the minstrel mask to make her stories more appealing to her audience, the readers of the White Sulphur Springs newspapers. Rose's writing constituted a "public enterprise," and so it was designed as a carefully crafted and strategic entry into the community's public sphere.[85]

Other documents, such as the sections of "Gone are the Days" not revised for publication in the newspaper, and especially those intended for private consumption such as personal letters received and written by Rose, suggest a lifelong and complex negotiation of racial attitudes and beliefs.[86] They show that Rose was a gifted negotiator, willing at times to play to white stereotypes of Black behavior and perform a particular version of race. Rose understood that she often needed to be accommodating, and used minstrel humor when necessary. She may have found a model for her survival skills in the Black community in White Sulphur Springs as she was growing up. She similarly used her abilities as a performer to make a place for herself in the town's public sphere. As the small business owner that she would become, she may also have been influenced by the achievements of African American business owners and entrepreneurs like Irvin Smith and Joseph Meek. Notably, Rose was also willing to stand her ground against prejudice when an occasion called for her to do so. In both her willingness to wear the mask when necessary and in her equal capacity for self-assertion, Rose took after her mother, her primary role model, from whom she learned the skills that would enable her to successfully navigate life in Montana.

CHAPTER 3

Anna Gordon's Quest for Equality

I would like to hear a little more of the inner life of that
dark mother and of the other wandering children. But
here there is scarce a serious word.

—W. E. B. Du Bois, in a review of *Born to Be*[1]

Anna Gordon, a mother of five children, worked constantly to
make a life and a living for her family in White Sulphur Springs, and
this burden was made especially heavy after John Gordon's death in 1893.
As her son Taylor Gordon explained in his 1929 autobiography, *Born to Be*,
"Mother was always hard pressed for money to keep her family going."[2] In
order to earn a living, Anna "took in washing and ironing and worked for
the wealthy people of the town. Washing and ironing were done by main
strength and awkwardness in those days. It was the wash board and irons
heated on top of the range."[3] Additionally, the family purchased water by
the barrel and heated it by burning wood. Her sons "helped haul the water
and helped saw the wood," but the hard work of laundering was Anna's
alone.[4] Anna provided much more than the basic necessities of shelter,
clothing, and food; she also insisted her children receive a proper education and were involved in community activities. Anna's determination
that the Gordon children partake in all that their town had to offer indicates that she would have had to negotiate race relationships—and likely
handle prejudice—and to teach her children to do so as well.

After two years of working away from home at a mining camp in nearby Castle, John Gordon returned to White Sulphur Springs "for a rest," though according to Rose, "he did not rest long." Rather, "Judge Gaddis of Fort Logan and some of the big ranchers wanted him to cook for them on the roundup." John then joined a cattle drive from Fort Logan to Livingston. After his season of working with the cowboys on the roundup, John "decided to go to Alaska, to the gold rush country." Following the mines from one boomtown to another had been lucrative in the past, but when John left home this time, the family "never saw him again."[5]

John never made it to the Alaska goldfields. Instead, he found a job with a Canadian railroad company, working as a chef in what must have seemed like safer and much more comfortable conditions than a frigid Alaskan mining camp. After some weeks passed without hearing from John, Anna came across a newspaper reference to a train wreck in Canada. As Rose would later recall, the family, not sure if John had been on the train or not, "wrote to police in Canada and a man of his description was among the dead." His death occurred just two months before Taylor's birth in 1893.[6] As Taylor later mentioned in his autobiography, "What little I know about [my father] is hearsay, I being the only one in the family that never saw him."[7]

The burden of John's death fell heavily on Anna's shoulders. As Rose described it, "Mother was heartbroken. She was then a widow and had to face the world alone with five children to support."[8] The emotional and economic stability that John provided were gone, and Anna's story throughout the rest of the 1890s was one of toil. She supported her family through a variety of endeavors, such as cleaning other families' houses, taking in laundry, and raising Plymouth Rock chickens and selling eggs and hens. Additionally, Anna—with Rose's help—assisted at private dinners and parties, eventually establishing a successful catering business. By the early 1900s, Anna had opened the Gordon Restaurant and Notion Store on Main Street, and some version of that establishment operated into the 1940s, with Rose taking over proprietorship after her mother's death in 1924. While Anna succeeded in ensuring her family's survival and well-being, this success came at a tremendous physical and psychological cost to herself.

We know some of Anna's story because Rose often wrote about her mother in the letters, columns, and other items that she published in the *Meagher County News* from the 1940s into the 1960s. Taylor also wrote about Anna and his early life in White Sulphur Springs in *Born to Be*. Although Taylor's book provided some of the Gordon family history, famed author and civil rights activist W. E. B. Du Bois remarked in a review that appeared in the *Crisis*, the literary publication of the NAACP, "I would like to hear a little more of the inner life of that dark mother and of the other wandering children."[9]

Reconstructing the "inner life" of Anna Gordon—her thoughts, emotions, feelings, and actions—is difficult. She was born a slave in Kentucky in 1853 and did not learn to read or write until her children taught her later in life. Thus, the sort of documents that might illuminate her inner life are sparse. Only two letters from Anna survive, but those letters, written during the time her husband was away in the nearby mining camp of Castle in 1889, provide some hints about how she responded to life in White Sulphur Springs:

> Dear Husband, I received yours of the 16th. I was glad to hear from you and sorry you are not feeling well this summer. I am tolerably well. The children are well. The Baby creeps a little now and is fat and Hardy. I guess you get tired of hearing of bills but I think I should tell you what I do with the money. Up to the first of May Anderson's bill was 30.00 dollars and I gave them 30.00 . . . and to the Druggist 5.00 and Wash Madison, gave the 5.00.
>
> We have no food bills standing. They are all paid.
>
> I wish something would turn up for you on this side. They say the road will be built to Neihart this Fall. Mrs. Meek is over to Barker. She sends her regards to you. We have had cloudy spells with no rain and everyone predicts a scarcity of everything this winter. No more at present from
>
> Your Affectionate Wife, Anna Gordon.[10]

This letter, written by one member of a couple who had been married for well over a decade and had four children together, seems oddly formal at first, from its "Dear Husband" greeting to its "your Affectionate Wife, Anna Gordon" closing, until one recalls that Anna could neither read nor write yet and needed to dictate her words to another person. Any suggestion of the emotions she might have experienced during her husband's absence is only hinted at in her comment, "I wish something would turn up for you on this side," intimating a longing for his presence. Likewise, her comment about the weather and the potential "scarcity" of the winter signals that she harbored otherwise unstated anxieties. The mention of household expenditures in the letter also suggests the difficulty she experienced paying the household bills and the import she put on keeping up with them.

The "fat and Hardy" baby she mentioned in the letter was their son, George, then just under a year old. The letter references Laura Meek, a local nurse and the wife of Joseph Meek, and Wash Madison. It is unclear why John instructed Anna to give Wash Madison, who worked as a coachman at the Higgins House hotel, five dollars, but the fact that Anna mentions him and Laura Meek in the letter suggests the couple's connections with the town's other Black residents.

John Gordon's desire for news about his fellow African American citizens is also evident in Anna's other surviving letter, dated September 1889, in which she provides him with bits of information about the community:

> Dear Husband, I received yours of August the 25th. It found
> the children well and I feeling some better. I was very glad
> to hear from you and I hope this will find you well. Out of
> the money you sent me I paid Anderson's 21.00 dollars....
> I bought shoes for the three children. I have Robert and Rose
> going to school.
>
> Here the weather is very threatening which makes one think
> of saving something for winter such as wood and vegetables.
>
> We will not need anything to wear after Robert has an
> overcoat.
>
> The Baby crawls where ever he wants to go and is very
> stout.
>
> Mr. Smith gave a Ball last week and Mr. Langham said to
> tell you the Band was improving very much.
>
> Write soon from your Affectionate Wife, Anna Gordon.[11]

This sparse letter tells us something about the African American community in White Sulphur Springs. The Mr. Smith who "gave a Ball" likely was blacksmith Irvin Smith, and Robert Langham (Langhorne) served as the cornet player of the town's "colored" band. The band had made its first public appearance earlier in the month when it played on Main Street before visiting "the houses of the colored people of town."[12] Smith's "Ball" may have been associated with the band's debut. A musician himself, John was certainly interested in hearing about the band's progress.

Anna's comment "I have Robert and Rose going to school" leaves much unstated, as enrolling her eldest son Robert and daughter Rose in the local public school would have been no easy task. The Montana territorial legislature had enacted a statute that required school districts to establish segregated schools for African Americans in 1872.[13] The measure remained in effect through 1895. According to historian J. W. Smurr, "when a colored boy asked to enter the public school" in White Sulphur Springs in 1881, nearly one-third of the town's citizens "threatened to withdraw their children," and the school board subsequently "prevailed on him to withdraw 'until other arrangements could be made.'"[14] In 1883, "four African American students were expelled to preserve the all-white local high school" in White Sulphur Springs.[15] Segregationist principles, however, were difficult to maintain in Montana, in part because some northern Republicans as well as elected officials of both parties "openly criticized segregated schools." Further, the small number of African American children in the state made segregated facilities impractical and expensive.[16]

Around the time of these students' 1883 expulsion, the Montana legislature, as part of a larger bill outlining educational policy, considered eliminating segregated schools in the territory. The *Rocky Mountain Husbandman* of White Sulphur Springs found that "the clause in the bill setting aside the present statutes as to the providing of separate schools for colored children is the most objectionable. It should, and we trust will, defeat the bill." While the paper claimed that all children should be educated, it qualified that assertion by noting "but not in the same school." This segregationist position aligned with the reasoning that school leaders had used to expel African American students. Eventually, *Husbandman* editor R. N. Sutherlin's friendship with the Gordons would result in the evolution of his beliefs about race. In 1883, however, his fears that the "mixture of races in schools will lead to their mixture in families" won out.[17]

Seeing that her children received a good education was of central importance to Anna Gordon. Years later, Rose explained how significant Anna's insistence on a good, public education was. Just months after the U.S. Supreme Court rendered the groundbreaking *Brown v. Board of Education* school desegregation decision in 1954, Rose, prompted by a proposal for a new school building in White Sulphur, sent a letter to the *Meagher County News*. In the piece, Rose presented her mother as a kind of early civil rights pioneer, whose struggles on behalf of her children were part and parcel of a longer battle that countless African Americans fought to secure their right to an education. According to Rose, the proposed new school:

> Brought back to me to the memory of my dear Mamma
> Gordon, who was not able to read or write. She was born
> a slave and all rights were denied her. She put forth a great
> struggle that her children might have an opportunity for an
> education. If she were alive today she would be the first one
> to want a school building. She loved her God, her liberty
> and her children and saw to their education. She worked
> for 50 cents a day in order to make ends meet. She wanted
> others to have the things she was denied.[18]

Rose's statement that Anna "wanted others to have the things she was denied" implies that she played an active role in making sure her children received an education on a par with their white peers. Securing a place for Robert and Rose in the local school may not have been as easy as Anna's statement in her letter to her husband implies. Rose was six in 1889, which many at the time considered the minimum school age, but Robert was two years older, meaning he could have begun school earlier than 1889. The documented history of segregation in Montana's schools might explain why Robert was not in attendance until 1889. It is unclear whether Rose and Robert attended school with the other children or if the district made other arrangements. As Smurr observes, "Whether the colored children were fully integrated" in White Sulphur's schools "before 1895 cannot be ascertained, as the practice of listing 'children of African descent' in the school returns ended in 1882, but the White Sulphur Springs experience was cited by a contemporary Helena newspaper as proof of the existence of segregation in other places, so the presumption is that the board refused to budge for a time."[19] Four African American children from the same family attended the public schools in White Sulphur by 1892.[20] It seems likely that those children were Robert, Rose, John Francis Jr., and George Gordon.

Anna Gordon's September 1889 letter to her husband implies that their children had integrated into the school system earlier than 1892. Although not conclusive, Anna's simple declaration indicates some sort of action took place to break the town's prior segregationist practice. Rose's writings about her school days reference her white classmates at least as early as second grade, so it seems probable that by 1890 the Gordon children were attending school in the same classrooms and at the same time as the other children of White Sulphur.[21] Whether this change came about as a result of a school board decision, Anna's insistence that her children be enrolled, evolving attitudes about race in the community, or the practical difficulties of providing separate facilities and teachers for so few students, remains unclear. Regardless, Rose and Robert were attending school in September of 1889. By 1892, John Francis Jr. and George had joined their older siblings.

The Gordon children thrived under Anna's devotion and advocacy, emerging as contributors to the town's lively community. Newspaper reports on activities sponsored by the school and the Methodist Episcopal Church, one of the first houses of worship built in the town, indicate that Anna Gordon was successful in her "great struggle" to secure religious and educational liberty for her children. The young Gordons seem to have participated on the same footing as their classmates in several activities. For instance, an 1894 announcement in the *Husbandman* of the events scheduled for "children's day services" at the church featured "Robbie Gordon" performing, or perhaps reciting, a piece titled "For We to Do." The same program included "Rosa Gordon" taking part in a "poetical dialogue" with several other girls.[22] Similarly, the December 31, 1896, edition of the *Husbandman* reported, "The Christmas exercise of the Sunday school children in the M.E. church Sunday evening was highly entertaining" and included recitations by "Misses Norma Monihan, Alvia Tullock, Rosa Gordon, Eva Hartfield and Edith Chapin [that] were encored by the large audience." Just a week earlier the newspaper listed a "Declamation" by Francis Gordon in the printed program for the same event.[23] Taylor is the only one of the Gordon children not recorded as a participant in the church's programs, in part because fewer reports of church activities were printed in the newspapers after 1900, when he would have been old enough to perform.

Anna "never missed church on Sunday" and was a "faithful church worker" who saw to it that her children also attended services in the humble brick building.[24] The Methodist Episcopal Church, Rose explained, "was her refuge." Reverend J. Hoskins, an early pastor of the church, baptized Robert, Rose, John Francis Jr., and George on October 21, 1891. The date of the baptism closely followed the death of Anna and John's infant son Arthur Gordon, an event that may have sparked her desire to have the rest of her children baptized together.

Particularly when it came to school and church, the children appear to have received equal access to participate in public performances. The family needed to stay vigilant, however, to ensure that they received fair treatment. The first school-related event that listed the Gordon children as participants was a "Program for School Entertainment, Friday Evening" from 1895 that included instrumental performances, recitations, and singing. The event also featured a play called "The Temple of Fame," described as a "grand affair" with "forty-six characters . . . [each] dressed in a different costume." The play required the costumed students to recite "his or her great deeds" in order to claim the "wreath of fame" as the one "deemed most worthy." Challenging for the wreath of fame were Benjamin Franklin, Robert Burns, Ruth, Cleopatra, Martha Washington, Peter the Great, and Daniel Webster, among other notable historic figures. In this program, the older Gordon children were cast as sidekicks for more significant characters. Rose Gordon was cast as Topsy and thus was paired with Harriet Beecher Stowe, while Robert Gordon played Friday to the drama's Robinson Crusoe.[25] What "great deeds," one wonders, could Topsy have claimed to compare with Ruth or Cleopatra?

It is striking to imagine Rose and Robert playing racialized and subordinated performance roles as Topsy and Friday—a comic fool and a servant—on the public stage as part of a school-sponsored event. From 1890 to 1910, the pages of local newspapers mentioned the Gordon children by name hundreds of times, but this 1895 school-sponsored program seems to be the only occasion when they took on such stereotypical roles in a public setting, leading to speculation about their mother's reaction.

Anna Gordon may have understood why her children needed to take part in this event, but it seems plausible that she knew where to draw the line. After seeing her daughter presented on the public stage at a school-sponsored event costumed as Topsy, Anna Gordon may have protested to the school authorities. While there is no documentation that such an intervention took place, this 1895 "Program for School Entertainment" marks the last recorded instance of the Gordon children performing in racialized roles at a school event. Given her goals for her children, it is certainly possible that Anna Gordon worked to ensure they appeared on equal footing with the white children of White Sulphur Springs and were not marginalized in the public sphere because of their race.

After his performance as Friday, Robert appeared as part of an entertainment event sponsored by the Monday Evening Club, one of the town's self-improvement groups, also known as the Literary Society. According to the program, Robert sang the hymn "Onward Christian Soldiers." The same program, however, listed a farce that included a character called "Gim Krow (colored)" played by the white J. W. Coad in blackface. Though racially insensitive material still appeared as part of public events, when serious parts were available the Gordon children took them—perhaps at Anna's insistence. This practice created a separation between the Gordons and the stereotyped images of Blackness popular in the era. The white citizens of White Sulphur might have enjoyed minstrel portrayals of white stereotypes of Blacks, but the Gordons performed an alternative embodiment of African American identity.

The Gordon children represented their community and expressed its values of education, patriotism, and honesty on the public stage as much as any of their peers did. For a school-sponsored celebration of George Washington's birthday in 1896, Robert recited "The School House and the

Flag" and Francis joined a group of five boys performing a sketch titled "I Would Tell."[26] At the town's 1898 Memorial Day event, Rose took part in a ceremony that began with a march down Main Street, where Joseph Meek served as the standard bearer for a small group of local veterans. Following a performance of the "Star Spangled Banner," Rose contributed a recitation.[27]

The local newspaper's descriptions of the roles played by the Gordon family point to their integration into the public life of the school and town. Among the school-sponsored public performances that they took part in were graduation ceremonies, important community events in small towns. With few students in each class, every graduate contributed an address prepared for the occasion as part of the commencement exercises. Having students deliver public speeches on topics of general interest added an important element to the town's self-image as a developing, progressive, and successful community: "The commencement exercises of the White Sulphur Springs High School which came off Friday evening last, . . . was the principal event of the past week," reported the *Husbandman* in June 1899. The ceremony, the paper added, "was a complete success and entitles the school here to take high rank among institutions of learning of the state." The report lauded each student's address, including Robert's, of which it noted, "Robert J. Gordon (colored) discussed here the practical question of 'Getting On in the World.' In this he showed originality and confidence in his own ability and acquitted himself splendidly."[28]

In a community that celebrated musical, theatrical, and athletic performances, the Gordons must have stood out for their frequent participation in all of those activities. Their involvement in the public sphere also extended beyond school and church to the town's many self-improvement groups. Rose as well as Robert took part in the Monday Evening Club. The *Husbandman* regarded the club so highly that it both reported on the previous meeting's activities and printed the events scheduled for the next week. On April 7, 1898, the newspaper noted that the club's regular slate of readings and recitations concluded after "Rosie Gordon sang a solo."[29] Throughout the several years that the literary society was active, Rose and Robert continued to sing, recite literature, and take part in debates and sketches.

Rose offered recitations and made other contributions to the March and April meetings in 1898. At the April 14 meeting, Rose appeared with the other "little ones," who performed recitations "with zest and animation."[30] Rose also gave recitations at a Memorial Day celebration and as a participant in "Children's Day" at the M.E. Church.[31] Robert Gordon "delivered a splendid recitation" at a January meeting of the Monday Evening Club the next year.[32] He continued to be a central contributor throughout the rest of the year, appearing at multiple meetings.[33] Rose's participation became more centered on her vocal skills, as she performed solos on several occasions.[34] As the *Husbandman* described one of her performances, "Rose Gordon's song of an inebriate's waif was catchy and loudly applauded."[35]

While Robert and Rose, in particular, excelled in music, theater, and athletics, George also received his share of acclaim in the newspapers, eventually appearing alongside his siblings. For instance, in 1902 the *Husbandman* reported the following: "Miss Rose Gordon and brother, George, are making decided progress in singing. Miss Rose sings soprano and George sings tenor. They appeared twice recently with success."[36]

There were limits to the Gordons' inclusion, however. The arrangement of the town's self-improvement societies made its class divisions particularly visible, as Rose would experience on multiple occasions. In 1899, the *Rocky Mountain Husbandman* clearly described the hierarchy of the town's self-improvement culture:

> Literary attainments of our town are receiving quite a rubbing up. The people, that is, we mean the society people, are plunging into the study of authors, stories and poems with the wildest enthusiasm. . . . These discussions alternate between three literary institutions of the town—the married ladies' society; the young gentlemen and young ladies' society and the public society, which meets every Monday evening under the name of the White Sulphur Springs Literary Society. The last-named institution gains much benefit from the other societies, which are not public, but many of the valuable papers are produced in the public assembly.[37]

While Robert and Rose participated in the public literary institution, there is no indication that they were allowed to join the "society people" who belonged to the private clubs. The various private organizations in White Sulphur—the lodges, athletic clubs, shooting clubs, and whist clubs, all of which were organized and maintained by white residents— did not seem to include the Gordons or other African American residents in their activities.

This does not mean that the Gordons were not in any way associated with community events in which whites predominated. For them, work— not enjoyment—was the constant backdrop of these public events. Around the turn of the century, Anna started a catering business, initially working at the behest of the town's elite when they had larger parties that required additional help. In time, Anna became the primary caterer for home parties, weddings, and balls, as well as for various events held at the town's auditorium. The catering business had its own travails. As Rose would later recall, the "real society" women would bring back plenty of fine dining ideas from the East. Those latest ideas meant more work for Anna and Rose, who often assisted her mother, in the work that private and public events created. "Miss Mamie Guitman" went to Boston every year "and brought back the latest in serving," Rose remembered, adding in an editorial aside, "What a headache."[38]

The other family members contributed to the household economy in other ways. When Taylor was old enough, he joined with his brothers to help the family by going hunting. Though George was never the most athletic of the brothers, he turned out to be a skilled fisherman. In addition to helping her mother cater for social events, which Rose did from an early age, she "always stayed out of school on Mondays" to aid her mother with the laundry, even though that meant falling behind in her studies.[39] Rose also worked as a babysitter, earning a dollar a night. While work cut into her education, babysitting added to it in other ways: "I went to homes where they had such wonderful books. I would read and they always left fruit and food for me to eat."[40]

By joining her mother in doing the work other women could afford not to do or could afford to pay others to undertake, Rose was able to observe the more privileged members of town society through a transactional lens. Rose and her mother participated in many of the town's turn-of-the-century social events, many of which took place in the town's auditorium, experiencing them from both an inside and outside perspective. Both her own and Anna's experiences shaped Rose's memories of White Sulphur Springs in the 1890s. Decades later, Rose's writing would provide a unique take on the history of the community in terms of not only race but also class and gender. Rose, as she often did in the pages of the *Meagher County News*, made clear the role that social class played in White Sulphur's early years. Both of the town's newspapers reported on high society events and the doings of the town's elite, but Rose's history tells a fuller story. She described White Sulphur as a "cultured Cowtown" where music was so important that the town's population of only eight hundred managed to have "10 grand pianos" among them.[41] In particular, the way citizens used the town's auditorium underscored the class distinctions and inequality that the newspapers' other contributors ignored. Taylor and Rose both noted the town's division of its citizens into the "high" and the "low" classes. Social activities similarly fell into categories of "haves" and "have nots." In an interview for a 1957 *Meagher County News* retrospective on R. H. Sutherlin, a major figure in local history, Rose pointed out the town's central divide: White Sulphur Springs "was a town of class distinctions," one "of formal balls and formal 12-course dinners" that excluded the less fortunate. For example, Rose remembered, "When Ernest Krumpe [the son of a prominent businessman] came home from the Spanish American war, the town tendered him a banquet with 500 persons seated and served in the auditorium."[42]

While White Sulphur Springs hosted formal twelve-course dinners and diverse musical performances, the town also offered gambling, drinking, opium smoking, and prostitution—activities that Taylor highlighted in *Born to Be*. Other Montana towns provided a similar range of entertainment in the nineteenth century. Within a year of its founding, the mining camp of Virginia City, for example, "was staging amateur theatrical performances and had organized a lyceum committee to engage touring musicians and lecturers," historian Joseph Kinsey Howard notes. Howard adds, "None of these innocent pursuits threatened the favorite position of gambling as a pastime or the dominant popularity of saloons."[43] The early settlers of Virginia City pursued both cultured civilization and unfettered vice, and White Sulphur Springs followed suit.

Higgins House exemplified this duality. Under its original owner, the dining room offered French cuisine, and subsequent owners added on a saloon and billiard parlor to appeal to a wider clientele. "In those days gambling was wide open," Rose explained in a 1963 article, "and the town was a lively place. Cowboys would ride in from Rock Creek, ride into the saloons on horseback and order a drink." She described the role Higgins House played in the town's social culture: "The hotel not only stood as a memento of the wild and wooly west, but an age of culture which existed here at one time. There were many distinguished guests registered at the hotel, from many foreign countries. They came to bathe in the spring water and gaze upon the beauty of Smith River valley. The hotel at that time was a place where grand parties were held."[44] From ladies and gentlemen in full evening dress attending gala events to cowboys riding their horses into saloons and ordering drinks without dismounting, the White Sulphur Springs of Rose's childhood had an ample amount of both virtue and vice.

By the turn of the century, White Sulphur was in the midst of a mining boom and offered eight saloons. Taylor observed in *Born to Be* that each saloon "had a gambling room."[45] Several brothels operated just downhill from the Gordons' house. Both Taylor and his brother George did odd jobs for the town's sex workers, carrying messages for them and supplying them with drinking water. Working as a "page" at Big Maude's Palace of Joy and wearing a blue suit with brass buttons supplied by Big Maude herself, Taylor witnessed many of the town's elite paying the brothel a visit.[46]

While the hotels, saloons, restaurants, and brothels offered social opportunities to visitors and residents alike, the Auditorium was the center for White Sulphur's large social events, many of which were elaborate affairs put on by and for the social elite. Rose and Anna attended almost every event that took place in the Auditorium, sometimes as members of the audience or as guests, but more often in Anna's capacity as caterer. Anna Gordon served the first supper given in the facility, as well as many suppers thereafter, including the New Year's Eve ball celebrating the arrival of the twentieth century. The *Husbandman* promoted this event, saying, "Mrs. Gordon will set a delightful luncheon of bread, butter, ham, pickles, cake and hot coffee for the ballgoers Friday evening at 25 cents each. . . . It will be well worth the money."[47] Anna knew much more about etiquette than many of the attendees of these private parties, and Rose remembered how some guests "would come to the kitchen and ask Mamma what to do." Although Rose admired the "linens, silverware, Haviland china, and cut glass dishes" that local and visiting socialites insisted upon using for fine dining on the frontier, she did so from a critical perspective, observing, "All this meant work, especially when you were shining up for a party."[48]

Reporting on a holiday ball sponsored by the Athletic Club, one of the town's elite social organizations, the *Meagher Republican* relayed that the club "is very grateful to those who helped the cause along by the purchase of tickets." They also offered thanks to many others who helped make the ball a success, including musicians and square dance callers, while singling out "the excellent supper served by Mrs. Gordon, assisted by her daughter, Miss Rose. . . . It was a veritable holiday feast, dainty and replete with innumerable good things."[49] When Rose recalled such events in her pieces for the newspapers, she sometimes echoed their views but often pointed out elements of these events that the newspapers failed to cover. Whereas the *Meagher Republican* described this event as a "dainty" feast, Rose detailed the hard work that took place behind the scenes.

For instance, the Auditorium, in addition to being overly large and expensive to build and maintain, had never been completed. One victim of the budget was the ceiling. One year, a rowdy local fired his pistol into the attic from the stage on New Year's Eve without damaging the ceiling because, as Rose noted, "it was never quite finished."[50] The size of the building combined with the unfinished ceiling made it impossible to heat effectively. Temperatures inside the structure were often not much warmer than the weather outside, although when Richard Ringling purchased the building, he tried to solve this problem by raising a circus tent inside.[51]

Cold or not, Anna Gordon cooked a midnight supper for one hundred people, all seated on the stage, for several of the New Year's balls. In 1905, the *Meagher Republican* reported, "On the outside of the 'big barn' the mercury went down to the forty [below] mark, while on the inside in close proximity to the red hot stoves the temperature was somewhere in the vicinity of zero." The article took special note "of the supper [for which] we have only words of praise. Mrs. Gordon is unsurpassed in her ability as a cook and caterer. It was no fault of Mrs. Gordon's that coffee was in greater demand than ice cream that night."[52] In an early draft of Rose's book manuscript, "Gone are the Days," she described the same event, observing that her "hands got so cold that I could not take money." The coffee "started to freeze in the cups," and "the joke of it was we had ice cream on a night like this." She then added, "I froze my feet going home and had a lame joint for many years."[53] Rose and her mother worked hard to survive, and throughout her writing Rose noted the toll exacted on their bodies.

Over time, the endless labor destroyed Anna's health. Rose put it bluntly: "Mamma carried on this hard work for years. She developed rheumatism from cold and exposure. She became quite lame in her feet. Walking to and from work was hard for her... [and] she became so lame for a while she could not got out to parties but did her laundry at home." When Anna took up catering work again, George and John Francis Jr. were old enough that on "cold winter nights" they could "go and get Mamma and haul her home on the large sled."[54]

Though physically demanding, the work that Anna and Rose performed was considered women's work. By taking on the appropriately gendered tasks—such as entertaining, childcare, and housekeeping duties—that the town's wealthier women outsourced to other women, Anna Gordon found an economic and social niche in White Sulphur Springs that provided economic stability for her family. Historian Glenda Riley has examined the types of work deemed appropriate for Black women in the West, noting, "Most commonly, black women worked as domestics in western areas," even when white women who worked outside their own homes "began leaving domestic work for retail, sales, and clerical work as well as the professions." For white employers, hiring Black women for domestic labor as cooks, washwomen, and maids seemed to be "logical and appropriate derivations of the roles black women had fulfilled as slaves."[55] However, "despite the odds against black women progressing very far beyond employment as domestics," Riley asserts, there were nonetheless cases where "black women earned reputations as skilled workers when they carried their domestic talents out of the home and into the public arena."[56] Using the avenues available to her, Anna Gordon did much the same.

With five children to provide for, Anna was in the difficult position of desiring higher social status while simultaneously having to participate in the town's underground economy of vice in order to make ends meet. Out of necessity, she offered her aid to the town's sex workers and to the down and out and itinerant, while still performing laundering, housekeeping, and catering services for the town's elite. "There were all kinds of women" working in the brothels, Rose recalled, "some handsome and others not so handsome." Regardless, "they would dress like queens and look like pictures." Rose remembered in particular one woman named Dolly, whom she described as "the most beautiful woman I ever saw." Rose's writing, however, offered insight into these women's lives beyond their appearances. They would often "come to buy eggs and chickens" from Anna. When they arrived, "Mamma always sent me out of the room," most likely to give the women free rein to talk, as "they always had troubles to tell."[57] The prostitutes sought out Anna's advice on matters of the heart and family concerns, but they also sought her out for medical cures and as a fortune teller, as Anna sold folk remedies and insights into the future. Taylor wrote that his mother "had a marvellous occult sense."[58] The women often "came up for Mother to tell their fortune with cards or tea leaves. She earned lots of money at that."[59] As a testament to Anna's capacity for empathy, when it came time for her to lend a sympathetic ear to another's troubles, she seemingly made no distinction between the rich and the poor, the women who worked the brothels, and those who returned from Boston with new ideas for setting tables. For the Gordon children, interaction with individuals at both the top and the bottom of town society became a central fact of their childhoods.

As they did about the town's economy of vice, the *Husbandman* and the *Republican* largely ignored the brothels and the women who worked there. Taylor, on the other hand, painted them as larger-than-life figures, colorful Western characters leading adventurous lives, selling their bodies but also surviving on their wits. Whereas Taylor romanticized the lives of the sex workers and the town's newspapers ignored them, Rose told a bleaker story that expressed her awareness of the costs of that particular branch of women's labor. She remembered, for instance, one woman called Morphine Ollie: "One day she came to our house to buy eggs. It was summer. She had on short sleeves. There was not a spot on her arms that had not been pierced by a hypodermic needle. I was young and asked her how she hurt her arms. She began to cry and told me she was a fiend. She said to me, don't ever be a fiend."[60] In considering the prostitutes, Rose pragmatically observed that while they may not have been a "moral asset" to the town, they played an important commercial role. The women were, after all, "great spenders," and "merchants missed their trade" when the brothels closed. Rose pointed out the hypocrisy of this turn of events, noting that valuing commerce over morality "has been the main thing since I have inhabited this 'pig iron world.'"[61]

Already marginalized by race, Anna Gordon found herself pushed to the economic margins after her husband died. The respectability and the financial stability that her husband's steady employment had provided no longer protected the family and necessitated that she expand her resourcefulness in order to maintain their well-being. Anna wanted her children to have an easier life than she had, and she desired to attain for them a kind of middle-class social status. Employed as a laundress and as a caterer for the wealthier families of White Sulphur Springs, Anna found in those families a model of respectability that she wanted for her children as well. The family's participation in the town's improvement activities, such as the literary society, was an important symbol of that status. As the *Rocky Mountain Husbandman* observed of one particularly well-attended event, "Among the audience were noticed many of our most prominent citizens and among those who took part were many of the children of the leading families."[62] Among the performers were Rose and Robert, who utilized their vocal, musical, and recitation skills to take their place on stage among those "children of the leading families."

Anna's devotion to her children's well-being went beyond ensuring their survival, and the physically demanding labor that she undertook on their behalf eventually took its toll on her. After a decade of back-breaking toil, Anna embarked on a new economic venture, opening her own store and restaurant in White Sulphur Springs. Her children helped out when they could, even though they kept busy making their own marks on the community. Both Anna's and Rose's standing in the town would grow in the decades that followed. Upon Anna's death in 1924, following years of failing health, the *Meagher Republican* both lamented the loss and celebrated her contributions to the community: "Mrs. Gordon has been a resident of White Sulphur Springs for forty-one years, and was a woman known in all the older homes in the town, where in many instances she ministered in sickness. She was universally respected and was a woman of unusual intelligence and force, as was evidenced by the large number of people who turned out to pay their last respects."[63] Rose, who lived out her life in White Sulphur Springs, would carry on her legacy.

CHAPTER 4

Casting Down Their Buckets
in White Sulphur Springs

A ship lost at sea for many days suddenly sighted a
friendly vessel. From the mast of the unfortunate vessel
was seen a signal, "Water, water; we die of thirst!" The
answer from the friendly vessel at once came back,
"Cast down your bucket where you are." A second time
the signal, "Water, water; send us water!" ran up from the
distressed vessel, and was answered, "Cast down your
bucket where you are." And a third and fourth signal for
water was answered, "Cast down your bucket where you
are." The Captain of the distressed vessel, at last heeding
the injunction, cast down his bucket, and it came up full
of fresh, sparkling water from the mouth of the Amazon
River. To those of my race who depend on bettering
their condition in a foreign land or who underestimate
the importance of cultivating friendly relations with the
Southern white man, who is their next-door neighbour,
I would say: "Cast down your bucket where you are"—
cast it down in making friends in every manly way of the
people of all races by whom we are surrounded.

—Booker T. Washington[1]

In "My Mother Was a Slave," a story Rose Gordon published in
the *Meagher County News* in 1955, she recalled a day during her
childhood when "a man drove up to the house with a load of wood and
started to unload it." He kept unloading even after Rose's mother explained

that she hadn't ordered any wood, and the man revealed to her that C. H. Sherman had sent the wood. "Dear Mamma came in the house, sat down and cried," Rose remembered. Sherman also "let the boys have a cow to milk so we had all the milk and cream we wanted."[2] Like the ship lost at sea in famed African American educator Booker T. Washington's allegory, the Gordons "cast down their bucket" in White Sulphur Springs, cultivating friendships, building community, and weaving their lives into the fabric of the town.

On September 18, 1895, while the Gordon family was still adjusting to life without John, Booker T. Washington delivered an address upon the opening of the Atlanta Cotton Exposition that catapulted him to national fame. His autobiography, *Up from Slavery*, followed in 1901 and cemented his status as a national race leader. Indeed, for much of the early twentieth century he was the most famous Black man in America. His exposition speech outlined the essentials of Washington's philosophy of "cultivating friendly relations with" one's neighbors, even if such friendliness meant compromising on seemingly essential rights such as voting, equal access to education, and civic equality in general. "Cast down your bucket where you are," Washington advised African Americans, rather than seeking to escape inequality in the South for the possibility of a better life elsewhere. "Cast it down in agriculture, mechanics, in commerce, in domestic service, and in the professions," he added. "No race can prosper till it learns that there is as much dignity in tilling a field as in writing a poem. It is at the bottom of life we must begin."[3]

In the speech's central metaphor, Washington observed, "In all things that are purely social, we can be as separate as the fingers, yet one as the hand in all things essential to mutual progress." Washington was willing to accept segregation "as separate as the fingers" as long as white Southerners would help Black people make some kind of economic progress. "Cast down your bucket," Washington enjoined white Southerners, "among those people who have, without strikes and labour wars, tilled your fields, cleared your forests, builded your railroads and cities, and brought forth treasures from the bowels of the earth." Washington's own Tuskegee Institute, as well as similar schools offering industrial education to African Americans and some Native Americans, aimed to teach the vocational skills necessary to create a readily available and tractable Black labor force during a national wave of labor unrest among white trade unionists.[4]

Critics referred to Washington's speech as "the Atlanta Compromise." W. E. B. Du Bois, another leading Black thinker of the time, memorably assessed Washington's approach in *The Souls of Black Folk* (1903), praising his dedication to thrift and patience but also adding, "But so far as Mr. Washington apologizes for injustice, North or South, does not rightly value the privilege and duty of voting, belittles the emasculating effects of caste distinctions, and opposes the higher training and ambition of our brighter minds,—so far as he, the South, or the Nation, does this,—we must unceasingly and firmly oppose them."[5]

As these national figures debated the best path for African Americans to take in order to survive, progress, and prosper in the new century, the Gordon family likewise developed strategies for thriving in a predominantly white society. By the end of the nineteenth century, many of their Black friends and neighbors had left White Sulphur Springs or were aging. The first few years of the twentieth century saw the deaths of longtime Meagher County residents Joseph Meek, John Wilson, Caesar Fields, and Irvin Smith. Although African Americans continued to live in the town, there would never again be a Black community as stable and active as there was from the late 1880s through the 1890s. Instead, every African American who came to Meagher County after the turn of the century eventually moved on, often to cities farther west where Blacks had greater opportunities.[6]

By casting down their bucket in White Sulphur Springs, Montana, the Gordons might not have exactly brought up buckets of the proverbial "fresh, sparkling water," but they did discover it offered them the means to make a home and to belong to a community where they could thrive. Undoubtedly their success was hard earned, especially after John Francis Gordon's death, but they were fortunate in where they had chosen to make a life. Dropping a bucket in the waters of many places in America in the late nineteenth century would have yielded an unpotable mix of racism, restriction, and violence, but White Sulphur had promise, and there the Gordons seized the opportunity to build a life for themselves.

The Gordons followed Washington's philosophy by "making friends in every manly way of the people of all races by whom we are surrounded."

They nurtured sustaining friendships with other African Americans in White Sulphur Springs and throughout Meagher County. Cultivating relationships with their white neighbors was also important, as those relationships contributed to the family's economic well-being and social standing. While Anna Gordon's culinary skills certainly contributed to her success, she also used her extraordinary people skills to build a successful business, the Gordon Restaurant and Notion Store.

The Gordons operated within an ever-present set of social limitations and expectations for African Americans.[7] In *Building Houses Out of Chicken Wings: Black Women, Food, and Power*, Psyche A. Williams-Forson writes that whereas "black men were considered a major threat to white American society" in turn-of-the century America, "images of black women as mammies, cooks, and caretakers were perceived as the salve to sooth the burdens caused by a burgeoning new society."[8] Focusing specifically on the stereotypical connections between African Americans and chicken consumption, Williams-Forson points out how Black women exploited those stereotypes for their own benefit: "Throughout Reconstruction and well into the twentieth century, black women continued to cook as well as sell chickens out of economic necessity," but, in so doing, "the trading and selling of these foods for commerce also provided relative autonomy, social power, and economic freedom."[9] The willingness of white Americans at the turn of the century to associate African Americans with a particular set of occupations made Anna Gordon's decision to emphasize her culinary skills as a means of establishing herself a strategic one. When Rose Gordon started advertising special chicken dinners at her restaurant in the 1920s, she would follow in this tradition, using the associations her white customers held about African Americans and poultry to build her business.

Anna Gordon's story seems to provide some evidence of Washington's claim that the "individual who can do something that the world wants done will, in the end, make his way regardless of his race."[10] She provided a service that her community desired, did it well, and, in the end, made her way in the world. For Anna to succeed, she had to "do something the world wants done," and her community had to allow her to provide that service. Even though the Gordon Restaurant placed her in direct competition with white business owners, the citizens of White Sulphur Springs provided sufficient patronage for her business to survive.

That was not the case everywhere in Jim Crow America. Many African Americans who could have done "something the world wants done," especially in the South, were rewarded not with success but with boycotts, burned businesses, violence, and even death. For example, in her scathing attack on late nineteenth-century lynchings in Tennessee, journalist Ida B. Wells-Barnett described case after case of Black individuals who could "do something well" but were instead murdered in public displays sanctioned by prominent white community members. In 1892, for instance, three Black businessmen in Memphis were lynched after opening a grocery store that competed with local white merchants. When Wells-Barnett wrote an editorial in the *Memphis Free Speech* denouncing the murders, a white mob destroyed the newspaper's office.[11] Wells-Barnett had put down her bucket in Memphis, but unlike the more fortunate Gordon family, she pulled up toxic mob violence.

This is not to say that White Sulphur Springs was not without prejudice, but the white townspeople appear to have been more flexible in their racial attitudes than whites were in many other parts of the country. And White Sulphur Springs was not the only Western town that accommodated Black citizens, nor was it the only one where several Black families settled and succeeded. In the biography *Showman: The Life and Music of Perry George Lowery*, Clifford Edward Watkins demonstrates that the Lowery family, Black settlers in the late nineteenth century in Eureka, Kansas, found an acceptance similar to that the Gordons experienced. Positive news items about the family appeared frequently in the *Eureka Democratic Messenger*, which also closely followed the rising career of the Black cornet player and bandleader P. G. Lowery. Eureka's tradition of acceptance dated back to before the Civil War, when it was an abolitionist stronghold. Those attitudes carried over into the postwar era.

Despite such progressive sentiments, Eureka maintained a segregated cemetery. Because of such practices, the family cemetery on Lowery's homestead was expanded to provide a burial site for other Black families who settled in Eureka. According to local lore, however, P. G. Lowery's stepmother was buried in the cemetery that locals generally reserved for whites.[12] Eureka's cemetery demonstrates that openness and prejudice could exist simultaneously in Western communities, which accepted some Black individuals as citizens and neighbors and excluded others. Like the Gordons, the Lowerys were perhaps particularly talented at cultivating good relations with their neighbors, which undoubtedly aided in their social and economic success. The fact that they were skilled musicians who regularly performed at town functions may have been a key factor in the town's willingness to accept them into the community.

Like her mother, who treated people kindly and received kind treatment in return, Rose Gordon was skilled at cultivating good relations with her neighbors. In the histories of White Sulphur Springs that she published in the *Meagher County News* and in her memorial tributes to the various citizens of the community, Rose documented her appreciation for the small acts of neighborly kindness that traditional histories often ignore: the care a neighbor put into tending her garden, the gift of apples during a harsh winter, the sympathetic word shared when one was needed. Building relationships with their neighbors helped the Gordons thrive as accepted members of a predominantly white community.

Several white residents of White Sulphur Springs and the larger Meagher County played important roles in the lives of the Gordon children. Newspaper editor R. N. Sutherlin created opportunities for Rose and Robert to participate in the town's literary and cultural events. B. R. Sherman assisted the Gordons in multiple ways, and his son, C. H. Sherman, offered Taylor the chance to become the cowboy he dreamed of being as a teenager. Margaret Coates of Martinsdale, who employed Rose to help care for her child, opened her home and library to Rose, while her sister-in-law, author-editor Grace Stone Coates, became Rose's lifelong friend and mentor.

Eleanor Armstrong Brewer had perhaps the most significance in the early lives of the Gordons because she brought them into the town's performance culture, providing them with music lessons and putting them on stage. As the African American citizens of Meagher County knew, participating in the local musical culture was an important way of establishing community belonging. Eleanor Armstrong arrived in White Sulphur Springs "to teach public school and give private musical instruction in the community," giving up a career as a concert pianist to do so.[13] She later married James Scott Brewer, who had founded Brewer's White Sulphur Springs, in 1892. He remained there after selling his interest, operating a successful livery and feed stable and one of the stagecoach lines. Brewer apparently still cut an imposing and attractive figure at the time of his marriage to Eleanor Armstrong, thirty-five years his junior. Their wedding brought out the descriptive best in R. N. Sutherlin, who reported that the day "dawned bright and beautiful and scarcely a speck of cloud fringed the horizon. There was an unusual bustle about our town, carriages and buggies flying every direction, and at half past nine o'clock the Presbyterian church, which had been decorated for the occasion, was well filled." The bride "was beautifully attired in a gray traveling suit while the groom wore black of a deep blue cast." James Brewer, Sutherlin continued, "has resided here almost continuously, and his genial social disposition and his manly, upright business characteristics has won for him the highest esteem of this entire community. The ROCKY MOUNTAIN HUSBANDMAN extends congratulations and trusts that every day of a long life may be bright and happy and full of pleasure as the marriage morning."[14]

Eleanor Brewer, who had been Rose's second grade teacher, gave up her teaching duties after her marriage. Leaving teaching allowed her to resume her performance career, and she frequently directed theatrical and musical events at the Auditorium. She also continued to teach piano to Rose privately. Rose exchanged services for her lessons, initially by helping with the Saturday afternoon cleaning and later by babysitting for the Brewer children, Ruth and Grayce, who like their mother became lifelong friends and correspondents of Rose's.[15] Brewer's daughters followed their mother into musical careers, with Ruth performing for a number of years billed as a "one-woman orchestra," displaying her versatility by playing multiple instruments ranging from banjo to trombone.[16] Brewer also taught and performed with the other Gordons, particularly George and Robert. She was a frequent duet partner of Robert, who played violin or viola.

During Taylor and Rose's childhood, the Brewer family made important contributions to White Sulphur Springs's remarkable performance culture, which also included mandolin orchestras, duets, solos, brass bands, and theatrical productions. Taylor Gordon's career grew out of this culture, as music and singing were central activities for his siblings and the townspeople in general. He was not the only resident to rise to national prominence as a singer. Kathryn Janie Sutherlin, daughter of the editor of the *Rocky Mountain Husbandman*, sang with the Chicago Civic Opera Company as a mezzosoprano, and the three Brewer women similarly became nationally known performers.[17]

The spectacularly talented Brewer girls' early performances in White Sulphur Springs sparked a statewide concert tour, which they followed with a national tour. The *Rocky Mountain Husbandman* reported that six-year-old "Grace Brewer will please the audience Saturday evening with her own compositions, as did the great Mozart in the seventeenth century, and if she continues to improve and develop as she promises she may in time be scarcely less renowned."[18] Even for the *Husbandman*, which was often hyperbolic in its view of the talents and prospects of the town's citizens, this was high praise indeed. Gifted with perfect pitch, Grace amazed the crowds by identifying each note played on a piano, even writing out whole songs on a chalkboard as they were performed. Her sister Ruth added dramatic readings, dancing, and singing.[19]

Sometime before 1910, the Brewers left White Sulphur Springs for Lewistown, where Eleanor worked as the music superintendent at the high school and led an all-woman orchestra. After their move, the Brewer women dedicated themselves to their musical careers. Beginning in 1911 and continuing well into the 1920s, the Brewer Musical Entertainers performed on the Red Path Chautauqua circuit, appearing in over ninety cities and towns each year. Grace Montana Brewer—the "Rocky Mountain Gem," as she was described in publicity materials—performed on violin and trombone, while sister Ruth Marea played piano and clarinet and gave dramatic readings. Eleanor managed the two star performers and provided their piano accompaniment.

The Gordons' friendship with the Brewers offers insight into the types of interracial friendships the family maintained in Meagher County. As a young man, James Brewer had worked as an overseer of enslaved people at a planation in Virginia.[20] How that affected his later attitudes toward African Americans is unknown, but the Gordon family's friendship with the

Brewers clearly centered on the Brewer women. Eleanor played several roles in Rose's life, serving first as her teacher, then as her employer, patron, and friend. Their shared interest in music, combined with Rose's fondness for children—especially girls, whom she claimed didn't have to work through the same "nonsense" that boys did—and willingness to provide childcare for the Brewers, created a bond between the two women. In keeping with the popular performance practices of the day, however, Eleanor was interested in and adept at performing racial masquerade. In what might seem an odd juxtaposition, at the same time that she was developing deep and enduring friendships with the Gordons, she also engaged in minstrel versions of Blackness onstage.

Married to the town's founder and prominent businessman, Eleanor Brewer had a high social standing among the town's elite. Thus, she participated as a guest at society events such as the town's New Year's Eve "Masque Ball." At the 1893 ball, "Mrs. James Brewer took the part of 'Topsy' and her antics were always attracting attention . . . and she even carried it out to walking with one foot turned over. . . . Her peculiar gait, adopted for the occasion, was stunning."[21] By the mid-1890s, Brewer had earned a national reputation as a songwriter, producing songs such as "Society Sam" and "Why Can't Girls Whistle." Her biggest songwriting successes, however, drew on popular racist tropes: "A Bad Nigger" and "De Hebbenly Heel" became popular minstrel songs, with the former performed by Richards and Pringle's Famous Georgia Minstrels, one of the earliest established "colored" minstrel groups.[22]

For the Gordons, succeeding in White Sulphur Springs meant being "agreeable" enough to play the minstrel role, dancing "jolly miggles" and performing the cake walk—a plantation-era dance that was appropriated by the minstrel shows—on request. It also required putting up with white neighbors pretending to be Black while acting out white stereotypes about African Americans. Racial masquerades of all sorts featured prominently in the town's social life, as they did elsewhere in America during this era. For the annual Masque Ball, the majority of participants chose "ethnic" costumes, with Irish and Asian stereotypes competing with blackface costumes. For example, the list of costumes for 1897 includes those for the following roles: "Daughter of Erin," "Squaw," "Shamrock,"

"Spanish Dancing Girl," "Nigger," "Jap," "Coon on Duty," "Coon off Duty," "Hot Coon," "Irishman," and "Ireland's Bonnie Son."[23] While serving ham, pickles, coffee, and ice cream to the ball-goers, Anna and Rose had to tolerate and interact pleasantly with their neighbors as they played "Nigger" and "Coon" roles with blackened faces.

The white citizens of White Sulphur Springs depicted Blackness not by imitating the work ethic and dedication to family demonstrated by their actual African American neighbors, but by performing such onstage antics as stealing chickens and singing songs about "Miss Ambolina Snow—the boys all love her so"—actions that reinforced white stereotypes about African Americans.[24] The town's athletic club, which sponsored the ball, also became a key sponsor and source of performers for a series of minstrel shows that Eleanor Brewer staged around the turn of the century. As part of the advertising for the event, the *Rocky Mountain Husbandman* reported, "Some onery [sic] coon broke up a prayer meeting by throwing a chicken at the congregation. Come see how it is done at the Auditorium July 4." The program for the minstrel show listed three acts containing performances of such songs and sketches as "Old Kentucky Home," "Little Alabama Coon," "The Parson in the Pulpit," "Pass Dat Bread," as well as Brewer's own "A Bad Nigger." The program concluded with a "Grand Cake Walk" in which couples paraded one by one while performing a high-stepping dance.[25] In the next issue, the *Husbandman* praised the production, saying, "The camp meeting, introducing guitar, banjo and vocal solos, also the chorus by company, reminded one of the genuine old southern darkies when religion takes hold of them."[26]

Did the town's white residents really think that the antics of their white neighbors, faces blackened, were reminiscent of "genuine old southern" African Americans? They certainly did not seem to question the appropriateness of those roles or the feelings that their celebration of the "Old South" might engender among their Black neighbors. Many of the performers were members of the town's elite, making them Anna Gordon's employers and patrons. Whatever feelings she might have had about seeing them capering on stage in blackface she had to keep to herself as she prepared to serve them refreshments. In her newspaper letters, Rose mentioned the minstrel entertainments, but emphasized the "fine voices" in the community back in those days, sidestepping the issue of blackface and tactfully—or tactically—ignoring the racist songs they performed.[27]

The enthusiasm for blackface entertainment that swept White Sulphur Springs around the turn of the century coincided with the disappearance of authentic Black performance in the town. By then, the "colored" brass band that the community had enjoyed in the early 1890s had dissolved, and nationally renowned groups such as the Fiske Jubilee Singers and the Midland Jubilee Singers, both of whom had performed there in the past, no longer visited the town. Rather than the serious presentation of spirituals, an authentic African American art form, the townspeople watched blackface performances based on white stereotypes of Blacks. In this way, whites pretending to be Black replaced a genuine African American performance culture in the town's public sphere and in popular imagination.

Although the Gordons still appeared in public as performers, they did not do so as self-consciously Black performers, as the town's cornet band—with their new uniforms and flashy bandwagon displaying a sense of racial pride and community belonging—had in years prior. Before the Panic of 1893 led to a downturn in the local economy, African Americans had participated in the public sphere as African Americans while forging an identity both as town members and as members of a particular ethnic group. Their public appearances evinced their pride in belonging to both groups, of participating in and contributing to local culture through distinctively Black activities such as singing spirituals. By 1900, however, "coon songs" had replaced spirituals, and blackface had eclipsed Black performers.

Adjusting to their white neighbors' newfound enthusiasm for performing in blackface, the Gordons took on non-racialized roles. Certainly, Robert J. Gordon's appearances debating the merits of the resolution "that the average young man of today has greater opportunities to make his life a success than his forefathers" with W. E. Harris in 1899 or singing "Onward Christian Soldiers" at the Monday Evening Club entertainment in 1900 seemed a far cry from minstrel show "stump speeches" and "Bad Nigger" songs.[28] That Robert took the negative in the debate, arguing that the forefathers of "the average young man" had greater opportunities, suggests that the race of the debaters was of no consideration. Robert, as an average young African American man, might have struggled to argue that his enslaved ancestors lived in a land of opportunity. Instead, Robert positioned himself as a raceless American citizen for the sake of this debate.

A talented musician, adept public speaker, and remarkable athlete, Robert was the most celebrated Gordon at the turn of the century. Taylor described in *Born to Be* an average evening in the Gordon household, where the family gathered in a front room:

> Sis reading the news, Bob, my oldest brother, playing the violin, banjo, Duolyne harp, or some other musical instrument from Sears, Roebuck and Company. (He had a mania for all new musical instruments. The more freakish they were, the better he liked them. But his best holt was the fiddle that he managed to play good enough to earn money with, playing for dances.). . . . We could hardly get into the place for musical instruments—piano, bass viol, horns—oh! I can't name them all. And drums too.[29]

Robert was perhaps even more versatile in sports than he was as a musician. Robert's presence meant that White Sulphur Springs fielded interracial athletic teams. The box score between two local baseball teams listed Robert as playing left field in a game that his team won forty-four to six. As the *Husbandman* reported, the two pitchers on the losing team were "each batted all over the prairie," especially in an eighteen-run ninth inning. Robert himself scored four runs and contributed on defense. "Features of the game," the paper noted, "were the pulling down of skyscrapers by Lincoln, Gordon and McCarthy."[30]

Robert's many talents featured prominently in the *Meagher Republican*'s account of the "Celebrated Glorious Fourth" of 1904, which they deemed "certainly a hummer this year and no mistake." Robert won the event's 220-yard foot race "by several feet," earning a $5.00 prize, and took "second money," or $2.50, in the 100-yard dash. Regarding the latter result, the writer suggested that "Gordon had previously expended some energy in the 220-yard run which probably contributed to his defeat." Yet running two races did not prevent Robert from pitching for the town's baseball team and doing so "at his best and [holding] the visitors down at critical stages of the game." To top off his athletic performances, Robert then demonstrated his musical skills, playing violin with the accompaniment of pianist Eleanor Brewer at the evening dance. For Robert, this Fourth of July was "certainly a hummer" indeed.[31] The public acknowledgment of his talents earned him, and by extension the Gordon family, a solid standing in the community.

Among his other athletic accomplishments, Robert excelled at bowling, and the local newspapers marveled at his success. "Robert Gordon made the remarkable score of 264 at the bowling alleys New Year's day. Three hundred is the largest possible score." Robert's score, the *Husbandman* continued, easily beat the previous alley record of 246. From the first day of the bowling alley's operation, Robert became associated with the new facility as both a skilled bowler and an employee of owner Frank Phelps: "The Phelps bowling alleys are now open and ready for patronage. The alleys will be under the care of Mr. Robert Gordon, and patrons are assured of prompt and courteous treatment at all times."[32]

Like Robert, the other Gordon children distinguished themselves in multiple ways that affirmed their membership in the community. In a letter to the *Meagher County News*, Grayce Brewer Allen remembered that when her mother, Eleanor, resigned from teaching, she "became active in putting on plays, musicals, dances, etc. in the Auditorium to help Bob Sutherlin pay for the building." Eleanor Brewer taught a large number of students, but Grayce recalled that "Rose and Bob Gordon were among the ones that will always be remembered vividly. Bob played so many instruments. He was a real genius. Then Rose and Georgie used to sing duets together. They enjoyed it and so did everyone." Nonetheless, she added that "strange as it may seem—Taylor never sang at that time. He may have been too young."[33]

Taylor had less of a presence in the White Sulphur papers than Rose, George, and Robert in part because he was uninterested in the kind of school-related activities those outlets provided. Not coincidentally, Robert, Rose, and George finished school, whereas Taylor did not. Like his brother John Francis Jr., who had "got cowboy-crazy and quit school," young Taylor wanted to be a cowboy.[34] By the time he was a teenager, though, he seemed to have found his own place in the community. In

1908, the *Meagher Republican* included an item noting that "C. H. Sherman, the cattle king of Smith river valley, started his herd for their summer range on Sheep creek this week, accompanied by Emanuel [*sic*] T. Gordon mounted upon the bob-tailed gray and followed by the faithful Teddy."[35] The next week's edition provided an update from Sheep Creek: "The cattle king, accompanied by Emanuel Gordon arrived Wednesday for the purpose of branding cattle."[36] Taylor seemed on his way to becoming a cowboy.

Although Rose was not the athlete her brother was, she was also an important figure in turn-of-the-century White Sulphur Springs and participated in key community events. She considered her 1904 graduation among the most significant events in her life and made strategic use of the occasion to assert a public identity inclusive of her African American roots. She was late finishing school, already in her twenties when she graduated, as years spent helping her mother make ends meet had prevented the timely completion of her degree. Rose nonetheless held the honor of being the valedictorian, and her commencement oration "On the Progress of the Negro Race" was a watershed event for the community. Rose was presented as both a symbol of African American achievement and a sign of White Sulphur Springs's social progressiveness.[37]

Friends and neighbors who witnessed Rose's oration mentioned her performance at this event for decades to come. In a letter to Rose in 1968, Dr. R. T. O'Neill wrote, "Nellie Stevenson, wife of Ike, used to tell me of the fine speech you made when you graduated from school there." After Rose's death, Laura French, in a letter of condolence to Taylor, remembered, "I can still see her as I did the night she graduated from high school. She was the only one who knew her essay by heart, and what a wonderful delivery. I was so impressed."[38] Grayce Brewer Allen, writing to the *Meagher County News* in the wake of Rose's death, recalled, "I remember when she graduated. I was about six years old and the graduation was held at the Auditorium. I do not recall who else was in the class, but I do know that Rose was the only one who recited her speech. She had the whole thing memorized and stood like a queen—confident, relaxed and beautiful."[39]

Rose was not as relaxed as she appeared, although her recitations with the Literary Society had prepared her well for public speaking. In "Gone are the Days," Rose notes that Caesar Fields, the elderly Black man who had thrilled and terrified the young Rose with his stories of life under slavery, inspired her to speak on the "Progress of the Negro Race." Fields's stories, Rose explained, "filled my heart with love for a down-trodden race"—a race that Rose herself belonged to. Despite her assertions of equal treatment in While Sulphur Springs during her youth, her description of the days leading up to her speech reveal an anxiety that stemmed from her sense of her own racial difference, perhaps compounded by the content of her speech, which drew direct attention to that difference.

Rose later wrote that when a teacher informed her that she would be the class valedictorian, her response was tempered by her awareness of being Black. "I did not say anything about it as I was the only colored girl in the class."[40] Her comment suggests that Rose sensed a contradiction between being valedictorian and being "the only colored girl in the class." Her silence on the matter may also have reflected her fear that others would protest her elevation to valedictorian, despite being based on her own academic achievement, over her white classmates. Rose's description of herself as no different from her fellow white citizens and her coinciding sense of distinct racial difference are unreconciled throughout her writing. Her awareness of her Blackness in a white community and her certitude regarding her equal treatment may have been an important coping strategy that helped her survive and succeed in this small Montana town.[41]

Memoirists construct themselves as autobiographical subjects through generic conventions, the vocabularies of selfhood available at their given historical moment, and the models of other autobiographers. In her reflections on her own life, Rose clearly used Booker T. Washington as a model on several levels, including as a "great man" whose story inspired imitation and as an influence on her understanding of race. *Up from Slavery* helped Rose place the meaning of her own oration into the larger context of both her life history and the progress of African Americans. Her graduation speech borrowed heavily from the events and the argument outlined in *Up from Slavery*. In depicting the story of her commencement speech in "Gone are the Days," Rose used Washington's narrative of his most famous oration, the Atlanta Cotton Exposition speech, as a model for building suspense.

"I felt a good deal as I suppose a man feels when he is on his way to the gallows," Washington wrote in describing his emotions as he journeyed to Atlanta to make that historic speech. He understood that the occasion marked "the first time in the entire history of the Negro that a member of my race had asked to speak from the same platform with white Southern men and women on any important National occasion."[42] Rose similarly described the anxious days leading up to her graduation oration, suggesting that the silent acceptance of her status as valedictorian pushed her into "a tight place." She recalled her emotions at the time, saying, "When I looked thru [sic] the curtain and saw the crowd, I was as nervous as a cat." Although Rose's memorization of her speech awed Grayce Brewer, Rose downplayed that aspect of her performance in her memoir. "As it was hard for me to see at night, unless the light was just right," she claimed, "I committed My Oration to memory, and had nothing to worry about except stage fright."[43]

Her anxiety paralleled Washington's storytelling, as his own unease at speaking before a large assembly of mostly white people provided Rose with a structure for understanding her own situation. The nervousness she described served as a literary device, and Rose's echoing of Washington's description of his own anxiety appears to be additional homage to his story. In contrast to other moments when Rose stood on stage, as with the Monday Evening Club, the fact that this time she planned to address issues of race was sufficient cause for apprehension. Like Washington, she stood before her fellow citizens as a "representative of Negro enterprise and Negro civilization" and used the occasion to both praise the progress of the African American race and "to say something that would cement the friendship of the races."[44] She also, like Washington, rose to the occasion in that moment. With a yellow rose in her hair and wearing a black silk lace dress made for the occasion by several of the women of the town, it is no wonder that Grayce Brewer wrote that she "stood like a queen—confident, relaxed and beautiful," even if in her own mind she was "nervous as a cat."[45] Unlike Washington, however, Rose did not express concern about how the white and Black listeners might interpret her speech in different ways. Nonetheless, her graduation oration marks one of the few moments where racial difference is brought to the forefront in her memoir, aware that she was asserting a Black identity in front of an audience.

By the time of Rose's graduation, the *Meagher Republican*, which had been suspicious of public schools and statewide efforts to professionalize public school teaching, had become one of their biggest boosters. The newspaper's politics may have shifted under the leadership of attorney Max Waterman. Having effectively run the *Rocky Mountain Husbandman* out of town by that time, the *Republican* no longer needed to take the opposite side of whatever issue the *Husbandman* advocated. The front page of the January 1, 1904, edition of the *Republican* was dedicated to "our public schools, which today rank among the very best of public schools in the state," and which are "fully equipped with modern apparatus and good library."[46] That year, the schools served a total of 226 children, and although the *Republican* broke that group down by age and sex, it did not mention race as a demographic category, although four of the five Gordon children were enrolled at the time.

In reporting on the 1904 commencement, the *Republican* observed that the ceremony rewarded the students for their "years of training in the public school [where] they have acquired the habit of industry and earnest individual devotion to the acquirement of their ambitions." The students would then not "rest idly" but "by persistent individual effort win success." The article noted that "the public school of today is a source of pride and gratification to the people of this community," particularly because "it was not many years ago that the scholars were crowded in a small and uncomfortable room, and the faculty consisted of one faithful teacher. There was no prescribed course of study, consequently little progress was made."[47] In the midst of both the transformation in primary and secondary education and the boosterism touting the town's progressive environment, Rose Gordon completed her final year of high school. Even given that context, it is still surprising to see a newspaper devote so much of its front page to Rose's valedictory address.

The paper dedicated its culminating description of the commencement speeches to that of Rose Gordon, who earned the reporter's highest praise: "One of the best orations of the evening was that by Miss Rose Gordon upon 'The Progress of the Negro Race.'" The article added that her "manner of delivery and handling of the subject was almost above criticism." Whereas the *Republican* quoted only a sentence or two from each of the other orations, a long quotation from Rose's speech took up an entire column:

> The fate of the black man was indeed a sad one, having been captured and dragged from their native homes on the dark continent, were driven to the coast and sold like cattle to brutal task masters, and were lashed with the blacksnake whip, leaving stripes upon them as deep as they were cruel in the sight of God. As said by the governor of South Carolina, "We owe an obligation to the black man. We brought him here; he served us well, we cannot forget his fidelity and we ought not to magnify his faults."[48] No human being ever rose on stepping stones of the dead to higher things, and no people can. The white man in the south can never attain his fullest growth until he has done absolute justice to the negro. The effect of slavery on the south made white people indolent and in some cases brutal. It retarded manufactories; their lands became worn out, and it discouraged education and enlightenment. The colored race accumulated the astonishing amount of wealth of $800,000,000 in farms and other property, while 43 years ago they did not possess their own person; and they have progressed in all lines of modern advancement. They possess many eminent men—eminent in art, law, literature, medicine and theology. As two colored statesmen I shall mention Bruce and Douglas; as colored educator, Booker T. Washington; as poet, Dunbar. The people of the colored race have shown themselves worthy of enjoying the full rights and citizenship of this country. They have fought and died for their country in the Civil war, the Indian war, and the Spanish-American war. The colored soldiers have won unstinted praise for their bravery, loyalty and fidelity. They have indeed been baptized into full citizenship by their blood shed in the defense of their country, and have earned the protection of that honorable emblem—the stars and stripes.[49]

Rose's arguments are familiar, particularly to anyone who has read Washington's *Up from Slavery*, and admirably condensed and forcefully presented here. Notably, she closed her oration with stirring patriotic sentiments. The "honorable emblem—the stars and stripes," plays on the imagery of whipping earlier in the oration, with the "stripes" of the dawning new age no longer a sign of cruel treatment but rather its opposite, the protection of full citizenship. Her comment that "the white man in the south can never attain his fullest growth until he has done justice to the negro" implicitly contrasted South and West, suggesting that in the West, civilization could indeed progress in ways unavailable to the rest of the country, which had yet to right its wrongs.

In reviewing over a hundred years of White Sulphur Springs's newspapers, I have not encountered another example of a high school commencement address receiving the kind of attention and accord given to Rose's speech. It is a truly remarkable and extraordinary moment in Montana's history. What is most notable is the placement of an African American member of the White Sulphur Springs community on center stage, not as an entertainer or athlete, but as a symbol of her own intellectual success as well as the community's progress toward the "Negro race." The narrative of progress offered in Rose's speech parallels the story that White Sulphur Springs consistently told itself through the pages of the *Rocky Mountain Husbandman* and the *Meagher Republican*. Rose served as the exemplar of the community's progress in avoiding many of the worst interracial problems elsewhere in the country. As the product of White Sulphur's new educational system and as a validation of the time, effort, and money put into that system, she also represented a "source of pride and gratification to the people of this community."[50]

After graduating, Rose relied on the friendship she had cultivated with Eleanor Brewer for her lengthiest exploration of the world outside her hometown.[51] Grayce Brewer recalled, "Rose was always dear to my mother and in 1904 when we moved to Lewistown, my mother got Rose a position with Mrs. Hoffman so they could be near."[52] Rose worked as a clerk in the Hoffman House hotel for six years, from 1904 to 1910, during which time she lived near enough to the Brewers that she could continue taking piano lessons from Eleanor. As devoted as she was to her family, she must have enjoyed the experience of being freed from caring for her mother and younger brothers and having an opportunity to live independently.

Even while Rose was working in Lewistown, she made frequent trips home to see her mother, coming by a combination of railway and stagecoach. First, she rode the reliably unreliable Jawbone Railroad one hundred miles to Dorsey, a stage stop near Ringling. From there, Rose took a twenty-mile coach trip to White Sulphur. "If you were a few days late" on the Jawbone, Rose later described, "it was quite alright and if the train ran off the track they would get a section crew and put it back on track and you were on your way again." Train travel on the Jawbone required both patience and courage: "You never heard of such a thing as blood pressure in those days," Rose later commented.[53] Though she ultimately chose to return to White Sulphur Springs permanently, her friendship with the Brewers helped her imagine other possibilities for her life.

During the span of time that the Gordons and the Brewers became friends, Rose met the Coates family of Martinsdale. This, too, proved to be an important and lasting interracial friendship that expanded Rose's world. Rose first became acquainted with the extended Coates family through William and Margaret Coates and their daughter Marion, who was born in 1900. Margaret suffered from debilitating headaches and employed Rose to help with housework and to take care of Marion, whom Rose adored and described as "sweet and angelic" despite her fondness for making mud pies while wearing white dresses.[54] As Rose described it, she was "what they now call a babysitter. But to me the babysitting sounds mechanical for I loved all the children I cared for."[55]

Through Margaret, Rose met Grace Stone Coates, then a teacher, and the two women remained friends for many decades. Born in Kansas in 1881, Grace Stone attended the University of Chicago before moving to Stevensville, Montana, where she and her sister, Helen, worked as teachers. In 1904, Grace moved to a teaching position in Butte, and six years later she married Henderson Coates and moved to Martinsdale, Montana, where Henderson operated a dry goods store with his brother John.[56] Grace taught in the Meagher County school system from 1913 to 1917 and later served as the county superintendent of schools.

Rose described Martinsdale as "a little town on the Milwaukee Railroad, thirty miles from White Sulphur Springs" and "surrounded by cattle and sheep ranches." An isolated railroad stop might seem an unlikely place to base a literary career, but Grace Stone Coates managed to build a successful life in letters there nonetheless.[57] Between 1926 and 1931, Coates published more than a hundred poems and stories. In 1927, she joined with H. G. Merriam as an assistant editor of the literary journal *The Frontier*, based at the State University of Montana in Missoula. Her well-regarded novel, *Black Cherries*, was published by Knopf in 1930. She also wrote articles for Montana newspapers and served as the Martinsdale correspondent for the *Meagher Republican*.

Grace Stone Coates would play an important role in the family's life for years to come, both as an early advocate of Taylor's singing career and, in time, as Rose's mentor. In the 1950s, Grace encouraged Rose's writing, suggested possible publishers for Rose's memoir, "Gone are the Days," and ultimately urged Rose to pursue newspaper writing as an outlet for the material from the unpublished manuscript. Rose's stories, she proposed, could be broken up, revised, and shaped for publication as columns and letters rather than as a complete book. She also encouraged Rose to go beyond the material in "Gone are the Days" and to say more about her own life story, saying, "Rose: Why don't you write—your true story, the bad and the good; a true life story. . . . You are overlooking a bet if you don't put your story on paper. I'll help you get it into print, a true bit of Montana."[58]

CHAPTER 5

Gone are the Days

White Sulphur Springs in 1910

Rose aspired to be a doctor, "but as I had no money I did not dare to think of it."[1] After the short stint of employment in Lewistown following her high school graduation, she enrolled in the nursing program at St. Peter's Hospital in Helena, but she had to abandon her training when Anna became ill in 1910. Living at home allowed Rose to care for her mother and help with the Gordon Delicatessen and Notion Store while her mother got back on her feet, even if it meant putting her own dreams on hold.

In many ways, 1910 was a wonderful year for White Sulphur Springs—an *Annus mirabilis*, the citizens thought. The town had witnessed many changes during the first decade of the twentieth century. For instance, the first graduating classes from the newly enriched public school system reflected the progressive changes taking place in the community. Nothing symbolized progressive change, however, like the arrival of the railroad, which generated optimism for a grand future for White Sulphur Springs. While many of the area's residents embraced the new decade and all its promise, Rose saw 1910 as the beginning of the end of the community she had known as a child. The year of Rose's return was also the year of Taylor's departure. His decision to leave signaled the future of the Black population in White Sulphur Springs: African Americans from all over

Montana would soon leave for elsewhere. At the same time, the loss of the town's older generation of African Americans created a void in the once vibrant Black community.

Without a doubt, the arrival of the Ringling Brothers—John, Charles, Otto, Alf T., and Al—in 1910 marked a moment of major change in Meagher County. The brothers had purchased the Barnum & Bailey Circus in 1907, and they now controlled the two largest touring circuses in the country. With the increasing fame and fortune that followed, John Ringling began seeking out other investments, buying stock in Madison Square Garden and acquiring properties throughout the United States. Both John and Charles, who often traveled with the circus, had their own private railcars. Because train was his preferred mode of transportation, John also built short-line railways.[2]

As Henry Ringling North writes in *The Circus Kings*, since John "routed the circus, he was as familiar with rail systems of the United States as a spider with its web," and would occasionally "discover a missing link that might be forged with profit."[3] Ringling found just that in White Sulphur Springs, forming the Smith River Development Company and bringing the area its long-predicted, long-promised railroad. In 1910, after purchasing some seventy thousand acres of adjoining real estate, he built a twenty-mile line between White Sulphur and the town of Broken Jaw, "whose grateful inhabitants," according to North, "rechristened their town Ringling—a great loss of picturesque nomenclature, but very gratifying to Uncle John." With "his usual geographical exactitude," Ringling named the line the "White Sulphur Springs and Yellowstone Park" railroad, a name that some joked was longer than the railroad itself.[4]

The citizens of White Sulphur Springs were ecstatic. The *Meagher Republican* devoted its September 2, 1910, issue of the paper to the town's brilliant future. The railroad, the paper argued, would bring an "influx of settlers" and "the coming of capital," as well as "the immediate development of the opportunities which have been so long neglected," particularly the town's potential as a tourist resort "advertised from coast to coast" for its healing mineral hot springs, which "German experts" had declared "superior to the Carlsbad caverns."[5] White Sulphur Springs seemed on the verge of an explosion of development.

Several land companies formed to capitalize on the expected growth. The Conrad-Stanford Company advertised real estate offerings in what the company called the "Carlsbad of America or Baden Baden of the Western Hemisphere" and declared the area "the nearest approach to the fountain of youth ever discovered by man." With a "Health Record Unsurpassed by any Spot on Earth," how could any wise investor pass on buying property in White Sulphur Springs?[6] The *Republican* predicted that an increase in tourism because of the railroad would result in more people seeking to settle permanently in the town and taking advantage of undeveloped agricultural land in the Smith River valley.[7] The flagging mining industry would also no doubt be revived.

R. N. Sutherlin, now publishing from Great Falls, could only watch from an envious distance, but he remained loyal to White Sulphur Springs. "We have just seen Joe Meeks (colored), the discoverer of the famous Joe Meeks mine at Barker," the *Husbandman* noted in April 1910, and "Mr. Meeks says the old town is booming. Thousands of acres of land are changing hands and people are pouring into the valley like fun."[8] The "dear old town," as Sutherlin frequently called it, "is going to hum."[9] After decades of predicting a railway arriving in White Sulphur Springs, Sutherlin could finally report without hyperbole that the project "is progressing and everything is looking well. The palmy days when White Sulphur Springs was the boom town of Montana have returned."[10] Later in the year the paper noted, "The dear old town of White Sulphur Springs was linked with the rest of the world in iron bands, . . . [and] we rejoice with the people there that the railroad, after nearly a third of a century waiting, has arrived."[11]

On October 30, 1910, the town held a massive parade and party to celebrate the completion of the twenty-three-mile-long White Sulphur Springs and Yellowstone Park Railway that connected the town to the Milwaukee Road at Ringling and, thus, to the wider world. Local leaders even invited "dear old friend" R. N. Sutherlin to drive the gilded spike celebrating the completion of the line.[12] The day also marked a visit by Eleanor, Grayce, and Ruth Brewer to their hometown. Eleanor's all-woman Brewer Orchestra joined with the all-male Culver Orchestra, also from Lewistown, for the occasion. The *Republican* reported of the performance that "it was a unique sight to see women taking their place beside men, and rendering equally good service on wind instruments." What better way to celebrate the triumph of progressive values in White Sulphur Springs than this shared public performance on the bandstand.

After enjoying the orchestral performance and listening to speeches by various celebrities and officials, the eight hundred people gathered at the event then witnessed a street parade organized for the occasion. This "representation of the 'old' and 'new' life of our community" was led by a group of cowboys, "followed by the band, then the freight outfits, the old Concord coach, the old steam woodsaw engine, and such other familiar signs common to the era just closed."[13] The parade closed with representatives of the new order: automobiles, trucks, and "other modern conveniences."[14]

The procession made literal the march of progress from old ways to new without expressing much sorrow for "the era just closed." Noticeably absent from this celebration of a new era was the elegiac mood that often accompanied later depictions of such symbolic moments: the arrival of "the machine in the garden," the harbinger of the fall of Paradise, or the close of an earlier era of frontier freedom. Instead, the community celebrated modernity as exemplified by the railroad and the presumed prosperity that would follow. Only Judge Cheadle, in his post-parade address, acknowledged that he "thought the railroad was not an unmixed blessing, that its advent would mean altered conditions not quite so pleasing to the older residents." The *Republican* framed Cheadle's remarks as an example of the "very amusing" qualities of his speaking style. Such notes of ambivalence did not match the newspaper's celebratory tone on what it called "this day of rejoicing."[15]

Ultimately, White Sulphur Springs continued to thrive, but as a small Western community rather than as the Carlsbad Caverns of Montana. The population did not "triple," as the *Meagher Republican* predicted. A mining boom did not follow the railroad, nor did the railroad bring more settlers or more visitors than already visited the town. Further, automobiles had already made White Sulphur Springs more accessible, with or without rail travel, thus undermining the perceived importance of the Ringling spur line. But in 1910, the town was full of optimism and excitement about its future.

In contrast, Rose's written reflections on the period do not celebrate the end of the era that resulted in a "day of rejoicing" in White Sulphur Springs in 1910. While looking back during the mid-twentieth century to the White Sulphur Springs of her youth, Rose Gordon often struck a melancholy tone in her tributes to "the grand old pioneers." The wistful title she used for her unpublished memoir, "Gone are the Days," exemplifies the sense of loss she witnessed as the community embraced change. For instance, Rose noted in her later writings that the departure of the *Rocky Mountain Husbandman* and editor R. N. Sutherlin had a negative impact on the town. The auditorium that he built, which was so central to the town's social life and to the Gordon family, fell into disrepair. To Rose, both Sutherlin and the Auditorium were "grand old timers" of sorts. The community's loss of these cultural anchors was emblematic of the changing, but not necessarily better, times in White Sulphur Springs.

In 1957, the badly deteriorated auditorium, which the *Meagher County News* described as "a wreck and soon to be a memory," was scheduled for demolition. The *News* used the occasion to reflect on Sutherlin's contribution to community life: "Sutherlin had tremendous love of the west, and visions of what it might become. . . . Sutherlin's dream was to provide a fit setting for music and art."[16] To a certain extent, that dream had been realized in the early days of White Sulphur Springs. But to Rose, such visible symbols of the pioneer settlers she celebrated no longer represented the possibilities of the future, but the failures of the past.

Rose had already paid tribute to the editor of the *Rocky Mountain Husbandman* long before the Auditorium was demolished. According to her, Sutherlin "wanted so much to see White Sulphur Springs become a beautiful little town. His effort failed and he moved to Great Falls but his heart was always here." Of the critics of Sutherlin's vision, she wrote, "So many strangers would ask why he built an auditorium in so little a town as this. I will tell you. Why, Mr. Sutherlin loved everything that was beautiful; the opera, literature. . . . People only made fun of him but not I. I was very young but loved the valley and wanted it to build up to a beautiful little town."[17]

Even a cursory glance at the *Husbandman's* pages clearly shows Sutherlin's vision of White Sulphur Springs as "a beautiful little town." The newspaperman had advocated tirelessly for the town's economic, social, and cultural progress, most notably through his support for educational reform. Even after the *Husbandman's* heated rivalry with the *Meagher Republican* essentially forced it to move to Great Falls in 1903, Sutherlin continued visiting and documenting daily life in the town for years.[18] "When he visited White Sulphur Springs," Rose described, "he always called on my dear mother and her family for he knew we appreciated the great effort he had put forth," both for the town as a whole and specifically regarding the Gordons. "The last time he came he was growing old," Rose wrote. She recalled his despair: "He wept like a child for he had not been happy in his new home."[19]

Sutherlin's tears and Rose Gordon's sympathetic regard for his failure to see his vision realized may have had more to do with twentieth-century race relations than with the delayed arrival of the railroad. During its twenty years of publication in White Sulphur Springs, the *Husbandman* regularly reported on the daily activities of the town's Black citizens, a rarity in Western newspapers. Sutherlin's friendship with the Gordon family was evident, as their activities—especially the accomplishments of Robert and Rose—appeared frequently in the paper. Even if Sutherlin's vision of what White Sulphur Springs could be was not quite multicultural, he nonetheless saw its African American residents as integral and integrated members of a thriving and accepting community. Such integration served as further evidence of the town's progress and made Montana different from the parts of the country that the Western pioneers, Black and white, had left behind.

By 1910, the town's remaining African American pioneers were an aging group, and the county was suffering an economic downturn that adversely affected both its Black population and the progressive ideals that had made the late 1880s and early 1890s the high-water mark for White Sulphur's African American community. Following the Panic of 1893 and the subsequent economic depression, references to Meagher County's African American citizens become fewer, suggesting that they in particular suffered from the economic slump. Meagher County in general reeled following the panic. As historian Marilyn McMillan explains, "White Sulphur Springs especially felt hard times because of the silver depression, particularly in the silver mining area north of the town. The resources from which the springs resort had hoped to draw on were gone: between 1890 and 1900, the county's population had declined to barely half its former size."[20] By 1900, Robert Langhorne had moved out of Meagher County altogether and was residing in Libby, in the far northwestern corner of the state. Other individuals mentioned often in the early 1890s newspapers— such as George Mason, Ernest Penny, and Wash Madison—had seemingly left Montana altogether or may have passed away by then.

In the early twentieth century, the *Husbandman* and the *Meagher Republican* detailed the impoverishment, illness, or death of the town's Black pioneers whose deteriorating health combined with general economic hardship contributed to waning Black participation in the town's public and cultural life. Millie Ringold fell on hard times shortly after the Panic of 1893. The county commissioner minutes record the following petition on her behalf: "A letter from E. R. Carroll was presented to the Board stating that the destitute circumstances of one Millie Ringgold [*sic*], a resident of Yogo, and the need for assistance. The Board instructed the Clerk to notify and authorize E. R. Carroll to purchases supplies of Chas. Lehman at [Utica] for her."[21] Although that assistance helped her survive, she was admitted to the county poor house on October 14, 1898. Likewise, John Wilson, the "enterprising gardener," managed to take care of himself until he was admitted to the county poor house on April 19, 1901, where he died just a few days later, on April 23.[22] The *Republican* reported in 1904 that seventy-five-year-old Caesar Fields, meanwhile, "died at the poor farm," where he "had been an inmate of the hospital for several years."[23]

Various newspaper reports noted the deteriorating physical and mental health of Irvin Smith, who was eventually "ordered confined to the state asylum at Warm Springs."[24] Ten years after the *Rocky Mountain Husbandman* published a glowing tribute to Smith on the occasion of his sixty-fifth birthday, his remarkable history as a Western pioneer seemed to have been forgotten, and he became just another inmate committed to the Warm Springs asylum.[25] According to the institution's records, Smith was committed because of "dementia" on December 6, 1907, and he died shortly thereafter, on December 21. His age at the time of death, according to the Warm Springs records, was ninety.[26] His son, Lee, continued to live in Meagher County with his family, but by 1910, Lee and his family had left White Sulphur for Harlowton, about sixty miles to the east.

In fact, most of the African American population of Meagher County had either shifted to Harlowton by 1910 or passed away. Belle Price, whom the 1900 census indicates operated a laundry in White Sulphur Springs, had also been admitted for a period to the county poor house by 1905. Although she remained in the county after her release, she, too, moved east to Harlowton by 1910, where she continued to work as a laundress.[27] Aside from the Gordons, Joseph and Sarah Meek were the only early Black settlers remaining in White Sulphur the year the railroad arrived. After Joseph died in 1912, however, Sarah moved to Helena.[28]

While the 1910 census recorded the high point in both the county and the state's African American population, what followed was a precipitous decline. The otherwise progressive decade heralded repressive changes for African American citizens in Meagher County and across Montana. Although Max Waterman, editor of the *Meagher Republican*, celebrated Booker T. Washington's visit to the White House in the pages of his newspaper, state representatives in Helena expressed fear of the possibility of racial integration and began instituting a series of laws that made it clear that Montana was no longer friendly territory for African Americans. In response, Blacks voted with their feet and began an exodus from Montana that has not been reversed.

Undoubtedly, the political changes in Montana's relationship with its African American citizens, such as a 1909 law prohibiting interracial marriages, contributed to Montana's declining Black population, as the more hospitable atmosphere of the late nineteenth century gave way to a political situation that reflected the deepening segregation of the country. Similar population changes occurred in nearby states as well. Wyoming's Black population grew from 940 African American residents in 1900 to 2,235 in 1910, but that number dropped sharply to 1,375 by 1920. North Dakota's Black population similarly fell from a peak of 617 in 1910 to nearly half that number by 1930. Only Idaho and South Dakota showed slight increases in Black population by 1920, and in both states, the numbers had dropped significantly by 1930.

As historian William Lang observes, however, there was "no single cause for the decline" in Montana's Black population. Unfriendly laws and an increase in discriminatory actions certainly contributed to that decline, but so too did World War I and the drafting of African American Montanans. Additionally, Lang speculates, it was "likely that blacks in Helena responded to the lures of war-related jobs in the Midwest and on the Pacific Coast."[29] Quintard Taylor writes, "By the second decade of the twentieth century, the center of African American life in the West was urban."[30] If African Americans living in Montana were on the move after 1910, that pattern was reflected nationally in Black population growth in cities such as Los Angeles, Denver, Omaha, Seattle, Tulsa, and others through the 1910s, 1920s, and 1930s.[31] Although the entire Gordon family was living in White Sulphur during the 1910 census, it was the last year all the family members were in one place. John Francis Jr., who had grown tired of the Montana winters, soon departed for Seattle. He never returned to White Sulphur Springs, not even for a visit. In 1919, George moved to Bozeman, where he lived and worked for the rest of his life.

Taylor could not wait for R. N. Sutherlin to "drive the gilded spike" that completed the spur to White Sulphur Springs. He had the "travelling blues," and he realized that he was not going to find the cure by waiting for the train to come to him.[32] On September 11, 1910, more than a month before the long-awaited railroad reached White Sulphur Springs, Taylor boarded a train bound for St. Paul carrying forty dollars and a cheap suitcase. He was on his way to the big city where Minnesota businessman L. N. Scott, one of Ringling's investors in the land company, had agreed to hire Taylor as his personal chauffeur.

Of the Gordon children, only Robert never left White Sulphur Springs to try his luck living elsewhere. Perhaps, like Rose, Robert remained because he felt a responsibility for taking care of their elderly mother, or he may have stayed because White Sulphur Springs was home. He appeared to remain a popular figure in the town, continuing to excel in athletics, especially bowling, and the newspapers continued to note his presence and activities. He participated in a "bowling contest pulled off at the alleys on Christmas day between the married men and the town boys," with the boys defeating the men, led by unmarried Robert's 179.[33] At twenty-seven,

Robert was hardly a boy, and his presence on the "town boys" team rather than the married men's team points to the limits of social integration in the town. While he participated in social activities, he did not necessarily do so as a peer.

Around the time of Rose's high school graduation, the paper reported, "A large party of young folks, on pleasure bent, stole a march on Ernest Abbott Saturday night at his spacious bachelor hall on the east side. . . . Mr. Abbott and Robert Gordon played the violins, accompanied by Miss Tillie Zehntner on the piano."[34] The context suggests that Robert was part of the "large party of young folks," especially as he performed as part of a trio that included the party's host and another guest. In any town, such social gatherings would be a respectable place for single men and women to get to know one another and for romantic alliances to be formed or further developed. Yet Robert's status at this and various other social gatherings is ambiguous. Was he there to earn money with his fiddle, as Taylor put it in his memoir?[35] Or was he there as a member of a group of friends? Whatever might have been the case, by 1909, legal efforts to forbid mixed relationships made the possibility of Robert being perceived as an eligible bachelor by his fellow partygoers even more unlikely. Without a doubt, after 1909, Robert would have been legally excluded from marrying most of the women of White Sulphur Springs solely because they were white. While interracial marriage would have been a social taboo before that year, the new anti-miscegenation law—titled "An Act Prohibiting Marriages between White Persons, Negroes, Persons of Negro Blood, and between White Persons, Chinese and Japanese, and making such Marriage Void; and prescribing punishment for Solemnizing such Marriages"— elevated the informal restriction to the category of legal prohibition.[36] "Montana has joined the Jim Crow Colony alongside of Mississippi, South Carolina, Texas, and Arkansas," wrote Joseph P. Bass, editor of the *Montana Plaindealer*, a weekly African American newspaper published in Helena. "God Help Us" was the *Plaindealer*'s headline when the law passed.[37]

By 1910, the closest young African American men and women would have been either sixty miles east in Harlowton or sixty miles west in Helena. The Gordons remained connected to those Black communities.

The *Montana Plaindealer* published occasional news about the Gordons, indicating that as the Black population dwindled in Meagher County, the family had reached out to members of Helena's Black community. "Mr. John Gordon of White Sulphur Springs," the *Plaindealer* reported in 1910, "was over on a business trip last week."[38] The newspaper noted the same year that "R. J. Gordon writes that he will be over from White Sulphur Springs to attend the fair."[39] Although Robert was the only sibling who did not live away from White Sulphur Springs for an extended period, he made frequent trips to Helena as a young man and was active in one of the Helena lodges for a time.

If the Gordon siblings had any interest in dating, they would have had to leave White Sulphur Springs to do so. George had several girlfriends over the years while living in Bozeman, which had a larger Black community. Robert, and for the most part Rose, stayed in White Sulphur Springs, and neither seems to have had any romantic relationships. Remaining in a town without a Black population beyond their family meant being single for the rest of their lives.[40] Not much information exists regarding John's life after he moved to the West Coast, as he was not much of a correspondent, and his extant letters are mostly from late in his life. None of the Gordons married, and although Taylor and George had relationships with women, none of those relationships resulted in marriage or children.

Taylor was a romantic, and much of *Born to Be* involves stories of his often ill-fated relationships. Rose, on the other hand, seemed ambivalent about marriage. "I have never had the heart to take the ship that sails out on the sea of Matrimony," she wrote in "Gone are the Days," adding, "from the time I was a young girl, there was always someone telling me, Your freedom is worth so much and if I only knew what it was all about I never would have married." As a result, Rose decided that "those women knew what they were talking about, so if you want any pointers on married life ask someone who has never been married, for they get the lowdown from folks who are unhappily married."[41] After 1909, the sea of matrimony might have been tough sailing anyway, given the legal restrictions on interracial marriage and the dwindling number of marriageable African American men in Montana. For Rose, however, unmarried life seems to have been a matter of her own choice.

There are some hints that Rose may have had, at the very least, a serious boyfriend during the time she lived in Lewistown. In October or November 1907, Mrs. Charles H. Sherman sent Rose a postcard that read, "Dear Rose, I just saw the notice of your marriage in the paper. Accept my best wishes. It was quite a surprise." Just a few weeks earlier, Robert had sent her a postcard with a caricature of an African American man and woman kissing beneath the moonlight on a park bench, with the comment, "My Dear Sister, This is a snapshot taken of your likeness at 12:30 AM."[42] There is no corroborating evidence of Rose dating or marrying, so it is possible that both these postcards involved jokes that only Rose and the sender would understand.

It is possible that Robert or Rose may have had same-sex relationships, but no evidence indicates that this occurred. Both certainly had same-sex friendships. Rose in particular established close friendships with several women. While working at the Hoffman House hotel in Lewistown, Rose became friendly with the Hoffman family, especially Mabel, the daughter of the owners. As Rose recounted, "I was sometimes inclined to be a little bit homesick for Mama and the rest of my friends at White Sulphur Springs, and had it not have been for Mabel I would have been very lonesome at times."[43] Mabel at one point sent Rose a comic—and anonymous—Valentine's Day card, which Rose worried over, as she couldn't imagine who could have sent it, until Mabel confessed that she was Rose's secret Valentine. "I was very happy for I knew Mabel meant no harm," wrote Rose. "Her black eyes sparkled when she told me what fun she had had picking it out at the store." Rose apparently saved the Valentine's Day card, as she quotes directly from it in "Gone are the Days." In other postcards to Rose, Mabel referred to her as "chocolate drop" and "dear angel of darkness," and at one point humorously observed, "[Y]our loving e-piss-tle (epistle, see?) of the 19th . . . was most tender as a porcupine in every respect."[44] The two young women had "many golden days together," according to Rose, who added, "I was heartbroken when her wedding day came."[45]

In a "description of the writer" that precedes the manuscript "Gone are the Days," Rose's dear friend Nell Butler claimed that to her friends, Rose was "a very jolly companion." She added, however, that "to those like myself who were interested enough to look deep within the Real Rose, one sees and feels something that is apart from the Miss Gordon of the Public[:] the soft, alluring mysteries of the Orient, deep, purple Nights, soft beat of distant drums, the intoxicating scent of hidden flowers, the intense, suppressed exaltment [*sic*] of the unknown and the feel of dramatic possibilities." To Nell Butler, this description captured "Rose Gordon as I know her."[46] What are we to make of the alluring mysteries of those "purple Nights," of Butler's poetic prose and its exoticism? Given the sensual description of the "Real Rose," one must at least consider the possibility that the intensity and intimacy of the relationship between the two women had a physical component. Yet there is no evidence that Rose's relationship with Nell Butler was sexual, and it could be that Nell, who was white, found Rose's blackness attractive. Still, the way Rose wrote about other women and the way they wrote about her suggests that Rose found sustenance and emotional fulfillment in her friendships.

For the African American population of Montana, 1910 marked the reversal of a demographic trajectory that had pointed upward since the 1870s. The early 1900s saw the African American community in White Sulphur Springs begin to disperse, and the new decade saw that community get even smaller. For the Gordons, 1910 was also a major year, as it marked the last time the family was all in the same place. By 1920, the only African Americans still living in White Sulphur Springs were Anna, Rose, and Robert Gordon. While the decades that followed would pose new challenges, Rose would meet those challenges head-on and create new opportunities for herself.

Mary Anna Gordon,
mother of Rose B. Gordon,
ca. 1885.   951-714, MHS
Photograph Archives

Rose B. Gordon in 1927.
951-716, MHS Photograph Archives

Robert James Gordon, the eldest of Rose's siblings. 951-715, MHS Photograph Archives

Anna and John Gordons' third child, John Francis Gordon Jr., pictured in 1907. 951-713, MHS Photograph Archives

George Washington Gordon, Anna and John Gordons' fourth child.
951-712, MHS Photograph Archives

Taylor Gordon, the youngest of the Gordon children, pictured in 1919.
Apeda Studio, photographers. 951-707, MHS Photograph Archives

The Springs Hotel in 1885. The natural hot springs drew visitors to White Sulphur Springs for leisure and recuperation.   951-686, MHS Photograph

The town of White Sulphur Springs in 1886. 951-670, MHS Photograph Archives

Southeast Main Street ca. 1893. Businesses from left to right are the Higgins House hotel,
J. MacDonald Harness and Saddle Manufacturer, Dr. J. M. Kumpe Drugstore, Baker and
DeLorimier Dry Goods, and John O'Marr's market. 951-695, MHS Photograph Archives

Robert Gordon (third from left, second row) and his school class, ca. 1894.
951-691, MHS Photograph Archives

The auditorium, located on 2nd Ave SE, pictured ca. 1895. The Gordon children performed in community events in the auditorium, and Anna and Rose frequently catered celebrations, especially New Year's Eve festivities. The Methodist Church, which the Gordon family attended regularly, is in the background. 951-677, MHS Photograph Archives

Taylor "Mannie" Gordon and friends, ca. 1903. As a young boy, Taylor worked as a messenger for the town's brothels.
Emmanuel Taylor Gordon Collection, PAc 82-19 F22, MHS Photograph Archives

Portrait of J. Rosamond Johnson and Taylor Gordon in 1927, around the time of their performance at Carnegie Hall. Taylor signed this copy for his brother Robert.
Apeda Studio, photographers. 951-710, MHS Photograph Archives

Rose feeds turkeys and hogs outside a ranch house, ca. 1908. On the back of the photograph, she wrote, "This is where I work [*sic*] last summer and I am going back nex [*sic*] summer. I wish you a happy news [*sic*] years." Emmanuel Taylor Gordon Collection, PAc 82-19 F06.11, MHS Photograph Archives

Rose Gordon and Maggie Jenkins pictured in front of Rose's Café, ca. 1925.
Emmanuel Taylor Gordon Collection, PAc 82-19 F06.08, MHS Photograph Archives

Rose stands in front of one of the locations of her restaurant, Café Gordon, next door to the offices of the *Meagher Republican* on Main Street. Emmanuel Taylor Gordon Collection, PAc 82-19 F06.07, MHS Photograph Archives

A business card for Rose Gordon's Kentucky Kitchen restaurant. Rose changed the name and location of her business a number of times over the years. Gordon Family Collection, Meagher County Historical Association, White Sulphur Springs

Rose Gordon and
Earl Fretwell in front
of Fretwell's Grocery
store, ca. 1938.
Gordon Family Collection,
Meagher County Historical
Association, White Sulphur
Springs

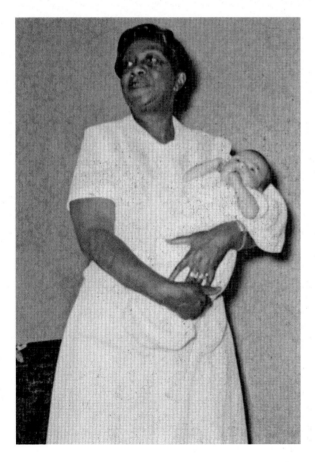

The College of Swedish Massage

CHARTERED UNDER THE LAWS OF ILLINOIS

Chicago • Illinois

Be it known that

Rose B. Gordon

has completed a prescribed course in Health Culture and has
passed a creditable examination in the Art of Scientific Swedish
Massage, Medical Gymnastics, Dietetics, Hydro Therapy, Swedish
Face and Scalp Treatment, Hygiene and the underlying principles of
Anatomy and Physiology in this institution and is awarded this

=DIPLOMA=

In Testimony Whereof We have hereunto subscribed our
names and affixed the seal of the College at Chicago, this
7th day of September A.D.1949

Rose's 1949 diploma from
the College of Swedish
Massage in Chicago.
Gordon Family Collection, Meagher
County Historical Association,
White Sulphur Springs

Wearing her nurse's
uniform, Rose holds
an infant in 1956.
Emmanuel Taylor Gordon
Collection, PAc 82-19 Fo6.06,
MHS Photograph Archives

Rose stands next to a 1950
Ford Custom in 1961.
Emmanuel Taylor Gordon
Collection, PAc 82-19 F06.05,
MHS Photograph Archives

Rose Gordon and Marvin Corkhill eat in a diner in 1965. Emmanuel Taylor Gordon Collection,
PAc 82-19 F06.01, MHS Photograph Archives

Rose and Taylor stand in front of their house in 1960, about a year after Taylor's return to Montana. 951-717, MHS Photograph Archives

Rose and Taylor Gordon at their kitchen table, ca. 1965. Rose passed away in 1968 and Taylor passed in 1971. Gordon Family Collection, Meagher County Historical Association, White Sulphur Springs

CHAPTER 6

Making a Living

In October 1911, the *Republican* informed readers that business at the "Gordon Delicatessen has been discontinued for the winter months."[1] After a spate of difficult health, Anna Gordon had closed her store and café, but with Rose's assistance, they were back in business in the Irwin Block on Main Street the next spring. An advertisement in the *Meagher County Republican* announced the newly reopened Gordon Delicatessen. The café served three meals a day and "short orders at all hours."[2] In 1913, after helping get the business back on its feet, Rose left home for Spokane, Washington, to pursue a medical career in massage and physiotherapy. Once again, however, she was obligated to cut short her education in order to return to White Sulphur Springs to help her mother, and this time she remained.[3]

Throughout the 1910s and 1920s, Rose helped her mother operate the Gordon Restaurant and Notion Store, putting her commitment to her family and her devotion to her mother's well-being above her own career aspirations. As Montana historian Marcella Sherfy observes, Rose "established a lifelong pattern" in which she balanced "earning whatever living the isolated community provided" with "pursuing as much medical training and work as she could, supporting and advocating for her family, helping her neighbors, writing, and singing."[4]

Each of the Gordon siblings was making his or her way in life. Like Rose, Robert invested in his home community, opening a tire garage to serve the community's growing number of motorists. George likewise had a local business—a cleaning service—until leaving White Sulphur Springs in 1919. By this time, John Francis Jr. had moved to Seattle, where he worked as a cook on a fishing boat. Meanwhile, Taylor, in a roundabout way, set off down a road that—by 1925—would lead to his "overnight" success as a singer of spirituals and provide him with opportunities to perform and travel with notable musicians such as the well-known vaudeville performer and composer J. Rosamond Johnson throughout the 1920s.[5]

Early in the 1910s, Taylor had worked as a Pullman porter on a West Coast route originating in Chicago, but he eventually settled into working at John Ringling's New York residence and serving as the circus magnate's personal porter on his private railroad car. For several years, Taylor traveled around the United States with Ringling. One afternoon, he was singing along to an Enrico Caruso record when he was overheard by a man who suggested he get in touch with the musician Max Bendix in New York. Bendix then introduced Taylor to conductor Otto Bartik. Although the connection ultimately did not pave the way for Taylor to work with Bartik, it sparked Taylor's interest in a singing career. A chance meeting with African American composer, conductor, and violinist Will Marion Cook resulted in a yearlong apprenticeship, after which Taylor studied at the recently established Colored Music Settlement in New York, directed at the time by Taylor's future performing partner, J. Rosamond Johnson. In 1919, Johnson resigned his position with the Music Settlement and returned to the vaudeville circuit where he had flourished as a performer earlier in the century. This time he took Taylor Gordon along as a member of his group, J. Rosamond Johnson and the Inimitable Five. After five successful years of coast-to-coast performances, the group disbanded. Johnson and Gordon then formed a duo, appearing on stage for the first time as specialists performing spirituals for concert audiences in 1925. Their partnership would last into the 1930s, after which the Great Depression and Taylor's declining mental health truncated his remarkable musical career.

The Gordons at home in White Sulphur Springs also continued to sing and perform for the public. Once again, friendships opened up new opportunities for them to showcase their talent. They became acquainted with Reverend J. Phillip Anshutz and his wife, Amy, who had moved to

Montana in 1907 from Omaha, Nebraska. Reverend Anshutz served as the Episcopalian minister for White Sulphur Springs and other Meagher County towns—including Martinsdale, where he, too, became good friends with the Coates brothers and their families.[6] He soon became an active part of the community, providing the invocation at the school's commencement and leading off the town's Fourth of July program. He was a popular speaker and an in-demand officiant at weddings and other community occasions.[7] The *Meagher Republican* reported on one of the early hunting trips that the minister made while embracing life in Montana: "While in the Musselshell country last week Rev. J. Phillip Anshutz was out hunting with a friend and secured his first antelope. Mr. Anshutz feels very proud of the animal which was a handsome creature, the head of which he has sent to Billings to be mounted."[8]

Amy Anshutz also participated in her new community with enthusiasm, becoming involved in women's clubs in several towns and actively joining in concerts. She sang, sometimes as part of a quartet, and played the mandolin, and she once performed "whistling solos" of "The Mockingbird" and "Dearie" at a Martinsdale event sponsored by the women of the Trinity Episcopal Mission.[9] Like his wife, Reverend Anshutz engaged in the local performance culture, and he showed a particular interest in African American entertainers. In 1910, he was one of a small group of individuals who organized a Lyceum course—a series of concerts and entertainments from traveling musicians and performers—at the Auditorium. The slate included the Midland Jubilee Singers, who, like many African American performers of the era, combined operatic skills and humor in their stage shows.[10] As part of the promotion for the concert, Anshutz wrote a column about the group: "The Auditorium was filled last year at their appearance and it is certain that it will be again this year. . . . The Jubilee Singers as it will be remembered are negro singers and performers. The program consists of comic and operatic music."[11] Anshutz's interest in supporting African American performers extended beyond traveling acts to working with local talent, especially the Gordon family.

Anshutz also helped stage a minstrel show that took place during the town's annual Harvest Festival one year. Several of the Gordons appeared in the cast, and in a letter to the *Meagher County News*, Rose remembered their participation in some detail: "We were six weeks getting ready for the great day. It was a lot of fun and real work too." According to Rose, the cast included her brothers George (tenor) and Robert (baritone). Although she does not mention Taylor specifically, he may have been among the "mixed voices" in the rest of the cast. To advertise the show, the cast borrowed a horse and wagon and drove the team around town while performing two of the numbers. "Tickets sold like hot cakes," Rose remembered, and the Auditorium was packed. "The following year," she observed, "a man from Kansas City was here for our show and wanted to take us out on a road tour but we were interested in other things."[12] In a later column in the *Meagher County News*, Rose described the "black-face minstrel" show put on by the Home Talent Folks and explained, "We decided to stay 'where bacon and eggs were easy to get.'"[13]

In 1911, Reverend Anshutz was promoted "to occupy the pulpit of one of the influential churches in the Episcopalian diocese of Montana" in Billings, and the Anshutzes left White Sulphur Springs.[14] He would eventually relocate to Brooklyn, New York, although he occasionally returned to Montana in the summers. Nearly a half century after meeting the Gordons, however, Reverend Anshutz—as well as the Coates family from Martinsdale—would provide essential aid when Rose worked to secure Taylor's release from a mental institution in New York.

While Taylor built a life in the wider world, Rose concentrated on her mother's restaurant and shop—variously referred to in the *Meagher Republican* as the Gordon Delicatessen, the Kentucky Kitchen, the Gordon Café, and the Gordon Restaurant and Notion Store—in White Sulphur Springs. Anna and Rose proved adaptable, changing the business's location, altering its name, and trying new things to grow their restaurant and their income. When they could afford to do so, the Gordons—especially Robert and Rose—purchased space in the *Republican* to draw attention to their businesses. Thus, the frequency of the businesses' advertisements suggests their success, as the absence of Gordon-related advertising in the *Republican* usually corresponded with hard financial times.

Advertisements and local news items kept the public informed on the status of the Gordon family's commercial enterprises. The *Meagher*

Republican announced on January 31, 1913, that the "Gordon Delicatessen has been moved into the Tal Reed building on Main Street, and meals are being served at the new stand." This move to a larger space reflected the enterprise's growth.[15] Throughout the entire year in 1913, the Gordons ran an advertisement declaring that the "Gordon Café" was open for business in the new building and serving "short orders at all hours."[16] Nearly the same copy ran for all of 1914 as well. That year, George Gordon started publishing a regular advertisement for a cleaning business: "Hello! Hello!! Call 101 the Cleaner, and have him call for your clothes, clean, press, and deliver them. G. W. Gordon."[17] Late in 1914, the Gordon Café became Traveler's Café, and advertisements for Traveler's, which otherwise featured the same text as prior versions, appeared weekly through 1915 in the *Republican*. In 1917, Richard Ringling settled in White Sulphur Springs to take care of his brother John's ranches. The following year, he married Aubrey Black, the daughter of pioneer settler Powell Black and a good friend of the Gordons, and the Gordon restaurant hosted their reception.[18] Soon after, Castle Mountain Gold Butter, a product of Ringling's ranch, became a staple at the café.

Rose's customers provided material for her writing and satisfied her interest in observing humanity in all its variety. Rose reported having met "many kinds of people, sheepherders, drunkards, thieves, gamblers and every class up to the millionaire" while working at the restaurant. Characteristically, she observed that she "found something good in them all."[19] Cattle kings, circus kings, miners, and lawyers all came through the restaurant, as did patrons who were in town seeking medical cures from the famous White Sulphur Springs water.

In a letter to the newspaper published in the 1940s, Rose related a story from her days as a restaurant operator to illustrate the healing powers of the water in White Sulphur Springs. The story also reveals Rose's compassion for others:

> I recall one case of a man who came to my café one evening
> to dinner. I filled a glass with cold water and took it to him.
> I saw that his hands were bleeding. I offered him something
> with which to wrap his hands. He said, "no, never mind." I
> thought it very strange.

>Dr. MacKay ... found that he had syphilis. The doctor
>came to my café and to other eating places and told us not
>to feed him with other people. No one wanted to feed him.
>He came to try the water for his illness, so they talked the
>matter over and decided to let him bathe in the mud bath
>which was just a little distance from the main spring. I knew
>what wonderful things the water had done. I told the doctor
>I would feed him in the back yard. I took great care that no
>one came in contact with anything I used for him. I kept his
>dishes outside in a little box, kept them sterilized, carried the
>food out and put it in the dishes.
>
>I never saw anything like it. The mud poultice soon began
>to heal the sore spots. He continued the baths for a long time.
>I kept on feeding him ... and I was glad to have the experi-
>ence of seeing what our water would do. He was here about
>seven months, and when he went away his skin was very clear.

When he returned seven years later to "take some baths in your good old
water again," his cure had been so effective that the restaurant served him
"in the dining room with the rest of the patrons."[20]

Their commitment to providing healthy food that pleased their customers kept Rose and Anna busy. They "did not like canned goods" and
preferred "things cooked from the garden, which made lots of work in
the summer season and winter season as well, for vegetables were kept in
root cellars in winter and had to be prepared."[21] They accommodated the
special tastes of regular customers, preparing favorite dishes, even certain
meals that "kept the place smelling with fish." They also prepared food for
customers with special dietary needs. "So many people came that were in
ill health. You would have thought we were running a hospital instead of a
restaurant." According to Rose, one customer was "surviving on soup and
Springs water."[22]

One set of customers, in particular, made an impression on Rose and
Anna. "Along with all the rest of my patrons," Rose wrote, "I shall not
forget the sheep herders, for in the fall we held the herders convention,
and they would all come in and being out at camp did not have all the
varieties of food that they liked, so they would come and have us to cook

everything they hadn't had in season: turkey, chicken, duck, lobster, and all kinds of salads." The sheepherding life was indeed a hard one. Rose recalled how one summer a gentleman named John invited her and Anna to visit his camp: "It was about 20 miles out [and] it was almost dark when we reached camp. . . . The sheep were on a hill just above the camp and of all the noise you ever heard. I said to the herder, my goodness, man, how do you stand that constant Ba Ba Ba?" When he responded, "You get so you don't notice," an incredulous and amused Rose replied, "Well, I guess when you don't notice, you are in the last stages, are you not?"[23]

Although the African American community in White Sulphur Springs had dispersed at this point, Rose nonetheless found ways to connect with other African Americans, even if their presence in town was temporary. Her ability to forge informal networks with other African Americans whose livelihoods also depended on pleasing white patrons and employers is evident in an anecdote about John Ringling's dining preferences. Once when John Ringling was in town, Rose, knowing that the Circus King and land developer was a multimillionaire, figured that he "would want something dainty." She recalled that after he had eaten his meal, however, "he said it was very nice," and then Ringling said, "I will be here tomorrow and will expect a real feed." An African American maid employed by the Ringlings responded to an inquiry from Rose regarding John Ringling's eating habits by advising that he liked "plenty of good solid food." Rose then realized that the "dainty" dinner she had cooked for him "was just an appetizer." The next day, Rose "cooked him corn beef and cabbage, corn bread and apple pie. He tipped and said the dinner was a real one."[24]

The family's restaurant was particularly busy when the county court was in session. Rose's writings describe several of the prominent attorneys and judges who dined there. Tellingly, her history of the town and of Montana in general includes several asides where she discusses important trials—in both White Sulphur Springs and Lewistown. Surprisingly, one of the most notorious trials in White Sulphur Springs receives no mention in Rose's writing whatsoever. Perhaps it was one that Rose wished to forget, as it resulted in the execution of three African American men in 1917. That outcome, even if the men were indeed guilty of the crime that had been committed, must have disturbed the Gordon family, being some of the few Blacks living in Meagher County at the time. Executions in the county were not unheard of, but they were rare, and the hanging of three men at the same time was highly unusual.

After being convicted of the October 1916 murder of Michael Freeman, Lester Fahley, Henry Hall, and Harrison Gibson were executed in February of the following year, "hanged on the gallows erected in the barn of the county jail at this place." According to the *Meagher Republican*, the crime itself took place when seven Black men boarded a freight train car where three white men—Michael Freeman, Earl Fretwell, and Claud Campbell—were already riding "and proceeded to hold them up."[25] The newspaper account does not say what sparked the violence. Instead, it offers racialized speculation: "For some reason the negroes became frightened or excited and commenced shooting," killing Freeman, forcing Fretwell off the train, and wounding Campbell, who escaped further injury by leaping from the moving train. Fretwell and Campbell flagged down another train and notified the authorities, who captured five of the men when the train arrived in Musselshell. Following a car chase, the authorities later apprehended the other two at a construction camp. After Campbell and Fretwell identified them, all seven suspects were convicted of murder, with four serving a range of sentences, including two life sentences, and three being handed down death sentences.[26]

The proposed execution elicited a well-organized attempt on the part of citizens throughout the state to have the sentences commuted. According to the *Republican*, these concerned Montanans favored that the men instead be given life sentences on the basis that they were illiterate and lacked "a true conception of their crime."[27] This campaign underscored the potential problems of the triple hanging. Governor Samuel Stewart also expressed concern "that perhaps the race of these men had been a factor," although he concluded, after reviewing the evidence presented at the trial, that was not the case and denied the request for clemency.[28]

The account of the execution in the *Meagher Republican* is disturbing, even as the writer praised the three men for showing "commendable bravery" and taking their places on the trapdoor without "weakening" or struggle. The *Republican* described the execution in detail:

The trap worked perfectly, and there was only a soft thud
as the three bodies came against the tautness of the ropes
at once. Each neck was broken, and only one man, Fahley,
moved in the least, a slight tremor going over him as his
muscles relaxed.

A large number witnessed the execution, some sheriffs
and deputies coming here from surrounding counties, and a
number from outside of White Sulphur coming especially to
witness it.

The bodies were cut down after eight minutes, previously
being pronounced dead. The three were almost immediately
taken to the graveyard, being interred in one grave.[29]

The article describes the sheriff at the scene calling the event "probably
the shortest hanging on record, the three condemned men standing on
the trap probably thirty seconds. The fact that none of the negroes weak-
ened, although one was biting his lip, facilitated the speed of execution."
Even when the *Meagher County News* revisited the event in the 1950s, Rose
offered no commentary to the newspaper on this grisly hallmark of White
Sulphur Springs's history.

In 2014, National Public Radio (NPR) investigated the story as
part of a series called the Race Card Project in response to a suggestion
from Carol Zachary, whose grandfather, Herbert Fleming, witnessed
the execution. According to the NPR investigation, Montana law legally
required Fleming, who served as the county auditor, to attend the hanging.
The invitation to the execution read, "Your presence is requested at White
Sulphur Springs, Montana, on the morning of Friday, February Sixteenth,
in the Year of Our Lord Nineteen Hundred Seventeen, to witness the
execution of Henry Hall, Harrison Gibson, Lester Fahley." It was accompanied by three photographs of the condemned men. As Race Card Project
curator Michele Norris observed of the large number of witnesses—over
sixty—at the execution, this event marked "the first legal triple-hanging in
the state of Montana. It was a pretty big deal."[30]

While there appears to have been no "miscarriage of justice" here, something still seems incomplete. Although race may have played no explicit
role in the sentencing of these men, it is unsettling that "the first legal

triple-hanging in the state of Montana" just so happened to involve three African American men. According to Fleming, the event "was awful."[31]

Later references to this execution signal that some Montanans remained uneasy about it. In 1963, a bill before the state legislature referenced it as evidence of the need for abolishing capital punishment in the state. M. D. Holmes, who had been a deputy sheriff in 1917, recalled the incident for the *Meagher County News* in 1963, describing it as "an unpleasant duty, and one he would not like to have to do again." The gallows used in the execution, the newspaper article revealed, was still in existence, as a barn had been converted for the purpose, with a trap being cut in the floor of an upper story. The barn returned to its original purpose after the events, but the modifications remained in place.[32]

Although both Rose and Taylor documented an earlier execution in White Sulphur Springs—that of Herbert H. Metzger, convicted of murdering and robbing a rancher at Sheep Creek—neither one wrote about the 1917 execution. A triple hanging of anyone was not the kind of local event that Rose paid tribute to in her writings, and yet no history of Meagher County is complete without mention of the incident. The fact that Rose never referred to it may indicate just how much it unsettled the remaining four African American residents of White Sulphur Springs: Rose, Anna, George, and Robert Gordon. Although there is no direct link between the executions of Fahley, Hall, and Gibson and the ongoing Black exodus from Montana, the triple hanging of three African American men could only have contributed to a developing sense that the state was no longer friendly territory for Black people.

Though their numbers had dwindled, the Gordons kept in touch with the dispersed African American population in Montana. After moving to Bozeman in 1919, George integrated himself into that town's Black community. Both Robert and Rose had multiple friends in Helena, Lewistown, and Great Falls, and they had visitors and boarders who came through White Sulphur Springs. Most African American residents of Montana had found other places to live, but for Robert, Rose, and Anna Gordon, White Sulphur was—and would always be—home.

During and after World War I, the Gordons undertook a variety of endeavors to make ends meet, from providing occasional room and board to visitors to George's cleaning business. When not helping her mother operate the café, Rose also offered massage and salon services. Starting in April 1917, Rose advertised "Face and Scalp Massage" and "Electric Massage" in the *Meagher Republican*.[33] Then, from December through August of the following year, Rose ran an advertisement for a "Beauty Parlor" located in Room 2 of the Wellman Block. The listed hours, 2:30 through 5:00 PM (between lunch and dinner), suggest that this endeavor may have been in addition to the café. The Gordons may have suffered financial difficulties during the war years. Between the 1918 influenza pandemic, which caused nearly weekly deaths in the town and drove Rose to volunteer as a health worker, and the resources directed to the war effort, earning a profit through the café alone may have been difficult. In addition to Rose's beauty parlor notice, Robert advertised a piano for sale, perhaps an indication of financial difficulty for a family that valued music.[34] Whatever the circumstances, the 1920 census listed Anna as proprietor of a lunchroom and Rose as a masseur in a beauty shop.

While his mother and sister made a success of the café and Rose branched out to massage therapy, Robert helped maintain the Gordon household with his own business, a used tire and tire repair shop that began operation in November 1919. The first advertisement for Robert's business appeared in an edition of the *Meagher Republican* that same month. Automobile travel—"motoring," in the parlance of the *Republican*—had become popular among Montanans, as an emphasis on road construction in the early 1920s made driving to and from White Sulphur Springs a viable alternative to the stage and the train. Later in 1919, the *Republican* reported that Robert had "taken over the vulcanizing plant" and would soon move it to a new location.[35] Not long after, he updated his equipment, and the paper's local news section noted in April 1920 that "Robert Gordon has just installed a new steam vulcanizing machine. The Springs Steam Vulcanizing shop is now prepared to take care of the trade in up-to-date fashion."[36] For years to come, Robert's advertisements would be a consistent feature of the *Republican*, running every week through 1927. "If you are running a car over these snow roads," a 1922 advertisement reads, "you must realize that every cut in the rubber is soon filled with snow, rocks and dirt. In a short time the tire is ruined. Save tires by having the repair made today."[37] The "Springs Vulcanizing Shop," with "R. J. Gordon, proprietor," offered retreading as well as "Gas, Oils, Grease, Second Hand Tires," and the ability to "Fix All Bad Tubes."[38] By 1925, Robert also helped customers repair or replace "Glass Enclosures."

Despite their hard work, the Gordons struggled continuously to keep up with the property taxes on their small home. In the 1910 census, the Gordons were listed as lodgers, with James B. Phelps as the head of the household. A friend of the Gordons, Phelps may have purchased the house and let them reside there until they could cover the delinquent taxes. They must have done so shortly thereafter, as Robert B. Gordon appeared on the state's delinquent tax list for failure to pay property taxes in 1913—an indication that the Gordons were once again owners rather than lodgers. Perhaps a reflection of better years at the café, seemingly none of the Gordons owed delinquent taxes between 1914 and 1916. In 1917, however, Anna Gordon's name was attached to the property on the delinquent tax list. The family was off the list again for the next three years, though that absence might indicate that they had lost possession of the house. The 1920 census lists Anna, Robert, and Rose—the only Gordon family members still living in White Sulphur Springs—as renters rather than owners of the house. This pattern would continue for the rest of Rose's life. The family's house and the parcel of land on which it was located would be repeatedly offered for sale by Meagher County pursuant of tax assessment but would go unpurchased, finally to be bought again by Rose Gordon for the cost of the owed taxes.

Many rural communities protected community members experiencing financial difficulties from foreclosure and eviction as Montana's economy plummeted following the onset of widespread drought in 1918. That the 1920 census again listed the Gordons as renters rather than owners suggests that the house was purchased on their behalf—possibly at an auction where the purchaser was the only bidder and thus able to buy at a low cost—and held until they could pay the delinquent taxes. It is also possible that the Gordons' interest in the property was protected in other ways, such as leaving the house unpurchased at auction. Certainly, there would have been ample opportunities for real estate investors to purchase the property and turn a profit. Yet the family's ability to retain the home over such a long period of time offers the possibility that the local community helped ensure they would be protected from eviction.

Ever an integral part of the town's social fabric, the Gordons continued to contribute to the community life of White Sulphur Springs through their musical skills.[39] The local popularity of minstrel performance had not waned in the early part of the twentieth century, and the Gordons, along with various friends and neighbors, continued to participate in minstrel shows at the Auditorium. Even after he moved to Bozeman in 1919, George performed in a charity minstrel show staged by the Bozeman Elks Lodge, his longtime employer, and often offered a vocal solo.

Traveling minstrel shows also continued to make stops in White Sulphur Springs. The Dixie Minstrels, "a troupe of colored singers and entertainers," appeared in town in August 1915.[40] The following year, J. M. Busby's World's Greatest Colored Minstrel Show, held "under canvas" rather than in the Auditorium, performed in late July with a noon parade preceding an evening performance.[41] In the fall of 1916, Tom Christy's All White Minstrels appeared at the Oddfellows Hall.[42]

For one noteworthy local performance, Rose and George Gordon joined with local residents Will Gehring, Max and Timothy Beebe, George Cruikshank, and Mrs. Roy Cox—all of whom were white—for a minstrel show for the benefit of the local Red Cross in June of 1917 as the country was preparing to go to war—a fact that made the final scene, involving a quartet gathered around an army campfire, particularly affecting, as it represented a scene "that may be enacted soon by thousands of American lads."[43] Traveling minstrel groups were either "All White" or "Colored" but not mixed, making this integrated minstrel performance in White Sulphur Springs particularly interesting. Although it seems incongruous to point to a minstrel show as a model of integration, performance spaces—on stage as well as in the audience—were often segregated in 1917. Similarly, the shows themselves trafficked in explicitly racist tropes. Blacks and whites did not perform together as a rule, with some exceptions. A single Black comedian such as Bert Williams might join the Ziegfeld Follies on Broadway, or a Black act might be included on a vaudeville slate, but Black musicians and white musicians or actors did not appear on the same stage together with any regularity. For instance, white dancers Vernon and Irene

Castle created a scandal when they insisted on having James Reese Europe and his all-Black orchestra accompany them at dance demonstrations on a national tour in 1913 and 1914. This decision raised the ire of the American Federation of Musicians, which did not admit Black members.[44]

Local performance spaces, especially in smaller towns where integrated performances might have occurred out of necessity in order to have enough participants to put on a show, may have offered more possibilities for onstage integration than nationally renowned stages could. Nonetheless, the joining of white and Black performers on stage in White Sulphur Springs from the late nineteenth century onward was more the exception than the rule in America during the period. Rose's stage performances were as integral to her creative expression as her writing was, and both were an important means of making herself useful to her community. Working on stage with her fellow townspeople in mixed-race productions was in keeping with her practice of cultivating friendly relations with her neighbors—a particular bit of Booker T. Washington's philosophy that the entire Gordon family put into practice effectively.

During the summer of 1922, Taylor Gordon, who had been traveling and performing throughout the United States and Canada, returned temporarily to Montana. He celebrated by joining his brothers and sister to put on a concert at the Auditorium, which was "attended by more than 300 people of the town and valley." The performers included vocalists "E. Taylor Gordon, George W. Gordon, Miss Rose B. Gordon, and A. W. Christmon," with musical accompaniment by Mrs. Halbert on the piano and "Robt. Gordon, violin," playing a program of popular songs and standards. The newspaper offered praise for the performance and gave a nod to Taylor's musical achievements, saying, "The solos and choruses proved delightful, especially solos by E. Taylor Gordon, who has been for several years on the principal vaudeville circuits of the country."[45] This winning performance was followed by others that were equally successful. Of those concerts, Taylor would write, "I made more money than I ever made at one time in my life."[46] After participating in the family's shows in Montana, Taylor returned to New York, and his brothers and sisters went back to work.

After some time as a member of the Dextra Male Chorus, Taylor rejoined the Inimitable Five, and he performed with them until the act finally came off the road in late 1924. Taylor continued his involvement with Johnson's various projects, culminating in the duo's debut on the Garrick Theatre stage in New York City on the night of November 15, 1925. With Johnson at the piano and Taylor as the featured tenor soloist, the dominant mode for classical music vocal performance, the two offered one of the first concerts devoted solely to the performance of spirituals using the piano and vocal format. They created an immediate sensation, and Taylor was soon on his way to stardom.

For Rose, however, the central event of the decade was not a happy one. After over four decades of anchoring her family, Anna Gordon died in 1924. That year, Rose later wrote, "brought me the greatest sorrow of my life." Anna had been "suffering from a bronchial cough almost all the winter and was not feeling her best," but the cough developed into pneumonia. In early June, what had initially seemed to be an insignificant illness, quickly overcame her. Although Anna was in her eighties, her death surprised Rose and the rest of the White Sulphur Springs community.[47] "There is something about a mother," Rose lamented, "that we expect them to remain with us always." In some ways, Rose's writings served as much as a memorial to her mother as a tribute to the White Sulphur Springs of her childhood, as though by writing Rose could keep her mother's memory alive both for herself and for the community.

The notice of Anna Gordon's death in the *Meagher Republican* lamented her passing and celebrated her numerous contributions to the community: "Mrs. Gordon has been a resident of White Sulphur Springs for forty-one years, and was a woman known in all the older homes in the town, where in many instances she ministered in sickness. She was universally respected and was a woman of unusual intelligence and force, as was evidenced by the large number of people who turned out to pay their last respects."[48] The Episcopal Church filled with mourners and flowers for her service. George traveled up from Bozeman for the funeral and stayed for several days to mourn with his siblings. The *Meagher Republican* does not mention Taylor, who may have had commitments with the Dextra Male

Chorus that prevented him from attending or had trouble arranging travel on short notice. After the funeral, a distraught Rose accompanied George back to Bozeman, where she stayed for a week before returning to White Sulphur Springs and her mother's house.[49]

The following months were difficult for Rose. From her mother's death in June 1924 until September 1925, the newspapers did not mention Rose. Although Robert continued to promote his vulcanizing business in the newspaper, after Anna's death no advertisements for the café appeared for nearly a year and a half. The business may have closed or been bought out, as several other cafés popped up in town after Anna's death. Then, in December 1925, the following notice for the Gordon Notion Store appeared in the newspaper:

> All Kinds of
> Christmas Candies and Toys
> Christmas Cards
> ROSE B. GORDON
> Main Street[50]

Just a few months before this notice appeared, Rose's beauty parlor began advertising "Scalp and Face Massage" and "Manicuring and Marceling."[51] That a year and a half passed between Anna's death and Rose's reopening of the Gordon store and café intimates how deeply her mother's death affected Rose.

Rose was going through her own transformation. Eventually, she would come into her own as the sole proprietor of the Gordon Restaurant and Notion Store, but first she seems to have taken a long period to mourn the loss of her mother. In June 1926, around the second anniversary of Anna's death, Rose advertised for the Gordon Notion Store for the first time since the previous December. The notice began to run weekly for the rest of the year.[52] The timing of her advertisement may have been either a coincidence or a conscious memorial to her mother's legacy. Either way, the placement of an ongoing advertisement for the family business signaled a new era for the restaurant and for Rose Gordon.

CHAPTER 7

Down for the Count and then the Comeback

Rose in the 1930s and 1940s

"Seats are fast selling," the *Meagher Republican* reported in April 1927, "for the American Negro Spirituals to be held here Friday evening, at the Auditorium, where Taylor (Manny) Gordon, a Springs boy, will sing, and Rosamond Johnson, another member of the company, who is an artist of national reputation."[1] Although this concert was scheduled with his sister Rose and brother Robert in mind, the whole town was eager to welcome Taylor home. "Everybody here knows and remembers 'Manny' as a boy," the *Republican* observed, "and are glad to hear of the success he has achieved."[2] Taylor Gordon and J. Rosamond Johnson were on a long tour across the country, traveling from New York to South Carolina and Alabama, through the Midwest, and out to the West Coast. Prior to performing in White Sulphur Springs, the duo had given a concert at Montana State College in Bozeman in part because Taylor wanted to perform in his brother George's adopted home. To the audience in White Sulphur, Taylor "was the same 'Manny' who went to school here: but he held his audience with the pathos of the folk music of his race."[3] Rose, at the insistence of her friends in the audience, joined Rosamond and Taylor on stage and sang one song, "which received enthusiastic applause."[4] This was likely the first time Rose had performed with her brother since their successful minstrel show in 1922.

The concert reflected the positive mood of the time, a sweet moment just before the Great Depression gripped the United States and ushered in a time of hardship for Rose and her brothers. Rose's survival philosophy of cultivating good relations with her neighbors would be tested by racial prejudice during these years. The work ethic she had inherited from her mother would likewise be challenged in these hard times, forcing her to shut down the restaurant. Even when the restaurant reopened in the 1940s, rationing and other disruptions related to World War II proved difficult obstacles to overcome.

Taylor's concerts in Montana came on the heels of a historic performance. On February 16, 1927, Taylor Gordon and J. Rosamond Johnson made their first appearance at New York City's storied Carnegie Hall as part of a benefit concert for the National Urban League and its New York and Brooklyn branches. "J. Rosamond Johnson, pianist and baritone, and Taylor Gordon, tenor, appeared at Carnegie Hall last evening," the *New York Times* reported, "in a program of American negro spirituals such as they have given in smaller halls here and in other cities." The performers "were enthusiastically greeted, their performance again giving to the old slave songs a devotional character of the music's actual origin."[5] African American performers at Carnegie Hall were a rarity in 1927; a concert showcasing African American music was even rarer still. The concert kicked off the duo's long cross-country tour. After they performed in the White Sulphur Springs auditorium, Johnson and Gordon headed back east. Following a brief stay in New York, they set sail across the Atlantic in mid-May. Over the next several months they became the first piano and vocal duo to give concerts devoted to African American spirituals in Paris and London, as well as elsewhere in England. Their concerts in England were so successful that they rented an apartment and stayed in the country, performing through November 1927.[6]

The Gordon siblings—Rose and Robert in White Sulphur Springs, George in Bozeman, and Taylor in New York—were doing quite well for themselves in the last half of the 1920s. Yet with the exception of George, whose position at the Bozeman Elks Club kept him steadily employed from 1919 until his death in the late 1940s, the Great Depression troubled the economic waters for the Gordons. By the end of the 1930s, both Rose and Taylor were barely making ends meet and struggling to survive. Likewise, their brother John Francis Jr., then living in Seattle, would have his own difficulties in the 1940s, but it is unclear how he fared during the Depression. In general, his work as a cook on commercial fishing vessels was lucrative, but he seems to have had periods of ups and downs.

Advertisements for the Gordon Notion Store, sometimes called the Gordon Confectionary, ran in the *Meagher Republican* weekly from 1927 through 1929, and offered "Ice Cream, Soda Pop and All Cool Drinks and Candy" as well as lunches and coffee.[7] The store also boasted seasonal specialties, such as "Easter novelties" and "Christmas-Time Gifts that you can afford to buy—and a fine selection of candies and notions for the children."[8] The ads suggest the store was doing a brisk business prior to the crash of 1928.

In New York, Taylor was doing quite well, performing with J. Rosamond Johnson while also starting to work on his memoir. In September 1929, the *Meagher Republican* reported that Rose had "received a few [advance] copies of the book, 'Born to Be,' written by her brother, Mannie Gordon, celebrated singer. . . . We have reviewed the book and will say in this brief sketch it is a surprise to us, not being what we anticipated at all. Instead of a musical sketch, it is more of a biography of Mannie's early life here and of his thoughts and ideals, his experiences and struggles." The same report declared Taylor's book "vitally interesting to every person in this valley, both newcomer and old timer."[9] By emphasizing that everyone might benefit from reading *Born to Be*, the *Republican* implied that those Montanans who had embraced the views of the Ku Klux Klan during the 1920s might find that Taylor's portrayal of a more egalitarian society offered a needed alternative to the racial animosity promoted by the Klan.[10]

In part a love letter to the White Sulphur Springs of Taylor Gordon's childhood, *Born to Be* clearly found a receptive audience in the editor of the *Meagher Republican*. By the time of the book's publication, Taylor's singing career had benefited from the expansion of radio networks that boosted his popularity beyond his hometown.[11] "Local people will be interested to know," the *Republican* reported, "that Mr. Gordon is on the air each Saturday evening, at 9:30 eastern time, and has signed up a year's contract to sing for the WABC network. Local radio owners will be on the lookout in the future for his programs, which already have been on the past two Saturday nights."[12]

Meanwhile, Rose's café had been doing well enough early in 1929 to move to a larger space in the Emery Building. As the *Republican* told readers that January, "The building next to the printing office is being remodeled this week and will be refinished inside to house the restaurant and notion store of Rose Gordon who will move to that location after a couple of weeks."[13] Receipts indicate that Rose paid for a variety of improvements to the Emery location, making payments to carpenters and other laborers for lumber, decorating, plumbing, and other work.[14]

To celebrate the move, Rose served "a big turkey dinner . . . as an opening event."[15]

In May, the business variously referred to as the Gordon Notion Store, the Gordon Restaurant and Notion Store, and the Gordon Confectionary put up a new sign proclaiming itself the Gordon Café.[16] "At the Gordon Café located in the heart of our city," the *Meagher Republican* reported, Rose Gordon, "manipulator of chicken," offered it fried, stewed, and boiled, and "is now serving a special attraction," a Sunday evening "chicken dinner de lux."[17] Later that year, D. T. A. Mackintosh, the editor and publisher of the *Meagher Republican* in the late 1920s, described a visit to the restaurant:

> Rose Gordon gave a Turkey dinner Saturday. . . . The editor
> and wife were guests of Rose and rise to say it was a real
> dinner—the turkey was juicy and tender, the fixings were
> complete and appetizing. Rose demonstrated her ability
> as a cook and caterer, having ample help in the kitchen
> and expert assistance in the serving. Aye, the dinner was a
> success and it took numerous turks to satisfy the demand,
> as the word went about and folks numerous, single and
> groups, came for the feast.[18]

The restaurant continued to thrive for the next couple of years. In 1930, Rose placed two advertisements weekly. One promoted the Gordon Café and the second touted what had become Rose's specialty—chicken dinners: "Spring Chicken, Fried to Order, Gordon Café."[19] By 1931, the latter advertisement had changed slightly to include a new specialty: waffles.[20]

Before the year was out, however, the Gordon Café was shuttered. Rose initially tried to salvage the restaurant by running the business out of her home. "After conducting a restaurant on Main Street for more than a score of years," Rose noted in a message printed in the *Republican*, "I am moving my place of my business to my residence on Lincoln street. And I wish to thank all in the city, for their kind patronage, and all those who have left the city in the years past. And last but not least, I want to thank all the little bright-eyed children who came to purchase all-day suckers. They will always be cherished as one of my sweetest memories."[21] The next year, Rose opened the Waffle Shop on Second Avenue in Great Falls. She made a go of the new location for a couple of years, but as the Great Depression settled in, not even a city with a larger clientele could keep her business afloat. Of her personal life in Great Falls, no revealing records remain, but an August 1932 letter to Rose from Amelia Ostby of Bozeman expressed "surprise you was back at the springs again, Rose I don't blame you in the least you have your home in WSS a roof over your head, I have heard Great Falls is down to zero, I was afraid when you went over there, you would have a hard time."[22]

By the next summer, Rose had opened another version of the Waffle Shop in White Sulphur Springs, offering, according to an advertisement, "lunches, meals, chicken dinner to order, east of Hotel Sherman, Rose B. Gordon, Prop."[23] It is not clear exactly how long she was able to keep the Waffle Shop going, but she did apply for permits to purchase liquor in July 1935 and again in 1936.[24] Starting in 1935 and continuing until 1942, however, she received employment assistance through the Works Progress Administration (WPA), working primarily as a seamstress.[25]

Robert Gordon's vulcanizing business followed a similar pattern. In 1929, the advertisement for his business cheekily asked readers to bring their "sick and sad tires to the Bob Gordon hospital where Robert will perform either a major or a minor operation as the tire may need."[26] Advertisements for the shop appeared continually in the *Meagher Republican* from 1919 through 1932 but ceased abruptly in January 1933. By that point, Robert may have begun working at the First National Bank as a janitor. Regardless, the Great Depression ended the family businesses that Rose and Robert had operated for years. While those ventures had not made them rich, they had helped them stay afloat in their small town. With the failures of the Gordon Café and the vulcanizing shop, Rose and Robert entered a period of economic struggle along with millions of other Americans.

At some point in the early 1930s, Robert moved from the family home to an apartment in the Wellman Building, where a bequest from the Wellman family enabled him to earn money by renting out another apartment space above him as well as the ground floor space for the post office. Comments in a variety of letters suggest that long-standing conflict between Robert and Rose provided the impetus for his move. One of Rose's correspondents observed the change in living arrangements and asked, "Is he nice to you now? I hope so, it is so trying on you all that friction. You have such a sensitive nature and tender feelings and no one knows better than I do just how you suffered. I hope you are very happy now."[27]

The Great Depression also affected Taylor's well-being. His radio contract was cancelled in the early 1930s, and that, combined with a falling out with J. Rosamond Johnson, undermined his financial stability. He still managed to earn money by launching a solo concert career and winning roles on stage, including small parts in *Gay Divorce* with Fred Astaire and in the Philadelphia production of *The Pursuit of Happiness*. However, when *The Pursuit of Happiness* ended its run in December 1934, Taylor's performance career essentially came to an end. By the time he left the stage, he had started exhibiting symptoms of the mental illness that ultimately led to his institutionalization later in life, as he became more and more obsessed with the idea that his creative work was being stolen from him. In time, he believed that multiple Hollywood films had been based on his unpublished writing and that other people were making money off his creative ideas while he struggled to survive.

After *The Pursuit of Happiness* closed, Taylor returned to White Sulphur Springs for the first time since he and Johnson performed there in 1927. In early July 1935, the *Meagher County News* announced, "Taylor Gordon to Give Concert Here." The newspaper reported that Taylor, who "came to White Sulphur Springs about a week ago and plans to remain during the summer," was "advertising a concert and dance which will be given in the auditorium."[28] The concert was a success, turning out a full crowd and drawing attendees from as far away as Helena, Bozeman, and Great

Falls.[29] Through the rest of the summer and into the fall, Taylor tried to jump-start his singing career with a series of Montana concerts, including a second one in White Sulphur Springs that featured a section devoted to solos by "guest artists" Rose and George Gordon.[30] He also performed a matinee concert at Gallatin County High School on September 27, where Taylor also spoke to the students about "the growth of Negro Music in America."[31] The high school event was followed by an evening "recital sponsored by the Women's club of Bozeman."[32]

Another concert was planned for the Eagles Hall in Helena, but a series of earthquakes thwarted those plans. The quakes started with a small shock on October 3, 1935, and continued throughout the month. The most destructive earthquake came on October 18 and damaged three hundred buildings, even collapsing a wing of the brand-new high school. Helena's residents were understandably leery of being packed into public venues during the ongoing tremors, and Taylor's concert was sparsely attended.[33] As a result, Taylor lost money he paid on the hall rental for the concert.[34] Ultimately, his return to the concert stage in Montana was not the beginning of the comeback he had hoped for.

Although he had planned to return to New York in November 1935, Taylor stayed and spent the winter on C. H. Sherman's ranch on Sheep Creek, helping foreman Frank Miller. Over the winter, Taylor sat at a typewriter and banged out a book-length manuscript that he called "Daonda." That manuscript would change the course of Taylor's life, but not for the better.[35]

Once the winter was over, Taylor once again tried to make a go of both living in Montana and maintaining a singing career. In May 1936, the *Meagher County News* informed its readers that "Taylor Gordon went to Great Falls Tuesday where he appeared in concert at the Methodist Church under the sponsorship of the City Federation of Women's Clubs and the Dunbar Society of that city."[36] The Dunbar Art and Study Club got its start at the Union Bethel A.M.E. Church as early as 1917 during World War I and by the 1920s was one of several women's clubs affiliated with the larger Montana Federation of Negro Women's Clubs. The Dunbar Club was the home club for Elizabeth Webb Hill, an active member since the early 1920s and a friend and correspondent of Rose, who was acquainted with the town's African American community. Taylor remembered the concert fondly. As he later wrote to Hill, "Great Falls is on my mind many a time. I hope many of the good people I meet there are still around. Also that the 'wooden manhole-covers'are not steel or nailed down. Ha ha. I'll never forget the one that floated up under my car, the night of my concert there, in 1936."[37] Rose's friendship with Hill continued to develop, and Rose herself maintained a periodic membership in the Dunbar Art and Study Club. Other concert endeavors were not forthcoming, and Taylor returned to New York with his "Daonda" manuscript in tow.

With his performing career seemingly over, Taylor had some success as an inventor of toys and maintained a Gordon Games shop for a couple of years with the help of investors. Yet his growing obsession with John Steinbeck, particularly his belief that Steinbeck had based *The Grapes of Wrath* on "Daonda," drove him to stranger and stranger behavior, including several weeks spent picketing outside Viking Press headquarters protesting Steinbeck's "theft" of his book. Previously, Taylor had submitted the "Daonda" manuscript to Pascal Covici, whose company had published *Born to Be* in 1929. Covici subsequently moved to Viking Press as an editor, and Taylor came to believe that he had passed the manuscript along to Steinbeck at some point in the 1930s. While Taylor would not have been the first African American artist whose work had been stolen or whose culture had been appropriated to benefit white creators and producers, he had no evidence to support this belief.

Around the same time that Taylor was preparing for battle with John Steinbeck, Viking Press, and the motion picture industry, Rose was having her own struggles. She applied for unemployment compensation in November 1935 and October 1936, and then several times throughout 1940 and 1941. In 1939, Rose received a letter from Grayce Brewer Allen, living in Philadelphia at the time, who offered to bring Rose out east to live with the Allen family and work as a housekeeper. "I believe it would be a wonderful chance for you to break away from your present condition," Grayce wrote, "and perhaps this is a stepping stone to something better." She noted that her sister and mother were relatively nearby in New York, where "Mannie has been down to see them several times, in fact, I do believe they see him pretty often."[38] Ultimately, Rose declined, not wanting to leave her

Montana home. "We were so sorry to hear that you could not come to our home," Grayce wrote in reply, "but then I understand your position exactly. You have a fine little place yourself, one that you have built up, and one that has so many, many wonderful memories around it."[39]

Those memories had occupied Rose's attention throughout the decade, during which she began work on her own book manuscript, which she called "Gone are the Days." In April 1934, she received a letter from Caxton Publishers in Idaho, responding to her query about a manuscript but noting that they would need to see the whole manuscript before committing to publication.[40] For the next fifteen years, Rose attempted to publish her memoir.[41] References in the manuscript to Marian Anderson's famous concert at the Lincoln Memorial on April 9, 1939, as well as references to events taking place in Europe before the onset of World War II, suggest that she continued to revise the book at least into the 1940s. Initially, Caxton Publishers seemed to have had an interest in the manuscript. However, they wrote to her in 1946 advising her that due to wartime shortages they were two years behind in their publishing schedule and the manuscript could not be published by them until they caught up on their backlog. Three years later, they wrote to inform Rose that they remained two years behind schedule.[42] In 1959, Grace Stone Coates contacted Caxton on Rose's behalf, but the company continued to insist that they were too far behind on meeting their commitments to consider new manuscripts.[43]

Rose received a notice in July 1940 from the WPA to work as a seamstress at the "Sewing Room" in White Sulphur Springs. The notice lists her wage class as unskilled, and, interestingly, her race is marked "w."[44] From Rose's accounts of the WPA experience, she was ultimately let go from the job because she was Black, and it certainly seems like her supervisor's racial prejudice made the experience unpleasant. In a letter to one of the WPA administrators, Rose explained that she "just received a 403 from the Billings office" notifying her that she had been taken off the job, even though White Sulphur Springs had a quota of ten positions and only seven were filled. When Rose called the Billings office, "they told me that I was very capable and that was why I was taken off," which, as Rose acerbically noted, "was a very nice compliment but it won't make your living in a town where there is no work."[45] Rose clearly recognized that the "compliment" was a backhanded insult, implying that the problem was not that she was too capable but that she was that particularly threatening type of individual: a smart and capable Black woman.

Although Rose's published writings rarely address directly any racial prejudice that she faced while living in White Sulphur Springs, her correspondence tells a different story. In one letter, addressed to a "Mrs. Moore," Rose directly acknowledged the racism behind her dismissal and indicated her awareness of the racial prejudice that surrounded her:

> You well know what kind of chance a colored woman would have getting an office job here if she were over smart. Or any other kind of job. I was valedictorian of my class but my color kept me from getting a position, so I was forced to do Domestic work in other women's kitchens, until I saved up enough money to start a business of my own and I learned how one should be treated by a Boss. I also employed help when I was in business. The Depression broke me as it did other people.[46]

Moore had apparently come to the sewing room to make a "little speech" defending her supervisor and referring to a "temperamental" employee. "That temperamental stuff was meant for me," Rose observed. She offered a different perspective on the incident that caused Mrs. Moore to intervene by speaking to the workers: "Mrs. Harding came into the sewing [room] one morning angry about something and was very unpleasant all day, which was nothing uncommon. Right out of the Blue Sky she bawled me out disgracefully and there was no need of it, and it hurt me so much it made me sick."[47]

Rose also wrote two different letters to Roy Ayers, then governor of Montana, though it is unclear if she mailed them. In one letter, she made no mention of race at all, but expressed a desire to have her name cleared with the welfare office. In a separate, more direct message, she underscored the racial context of the WPA conflict, writing, "Hoping you can advise me about the [affair]. [From] what I can hear whispered, it is Racial on the part of the Supervisor."[48]

As African Americans in the West, the Gordons were not alone in feeling the effects of the Great Depression. Quintard Taylor observes that the Depression "ravaged Western black communities throughout the 1930s," with Black unemployment more than double that of white workers in many cities. Further, for African Americans in many parts of the West, "New Deal agencies did not guarantee public employment or relief," and many, including the WPA, discriminated against Black workers.[49] Although there were regional differences in how the New Deal agencies treated African Americans, Quintard Taylor's documentation of WPA discrimination lends credence to Rose's belief that racism caused her difficulties with the agency.

In 1941, Rose reentered the restaurant business. "Rose Gordon is advertising this week the opening of a café," the *Meagher County News* reported, "to be known as Rose's Place." Rose's paid advertisement made a more triumphant announcement. "The Rose returns to Broadway," it declared, and then it asked the question, "All Prize Fighters stage a come back, why not the Cooks?" The next week, Rose sent the newspaper a card of thanks, saying, "I wish to thank the people of White Sulphur Springs for their patronage on Easter Sunday. My come back was great. I found myself still able to take it on the chin."[50] Rose's Café, the establishment's formal name, remained in operation through 1944, although it closed for various periods of time and reappeared in different locations. In 1941 and 1942, Rose's Café was only open for business during the summer season, with Easter Sunday as the traditional opening day.

In September 1942, Rose completed the standard Red Cross Home Nursing course through the Meagher County chapter of the American National Red Cross. She then closed the restaurant and moved to Great Falls, where she worked as a nurse at the O. S. Warden Home, a facility that housed a number of servicemen among its patients.[51] A couple of months later, the *Meagher County News* printed a letter that Rose wrote to her hometown from Great Falls about seeing the B-17 bombers training from the newly constructed Great Falls Army Air Base :

> It is a beautiful sight to see the large bombers flying in for-
> mation. I saw ten one day. I see lots of soldiers here. There

are thirty-four of them sick in the hospitals. The people call
on them and cheer them all they can. Many of them from
warmer climates are very despondent. They have not really
experienced any cold weather yet. These camps having to
be prepared in so short a time places a great hardship on the
boys. I passed by the U.S.O. the other night and every boy
was writing a letter, I said to myself if you boys miss home as
much as I miss my dear old smith river valley it is too bad for
you all.[52]

Whether because her employment in Great Falls did not last or Rose's
homesickness for the Smith River valley got the best of her, Rose returned
to White Sulphur Springs and her café in 1943. Wartime shortages, lean
budgets, and the shifting workforce made it difficult for Rose to operate
her restaurant cost-effectively, and hers was not the only business that
suffered. The *Meagher County News* reported a year earlier that "Frank
O'Dell closed up his restaurant on Thursday of last week. So many people
have left the community that his restaurant business has slackened to a
point where it is no longer profitable to operate."[53] In addition to draftees
and volunteers for the armed services, wartime manufacturing in other
states drew temporary workers away from Montana's small towns for long
periods. In 1943, upon learning that Working's Store, the Western Bakery,
and the W. G. Woodward store, all of which had "been operated over a
term of years," planned to close permanently, the *Meagher County News*
reported, "Local people realized how deep the war has bit into small town
business."[54]

In an effort to survive, the town's restaurants changed locations and
owners frequently during the war. In 1942, Annie Berg bought out Frank's
Café, which Frank O'Dell had operated, and renamed it Victory Café.
Berg moved her business to a larger space in the Woodward Building the
following year and renamed it the Rainbow Café. Rose then reopened her
restaurant in the space that Berg had vacated on August 25, 1943. As the
Meagher County News noted about Rose's return to the restaurant business after an absence of nearly a year, "Rose has been in the restaurant
business in several different locations in White Sulphur Springs during the
years past."[55] In September 1943, Rose started running an advertisement

for Rose Gordon's Café, which appeared continuously through October 1944. In a ledger, Rose recorded that she served 264 patrons, accounting for $692, during the last week of August 1943. By Christmas of that year, Rose was doing well enough to hire two extra workers to help her out.[56] In June 1944, Rose changed locations again, "to the building formerly occupied by Everett Hawthorne's barbershop."[57]

Rose nonetheless found turning a profit during wartime difficult. In October 1944, the *Meagher County News* reported, "Mr. and Mrs. V. E. Wood completed a deal on Tuesday of this week whereby they became the owners of Rose's café."[58] With that sale, after nearly forty years of preparing meals for visitors and citizens of White Sulphur Springs, Rose Gordon retired permanently from the restaurant business.

Retirement, however, was not the end for Rose as a businesswoman, but the beginning of her comeback. After the sale, Rose concentrated on the healthcare services that she had been offering sporadically throughout much of her life. From 1944 to 1968, she made a successful living as a massage specialist, physiotherapist, and private nurse. She had wanted this career from a young age, and the sale of the restaurant and her subsequent retirement gave her the opportunity to make that dream come true. She began purchasing equipment for Rose's Massage Parlor in 1945. Four years later, she enrolled in a correspondence course offered by the College of Swedish Massage, and she purchased a massage table, which was installed in the Gordon home. In 1947, a continuing advertisement started to appear in the *Meagher County News* offering "Body Massage"—and later, "Electric Massage"—at Rose's Salon of Health and Beauty, by appointment.

Rose coordinated her efforts with local physicians and worked out of the newly built Mountain View Memorial Hospital roughly every other day—usually Monday, Wednesday, and Friday. After a sawmill opened in White Sulphur Springs in the early 1950s, she treated injured workers referred by Montana's Industrial Accident Board, seeing from four to six patients at the hospital each day. Her appointment book, kept from 1957 to 1967, indicates that she maintained a busy schedule until almost the final year of her life, frequently recording multiple one-hour appointments a day.[59]

Several of Rose's books and ledgers, labeled "Therapy Treatment Accounts, 1945–56," reveal the growth of her healthcare business. It began to take off in 1949, when her client list expanded. Both massage and nursing provided her with a steady income, and sometimes she earned a bit more through the charge of room and board for long-term care: four months for Art Jenkins, thirty-four days for Frank Williams, nineteen days for Nora Buckley, and twenty-one days for Jennie Smiley. Rose listed board separately for many of the patients, as her nursing care often included preparing food for them as well. Sometimes her care involved all these services, as in 1954, when she charged Bernard Weatherhead for nursing, board, and room, as well as additional payments for therapy treatments, from March 14 through July 3.[60]

Rose also offered end-of-life care. As part of those services, she wrote letters at the behest of the patients to their family members and friends, who otherwise would have no opportunity for a final word. Much of the correspondence addressed to Rose from this era consists of letters of thanks from the grateful recipients of those final messages. One writer, Della M. Stephens, replied to Rose and asked her to send her photos of her brother's headstone: "I am so glad that his grave is not far from your people's graves. I am also thankful that I can contact you personally in regard to my brother's grave if it should need keeping up or care in any way." She later wrote to thank Rose for "placing flowers on my Brother's grave. . . . I hope you will excuse this long letter Miss Gordon but some how I feel I have found a real friend in you."[61]

While Rose's healthcare business was largely successful, receiving full compensation for her services was not a guarantee. In September 1952, Rose provided nursing care for two weeks for Nora Buckley, staying with the dying woman in her room at the Broadwater Hospital in Townsend, Montana. For that care, she charged a fee of $30.00 a day. After her death, Buckley's husband refused to pay Rose. In October, Rose filed a creditor's claim against Buckley's estate for $571.94, including reimbursement for phone calls Rose made on the woman's behalf. In December, she received notice that the executor of the estate agreed to allow payment of $250.63, but "rejected and denied" the balance of the claim.[62] Rose worked with a local law firm to receive full payment to no avail, even though her attorney, Joseph T. Wilson, verified Rose's work with Dr. Nash, the attending physician, which he passed along to the estate's executor. Wilson assumed that if the judge "cared about doing justice in your case, he would then consent that the claim be brought up for re-consideration." But the judge did not, instead informing Wilson that he would only be able to change his order if all parties came to an agreement. As Wilson informed Rose, "Under the circumstances, there seems to be nothing that we can do, and about all we can say now is that we think you had a raw deal and are sorry that we cannot do something about it."[63]

Rose was not the only Gordon to get a "raw deal" during this period. Although Rose's postwar prospects were generally improving, John Francis Jr., living in Seattle, had his own financial difficulties. In October 1947, he wrote to his brother Robert:

> I have been on the shelf for the past year. I worked too hard during the war but what's the use of working so hard when you have to spend it all for Doctors? Well Seattle is sure a place there is lots of colored people here but not no work. Lots of them have bought homes and it's going hard for them to make payments but I guess by the good will of God they will be able to make the grade.
> I worked for a Greek at the US Hotel but he won't pay me my overtime so I will have to take it to the labor board. I have quite a sum coming. How is George? I wrote him but he hasn't answered yet I guess maybe he is busy. What are you doing to keep yourself busy in WSS. Has the old town grown much? I sometimes long to see it, but it is so cold in the winter, so hot in summer.[64]

Either John Francis's appeal to the labor board did not bring the sum he was expecting or the money did not last. Within a few months, he again queried his brother for money. Robert's negative response elicited a letter of apology from John Francis: "Bob I am sure sorry that you think I thought money grew on trees but whatever I get from you I will pay with interest. It's my fault I am in this shape but with some help getting back my strength I think I will make the grade."[65]

Although nothing in these letters directly suggests a racial context, an African American man or woman seeking legal recourse from a white employer faced an uphill battle in the 1940s. John Francis and Rose had not been paid money they were owed and had to seek redress from government officials or agencies that were not sympathetic to their claims. In some ways, the injustices that John Francis and Rose experienced bring to mind Taylor's belief that John Steinbeck and Viking Press had taken advantage of him. In Taylor's case, the understandable sense of grievance he felt developed into delusional fantasies of unfair treatment as a result of his mental illness.

All the Gordons were deeply concerned about Taylor, and their apprehension was exacerbated by the strangeness of his condition and the distance between Montana and New York. Before his institutionalization, they did not so much worry about Taylor as express an occasional sense of irritation with his behavior, especially when he asked them for money. "So Mannie is a hay seed," George wrote to Rose in 1939, "quite a swell dish for a famous tenor . . . wasting a beautiful talent simply because of the lack of Human Knowledge, I mean real knowledge of courtesy." Even in his frustration, George could forgive Taylor's behavior. "Oh well," George allowed, "he is still younger than we are."[66]

But Taylor's behavior became much more disturbing than asking for loans. Shortly before the police took him to Bellevue Hospital in July 1947 following a call from his landlord, the *Meagher County News* published a letter from him. An earlier discussion in the paper about building a hospital in White Sulphur Springs, which eventually became Mountain View Memorial Hospital, occasioned his message, which read:

> When I was with John Ringling I had my hopes built high in seeing such a building standing in the park and people from different parts of the world coming to take the baths, but you know how that trial balloon cracked up.
>
> It was not until I was snowed in, in the mountains on Sheep Creek, in 1936 that I really got the yen to see that dream come true, and I am now about as close to it as I will ever be.
>
> The manuscript "Daonda" which is the father of "Grapes of Wrath" has earned millions, and during the passed [*sic*] seven years I have battled diligently, to a success, in convincing to the people of these United States, that truth.
>
> So upon this day after going through one of the most hectic "I Q" (Intelligence test) ever given in the history of

this nation we find, I passed, and how; God only knows, for I didn't know that so many people had so little faith in the laws of the nation or God.[67]

After a paragraph observing how the hospital would be important not only to White Sulphur Springs but "the people of the west," Taylor then offered, "When the money that is rightly mine, is given to me, I will turn it over, all except my share, to proper authorities who will see that it is well spent right and obtain the necessary personnel and facilities, to open the hospital." Although based on his fantasy that he would one day be compensated for a manuscript that Steinbeck allegedly stole from him, the letter is otherwise coherent and fairly amusing. At one point, he kids with editor Fred Ward, an advocate of building a hospital in town: "I know you have had many a hot flash regarding such a building during the years you have been the editor of the Meagher County News, better known as the 'RAG,' Ha, Ha!"[68]

Yet Taylor's letter also includes a strange reference to the "hectic" IQ test. He also closed the message curiously: "I have been waiting since the war to send a lot of people some post cards and I wanted to mail them the day I left, but now I am changing my mind; that's a good laugh too. I can't leave any openings for anymore ALIBIES. So if you learn I have mailed some, to some one that might have died or not there just remember that I took the names out of the Rag of January 22, 1947. A lot of water could run over the dam since then." The specific reference to the January 22, 1947, edition of the *Meagher County News*—which may just be the edition that made it to him in New York—is certainly odd, especially as it seems to have provided him with a list of names for sending postcards that he had not yet sent.[69] In his other writings, he uses the words "alibi" and "tail" interchangeably with both words usually written in all caps, referring to his belief that he was being followed or tailed.[70] His exact meaning is difficult to determine, but it is easy to see why this letter might have given his siblings cause for concern.

The other Gordons certainly recognized that Taylor was mentally ill, but they also seemed to believe that his accusations of plagiarism were at least plausible. In September 1947, after Taylor had been two months into his commitment, George Gordon wrote to Bob: "I wired NY for information in regard to Mannie and soon as I hear I will give you the dope. That article in the paper was a bad sign to me although I believe he is right in that respect. I hope he is still alive, but a nut in a big city is in bad if no one looks after him. Of course, a crazy man is dead anyhow. But I want to hope he can see the light again."[71]

After a brief stay in Bellevue Hospital, Taylor was confined to Manhattan State Hospital on Ward's Island. Rose queried the hospital director, who sent a letter to her in September 1947 stating, "Your brother was hospitalized because of his strange behavior and delusional ideas." The letter also informed Rose that the doctors thought it advisable "that he receive shock treatment" and enclosed a permission form for her to sign.[72] In a sequel to *Born to Be* that Taylor wrote during the last years of his life, he described a conversation he later had with his brother Robert, who told him that he and Rose had discussed the request and decided not to grant permission.[73] While Taylor was released in 1948, he was by no means cured of his delusions. He visited White Sulphur Springs in 1949, then returned to New York against Rose's advice. In May 1952, he was hospitalized again, and he remained in a mental institution for seven years, mostly at Central Islip State Hospital, until released to Rose's care in the winter of 1959.

Taylor's illness was just one of the tragedies the Gordons faced in the postwar era. Both George and John Francis died prematurely, George in 1948 and John Francis in 1952. According to his obituary in the *Bozeman Courier*, George Washington Gordon, "the steward at the Bozeman Elks club for 29 years, died early Tuesday morning at the Bozeman Deaconess hospital after a four month illness."[74] The October 22, 1948, obituary and a report on the funeral in the *Meagher County News* noted that following George's memorial service in Bozeman, his body was buried in the Mayn Cemetery in White Sulphur Springs, where a graveside service was held. In Bozeman, the "members of the Elks lodge sang 'There is no Night' and 'Lead Kindly Light,'" the report noted. "The coffin," it continued, "was banked with a floral tribute given by the Elks lodge and the people of Bozeman who had known George during the 29 years that he had lived in that city."[75] In a letter to John Francis, Rose wrote, "We lost our little Brother

George in Bozeman he had cancer was in the hospital for 4 months. Dear little fellow he was so kind to me I miss him very much. The Elks were grand to him they paid his hospital bill—they were grand to him, he suffered so much. I went back and forth for four months."[76]

George had found a home in Bozeman, and, through his employment at the Elks Club, a steady income, friends, and appreciative employers. Contributors to *The Antler*, the Bozeman Lodge's newsletter, regularly expressed their appreciation for his work.[77] For example, after George's service at a "Stag Night Dinner" in 1948, Art Duntsch wrote to thank him for the "splendid" dinner he "so graciously prepared and served." Duntsch added a heartfelt note of appreciation, saying, "These fellows really enjoy your feeds as you already found out personally the evening they greeted you with a round of applause."[78] George had also played "a star part in many of the Elks' Minstrel shows in Bozeman," a yearly event to raise money for charitable causes in Bozeman and Gallatin County.[79] In addition to participating in other parts of the show, George usually contributed a solo.

George Gordon's hometown paper had followed his life even years after George moved to Bozeman. In 1945, the *Meagher County News* reprinted a celebration of George from *The Antler*. As the dialect sections of the article suggest, the Elks' fondness for minstrel humor was not restricted to the stage:

> Much has been said about the so called "indispensable man" pro and con—but it behooves the editor to bring forth and give credit to one fellow who is almost indispensable as far as Bozeman Lodge No. 463 is concerned. This fellow is none other than our George Gordon, whose official title we might say is assistant steward in charge of Elks' feeds and lunches. Stag night or Ladies night, —whatever it might be, George struts his stuff . . .
>
> Those on the outside will really never be in the know just why the boys of Elkdom in 463 are so full of pep and vinegar until one gets on the inside and partakes of George's sumptuous feeds "and boss what ah means they are sho' some spreads." In short these added features are part of the drawing card to the local club—and George deserves considerable credit for his part of the program.[80]

George had made himself a part of the community by following, as did Rose, in the steps of his chef father and caterer mother as well as by contributing his musical skills. In contemporary terms, George was adept at code-switching, meaning he could employ different social languages depending on the situation. He could perform skillfully in the kitchen but ably shift to the role of minstrel performer at fundraising events. He likely employed some combination of the two in his interactions with club members. George, like the other Gordon family members, understood the necessity of sometimes wearing the mask of minstrelsy. He was also graciously accommodating when his white employers adopted the fractured dialect of minstrelsy while they sincerely praised the contributions their African American employee made to the club.

Like Rose, George had also made himself a part of his community through kind and neighborly behavior. In an undated letter, a woman named Lulu, having heard about his illness from a notice in *The Antler*, wrote to George from Boise, Idaho, where she had moved: "Don't think it said what your illness was but hope it isn't anything serious. I'm sure you remember us as we lived across the street from you in Bozeman, the one that had the crippled boy that you tried to learn him to sing. He is working in Spokane running a theatre now."[81] In Bozeman, George had cultivated friendly relations with his neighbors. They expressed appreciation for his contributions in various ways, the Elks Club paying his hospital bills being one example, but also through sharing remembrances of his kindness.

After an article about Taylor and Rose appeared in the *Helena Independent* in 1967, Beatrice Simms, a former resident of Bozeman, wrote to Rose to share her memory of George: "My husband Jim and I lived in Bozeman, Mont, after we married in Helena. He worked at the Elks home in Bozeman. Your brother George came to Bozeman and worked at the Elks home too. He kept company with a very good friend of mine Eva Robinson, and we all became very close friends for years. You come over to Bozeman and stayed with Eva. That's when we first met."[82] During his hospitalization, George also received get-well wishes from Elizabeth Hill in Great Falls and a card from the Butte Branch of the NAACP, indications of the web of relationships he had established with Montana's widely dispersed African American community.[83]

In November 1948, shortly after George passed away, Taylor was released from an institution in New York. He was again committed to a mental institution in May 1952, just a few months before his brother John Francis Jr. died of a heart attack. As John Francis's obituary in the *Meagher County News* noted, "Mr. Gordon became a cook, and was employed by the United States Steamship lines. This job took him to all the major ports of the world." As a young man, "he worked on various ranches in this county, including the Buckingham and Hanson ranches. He was known to his friends as 'Sambo.'" There is no indication, however, that he was known by this racially marked stereotypical nickname in Seattle. He referenced the name in his letters to family members, signing off as "Sam," although usually enclosing that name in quotation marks, perhaps suggesting an ironic distance from a name he had left behind in 1912 when he moved away. Although John Francis never returned to his hometown, the newspaper reported that his body would be "cremated in Seattle and the ashes brought to White Sulphur Springs."[84] White Sulphur Springs might have been too hot in the summer and too cold in the winter for Sam's tastes during his lifetime, but he finally made his way back after death.

There had clearly been some distance between John Francis and his family members, but the frequency of letters between him and his siblings seems to have picked up around the time of George's death and thereafter. Rose was particularly close to George. They had been singing partners, and she had visited him often in Bozeman. In one letter to Taylor, Rose noted that "George kept his illness to himself." Although he "suffered terrible" from the progress of cancer, "George did not want to worry anybody about his illness."[85] Like Rose, George put his concern for the feelings of others above himself. The Gordons' renewed correspondence with one another following George's death suggests that their shared mourning brought the siblings closer together during the years between his passing and John Francis's, even though they could not give John Francis the homecoming they might have wished for him during his lifetime.

CHAPTER 8

Rose's Civic and Community Life

In December 1951, Rose left wintry Montana and traveled to sunny Los Angeles. Her three-week trip included visits to Ruth and Grayce Brewer and their mother Eleanor, Rose's second grade teacher and longtime piano instructor, as well as several other former residents of White Sulphur Springs who had migrated to southern California. The trip occasioned one of her many contributions to the *Meagher County News* in the 1950s. She enjoyed "a fine time" traveling on a train filled with other Montanans.[1] "I thought of the old Jaw Bone train," Rose mused. "I have reached the promised land of sunshine and flowers," she wrote, but only after the Union Pacific train struggled through snow-covered Utah, taking thirty-six hours to make the trip from Salt Lake City to Los Angeles. As Rose described it, "I had the urge to take off my overshoes." When the train reached Riverside, Rose was delighted to be greeted by the orange trees for which that town is famous. "Such a sight in December," she exclaimed. "Those large trees of the desert and their large yellow blossoms were beautiful."[2]

Greeted at the depot by Ruth and Grayce, "the children I baby-sat for years," Rose and her old friends started catching up immediately. "I have not managed to get away," Rose wrote. "We had so much to talk about. Mrs. Brewer is not well but has that same grand spirit. I think we have just about got them all about talked over."[3] The following week, she highlighted one of the adventures of her trip: "We will shake hands with the grand old Pacific ocean."[4] While Rose was in Los Angeles, she saw the sights—from Grauman's Chinese Theatre to the view from Hollywood

Hills. She made special note of the city's multicultural environment: "I saw a colored Catholic priest and his parish of children out playing. He was instructing them. All races side by side in many large places." Even while observing that "the sun is beautiful today," Rose began thinking about her return to White Sulphur Springs: "I hope the Union Pacific is feeling better when I start home. The snow almost got her down."[5]

After Rose's return from California in late January, she started to experience health problems that would bother her throughout the rest of her life. In February 1952, she was admitted to the hospital in nearby Broadwater County, as Meagher County had no hospital. Robert wrote to Rose, "Dear Sis, I received your letter and am glad you are improving. Of course, when one gets high toned enough to go to California, he or she must expect some kind of reaction, good or bad."[6] In a letter to John Francis, Rose explained that her hospital stay was due to a "bladder attack," but the X-rays showed no stones and she was told to "keep on a diet."[7] The *Meagher County News* reported the next month that she was "home again after a term in the hospital in Townsend as a medical patient. She is feeling much better."[8] Rose would be hospitalized periodically throughout the remainder of the decade. The *Meagher County News* again mentioned that she had been discharged from the hospital in Townsend in 1955. She was also listed as a hospital patient in October 1959.[9]

Despite her occasional bouts of illness, and a journey every now and again, the final decade and a half of Rose Gordon's life followed the pattern she had established in the late 1940s and early 1950s. During these years she served the community as a nurse and massage therapist and continued to develop her role as the area's "heart and historian."[10] Rose was also involved in several organizations both in and outside of White Sulphur Springs. She became a highly visible member of multiple groups, joining the statewide Montana Federation of Negro Women's Clubs and the Montana and Meagher County historical societies, becoming an officer in the state's massage therapists' organization, and emerging as a prominent voice in the *Meagher County News*.[11] Her engagement with these organizations and her connections with the extended African American community in Montana prompted her to become politically active in issues affecting Montana's Black population. Another notable feature of

Rose's life in the 1950s and 1960s was Taylor's nearly decade-long confinement in New York state mental institutions and Rose's ongoing efforts to get him released.

🙢🙠

Beginning in the 1940s and continuing into the 1950s, Rose was actively if intermittently involved with the Montana Federation of Colored Women's Clubs, attending meetings at the Great Falls chapter of the group's Dunbar Art and Study Club with her friend and frequent correspondent Elizabeth Hill. Club records list Rose as being a member in 1945 and 1946. In 1938, she had joined a letter-writing campaign that the Federation organized in support of an antidiscrimination bill before the Montana legislature. When that bill failed and was taken up again in 1951, she sent a letter to Myron Tripp, the legislator who introduced the measure, thanking him and observing, "I am praying for the day when people will learn that the people of the earth are God's people; and no race has the right to dominate the other."[12] She attended the twenty-sixth annual statewide convention of the Montana Federation of Colored Women's Clubs in Anaconda in July 1947. She likewise attended the group's thirtieth annual convention four years later in Great Falls. Rose's active involvement with the Montana Federation of Colored Women's Clubs may have led her to develop a more assertive and actively political stance on many issues.

African American women's participation in service-oriented women's clubs is another area of Western history that needs further investigation. Importantly, clubs served multiple functions, from offering a social network and providing educational opportunities to lending support for social and legal justice for Blacks. Because the General Federation of Women's Clubs had "a long-standing policy of accepting black women's organizations only as segregated locals," as historian Glenda Riley has pointed out, African American women "formed a parallel organization, the National Association of Colored Women, in 1896, and by 1915 it had fifty thousand members in twenty-eight state federations and over a thousand individual clubs."[13]

The Montana Federation of Negro Women's Clubs was organized at a meeting in Butte, Montana, on August 3, 1921. Representatives of seven of the existing local women's clubs attended: the Clover Leaf Art Club (Butte; established 1921), the Good Word Club (Anaconda; established 1921), the Mary B. Talbert Club (Helena; established 1921), the Mutual Improvement Club (Kalispell), the Pleasant Hour Club (Helena; established 1916), the Pearl Club (Butte; established 1918), and the Phyllis Wheatley Club (Billings; established 1920). Although not represented at the meeting, Rose and George Gordon's friend Eva Robinson had also organized the Sweet Pea Study Club of Bozeman in 1921 and served as its first president. The Great Falls Dunbar Art and Study Club, established in 1920, was also absent from the meeting, but joined the federation in 1922.[14] Like some of the other women's clubs, the Dunbar Club built on an already established tradition of community service centered around the Union Bethel African Methodist Episcopal Church. While the church had resided in the same location since 1891, its congregation dated to 1884, just one year after Great Falls itself was founded.[15] In 1948, the statewide organization voted to change its name to the Montana Federation of Colored Women's Clubs.

Riley observes that the primary concerns of African American women's clubs involved "meeting the needs of the black community—promoting racial self-help and raising the standards of women and families to counter prejudice and accusations of immorality."[16] On behalf of the member clubs, the Federation made annual donations to national organizations, including the Anti-Lynching League and the NAACP.[17] In 1951, the organization established the Claudia Bivens Scholarship Fund, an annual grant award to a Black Montanan attending college either in-state or out-of-state. The Federation also organized letter-writing campaigns, like those that Rose had participated in, and other actions supporting or opposing proposed legislation in the Montana state legislature.[18]

Local clubs in Montana demonstrated their commitment to the Black community in multiple ways. For example, in 1921, the Mary B. Talbert Club succeeded in placing two books by African American writers on the shelves of the Helena Public Library: W. E. B. Du Bois's *Dark Water* and Maud Cuney Hare's biography of her father, Wright W. Cuney. Previously the library only had one volume authored by an African American writer: a collection of Paul Laurence Dunbar's poems. In a 1926 letter to the

Federation, Katherine Smith, president of the Good Word Club in Anaconda, reported that, among the club's yearly activities, "we have visited the sick, eased the dying, and helped those in distress." Smith highlighted one particular action taken by the club: "Last week we had to step forward and get a lawyer to protect one of the women of our race that had had a little trouble and the law had threatened to take her babies and send her to prison." Through the efforts of the club women and their lawyer, the woman was released.[19]

Rose maintained friendships and correspondence with several women who were active in African American women's organizations at the local, state, and national level, most notably Eva Robinson in Bozeman, Octavia Bridgewater in Helena, and Elizabeth Hill in Great Falls. She knew Robinson through her brother George, who had "kept company" with her for several years. Rose would often stay with Eva when she visited George in Bozeman. Octavia Bridgewater was a nurse, and their shared work in healthcare connected the two. Elizabeth Hill was a massage therapist, and, in addition to coordinating with one another on civil rights issues, she and Rose joined with other masseuses in the late 1950s and early 1960s to form a professional organization.

Bridgewater and Hill were central figures in the Montana women's clubs, both in their local chapters and as active members of the state Federation. From as early as the 1920s until the Federation disbanded in 1972, each of these women held a variety of officer and committee chair positions, and Hill served as Federation president for several years from the late 1960s onward. As early as 1927, Bridgewater helped organize the group's annual convention. As the newly elected chair of the Federation's music department, she wrote to the Clover Leaf Art Club in Butte to send them the program she put together for that year's convention.

Octavia Bridgewater grew up in Helena, and, like Rose Gordon, lost her father while she was a child. Her father, Samuel Bridgewater, was a "buffalo soldier," a member of a unit of segregated army troops stationed in the western United States. A veteran of the Spanish-American War who had been wounded in the Battle of San Juan Hill, he was originally posted at Fort Huachuca in Arizona. In 1903, he transferred to Fort Harrison, near Helena. Octavia's mother, Mamie Bridgewater, raised their five children on her own after Samuel Bridgewater died in 1912. Mamie was one of the founders of the Pleasant Hour Club and remained active in the club into her seventies.[20]

Octavia Bridgewater graduated from Helena High School in 1927, at which point she had already been an active member of Helena's Pleasant Hour Club for years. The following year, a report submitted by the club historian to the Federation acknowledged, "One of the faithful members of the Club, left this year in the person of Octavia Bridgewater. She went to New York City to take up nursing as a profession. We wish her God's speed."[21] In New York, Bridgewater studied at the Lincoln School for Nurses, an institution dedicated to training African American nurses. In 1930, she returned to Helena and worked as a private duty nurse, as Helena's hospitals did not hire Black nurses at that time—a situation that did not change until after World War II, when Bridgewater broke the color barrier.[22] After moving back to Montana, she also rejoined the Pleasant Hour Club. In 1940, she became "the first negro nurse to enroll in the Red Cross Nursing Service in Montana," with the goal that she would eventually serve with segregated army units after completing her initial service.[23] Bridgewater began active duty in 1943, serving for two years and earning the rank of first lieutenant. When she returned to Helena after the war, she worked as a maternity nurse at St. Peter's Hospital.[24]

When Rose attended the thirtieth annual convention of the Montana Federation of Colored Women's Clubs in 1951, Bridgewater was then treasurer of the Federation. If Rose had met Bridgewater before, the 1951 convention cemented their friendship. By 1952, the *Meagher County News* noted that Bridgewater had made her first visit to White Sulphur Springs and was staying with Rose.[25] That friendship continued for the remainder of Rose's life. In 1964, the *Meagher County News* reported, "Rose Gordon was a business caller in Helena on Tuesday and was a guest of Octavia Bridgewater."[26]

As was the case with Bridgewater, Elizabeth Hill's involvement with Black women's clubs originated with her mother, Frances Peterson. Born in Iowa in 1874 and spending much of her life in Nebraska, Peterson arrived in Montana in 1922, where she was an active member of the Seventh-day Adventist Church as well as being involved with the Dunbar Art and

Study Club.[27] Like her mother, Hill was an active member of the Dunbar Club as early as 1924, when her membership is noted as Mrs. Elizabeth Webb.[28] She later married Burr Hill and is listed in Dunbar Club minutes as Elizabeth Webb Hill after 1936.

Rose's involvement with women's clubs was intermittent, but at the very least they provided her a means of making connections with other African American women. Indeed, Rose built a support network of Black women friends with whom she visited and corresponded throughout her life. For instance, Rose came to know Lulu B. McCabe of Billings at the Federation's 1947 meeting. At the time, McCabe was listed as the organization's second vice president and—as with Hill and Bridgewater—was a central figure in the organization throughout the twentieth century. Perhaps due to the longer distance between White Sulphur Springs and Billings, McCabe was not as intimately connected with Rose as Hill and Bridgewater were. Nonetheless, after the 1947 meeting she wrote to Rose to say, "I enjoyed my vacation at Anaconda where my usual friends greeted me and also several new ones, you being amongst them. I saw your friend Mrs. Chase yesterday and she rejoiced to hear about you as she grew up with you and other members of your family. She would like so much to see you again. Couldn't you come over to Billings soon?"[29] By 1947, Eva Robinson had moved from Bozeman to Salt Lake City but returned to Montana for the 1947 Federation meeting. She later wrote to Rose, "I have been trying to write you ever since I have been home from the Federation. I was so glad to see you and all the dear old friends. . . . I thought the State Federation was just perfect, no unpleasantness, no signs of anyone being mad or upset."[30]

Given the timing of Rose's active participation in the women's clubs, it seems reasonable to suggest that the model of activism they presented contributed to Rose's decision to throw her own hat into the political arena. As she became a more frequent contributor to the *Meagher County News*, she commented on political and social concerns more often. Her letters to the editor in the late 1940s addressed critical local issues and town governance. In 1947, for instance, she protested the newspaper's decision to stop publishing the salaries of public employees, arguing for transparency in local government—especially concerning budget issues.[31] The following year she commented on the maintenance and upkeep of the Mayn Cemetery, advocating that the city government take on a responsibility that had been paid for solely by a private individual who had since died.[32]

In 1951, Rose decided to run for mayor of White Sulphur Springs. Marcella Sherfy argues that she did so because she was "frustrated by slow attention to community problems."[33] Quixotic as her election campaign may have been—she was a political neophyte running against an experienced incumbent—her decision shone a light on the prejudice that at other times remained less visible in the community. At one point during the campaign, Rose received an anonymous letter—or, more correctly, a letter signed "Annonomus [*sic*]"—threatening that even if she won the election, no one would serve with her: "I doubt very much if, any of the incumbent councilmen . . . would even accept their office, with you as mayor." Just in case Rose might miss the implications, the writer clarified, "This Miss Gordon is due to your color," and ended the letter by saying, "I suggest that, you withdraw your name from the ballot for no one will serve with you."[34] Unsurprisingly, Rose lost the election to Elmer Schye, 207 votes to 58.[35] Although soundly defeated, Rose made a good showing for an inexperienced candidate, let alone an African American woman running for mayor in a rural town that had only two registered Black voters: Rose and her brother Robert.

After the election, Rose published a letter explaining her decision to run for mayor:

> I was born in Meagher county and have always had a deep
> regard for White Sulphur Springs. I filed for office because
> any one regardless of race, color or creed has a right to file for
> office. We vote for whom ever we wish to. I was in business for
> many years on Main street. They came into my place of busi-
> ness from the smallest county office in town to the governors
> of the state and the senators who were elected to congress to
> get me to do what I could for them. . . . My hobby has always
> been people. I love to study them and watch their reactions.[36]

Whatever originally motivated her to run for office, this letter reveals that she shared the same belief in civil rights as other African Americans across the country did and that she ran for office as a way of exercising her right, "regardless of race, color or creed," to do so. Her decision to become a mayoral candidate, taking place when she was most actively involved with the Montana Federation of Colored Women's Clubs, may have been partially inspired by that affiliation. She shared her experiences at the organization's 1951 meeting, where, according to the secretary of the Federation's records, "Miss Rose Gordon of White Sulphur Springs spoke on her filing for mayor and how the town people supported her."[37]

Rose occasionally expressed contradictory opinions on race and on the issue of civil rights. In a 1957 letter to the *Meagher County News*, she worried that the larger civil rights movement had "a vicious purpose to destroy not only the rights of the negro, but the rights of all American citizens."[38] Written a few months before the Civil Rights Act of 1957 became law, and perhaps inspired by the turmoil and activism leading up to that legislation, Rose seems to have been concerned about possible communist influences in the civil rights movement and expressed skepticism about the wisdom of using legislation to change social attitudes. A year later, however, she wrote to Taylor, "Well, I guess the South will secede from the Union. When they told the Negro to go back to Africa, they don't know who Africa belongs to. They are a bright lot down south. There is a bunch of them here from N.C., timber workers. A stupid lot, they are all broke, came here from Livingston, the timber has a terrible lot of riffraff with it."[39] In terms much more blunt than she ever used in her published writing, Rose expressed no sympathy for white Southerners' backlash against civil rights legislation and activism. The letter also suggests another reason that Rose consistently contrasted White Sulphur Springs's past and present when it came to racial attitudes: an influx of Southern workers that seems to have altered the racial climate of White Sulphur Springs. That Rose's therapy practice often involved treating injured timber workers may have also brought her into closer contact with prejudiced attitudes and caused her to be more assertive.

Although Rose had her difficulties, the final decades of her life stand in sharp contrast to her brother Taylor's downward spiral. In the same letter in which he teased his sister about her California adventure, Robert also noted, "Got another one of those letters from Taylor, only a little more to his satisfaction, that is as he writes."[40] All the Gordon siblings would receive "one of those letters from Taylor"—or more accurately, one after another—as the decade went on. Taylor wrote letters to everyone he could think of: family, friends, and acquaintances; columnist Walter Winchell; Federal Bureau of Investigation director J. Edgar Hoover; President Eisenhower; and many more government officials, political leaders, and public figures.

In letters he sent to Rose and Robert, Taylor continually tried to explain his situation, outlining the conspiracy that he believed led to his institutionalization. Although correspondence between the siblings reveals that they recognized Taylor's illness, they carefully acknowledged the validity of his grievances in their letters to him. They certainly thought it possible that Taylor's "Daonda" manuscript could have been stolen by John Steinbeck and Viking Press, but his story kept getting more and more far-fetched. Rose and Robert eventually found themselves entertaining Taylor's belief that he had been recruited by the FBI to engage in activities that he never entirely explained.

In 1953, Taylor wrote to Robert from the Manhattan State Hospital, "I know some people thought I'd be a 'natural' for their 'incredible plot.' What they did not know was that I knew they were a 'frustrated lot,' or else they would not have joined in any such idea . . . I know you are familiar with what I mean, although much has been kept from you." He ended the letter, "I have written Steinbeck and gang to call off the dog, and only silence on anyone else's part will prove a point."[41] Here, Taylor seems to refer to several of his ongoing delusions: the theft of his manuscript by Steinbeck, his belief that "Steinbeck and gang" had plotted to persecute him, and his belief that this persecution involved a broader plot involving multiple individuals acting against him so they could record and broadcast his actions for the entertainment of a watching audience. As his hospital stay continued, his delusions shifted toward the plot involving FBI recruitment, and his progressing illness altered the way he remembered the past. Although letters and other documents written in the late 1940s detailed the actions of the "Steinbeck gang," they did not mention Hoover or the FBI. By the 1950s, however, when he retold those earlier experiences, suddenly the FBI assumed a major role.

His siblings played along as best they could, seemingly with the intention of calming Taylor down. Resisting or questioning him only seemed to make him angry and made him believe that Robert and Rose were part of the conspiracy. Along these lines, Robert wrote to Taylor in 1955, "Bro Tayler: I received your letter, and the one that you wrote to the Director of the Bureau, and that cleared up some of the trouble that keeps you in there. I thought all the time it was a click, but you never told Sis and I about the cause. I am sorry for it is a sad plight, but I think that there will be something done very soon."[42]

Between 1952 and 1959, Rose took the central role of communicating with hospital administrators. Although she sometimes wrote to her brother that she wished he had stayed in Montana rather than returning to New York, Taylor asserted that his location would have made no difference to his dilemma: "As to my friends here, I know lots of people, but when the chips are down you can't tell who will stick with you. I stayed away from many people because I did not want their homes bugged. Every place I went was under watch when I returned in 1949." Why, Taylor suggests, would he stay in Montana when he was under surveillance there as well? Why would he have been able to trust his Montana friends any more than his New York ones? In his letters to Rose and Robert, Taylor repeatedly requested that they come to New York and retrieve him, as if that would guarantee his release. Later in the same letter, he observed, "I can tell by your letter you are not coming," before noting, "I have not been visited by your minister friend. I am feeling fine and if the President makes the decision I feel he should, I'll be home soon."[43] While the president did not acknowledge Taylor's letter, Rose's friend from many years past, Reverend J. Phillip Anshutz, responded to her requests that he check on Taylor. Anshutz's appearance would set in motion the events that eventually earned Taylor his release and his return to White Sulphur Springs.

In 1957, Reverend Anshutz, the Episcopalian minister who had served in White Sulphur Springs nearly five decades earlier, had been informed of Taylor's condition by Marion Coates. Through correspondence with Rose, Anshutz eventually located Taylor. Anshutz did not immediately recognize the adult Taylor—who was much taller than the teenager who had performed in the Auditorium shows—but Taylor recognized him:

Then he told me all about himself and frankly answered all
of my questions that I put to him in my effort to help him.
As a matter of fact, I cannot see why he is there. He speaks
as rationally and coherently as any of my friends speak to
me, although of course there may be some subtle disorder
of which I know nothing and which further investigation
would disclose.

I was particularly sorry when Manny told me that for the
28 months he has been a patient in the hospital he never has
had a single visit from anyone until I came. . . .

You may write me just as much as you wish and I will do
everything possible in my power to help you and Manny. I
feel very keenly the situation that he is faced with and I can
well understand how he may have been railroaded to the institution and not had a friend at court to speak on his behalf.[44]

After meeting with Taylor at Central Islip, Anshutz wrote to Rose that
they had "reminisced over the old days in the West." He added, "It scarcely
seems possible to me how that it was almost fifty years ago that I took him
under my wing and developed his theatrical ability in the giving of those
shows in Sutherland's [*sic*] Auditorium on the hill. I have always liked
Manny and his forthrightness and openness, and you may be sure that
I will do everything that I possibly can to bring light to the situation."[45]
Anshutz never wavered in his initial assessment that Taylor was not dan-
gerous, although his further investigation revealed the extent of Taylor's
obsession. Still, Anshutz felt that Taylor's delusions were not sufficient
cause to confine him.

Although Rose was unwilling and unable to travel to New York on a
likely fruitless mission to retrieve her brother, she coordinated a letter-
writing campaign involving Taylor's friends and correspondents. They
wrote to Taylor with the same mission: to try to have him realize that
continuing to press his vendetta against Steinbeck was counter to his
desire to be released. Rose also consulted lawyers in Montana for advice
and regularly wrote to hospital administrators seeking information on
Taylor and ways to secure his release from state custody.

Anshutz reported back to Rose regarding his visits with Taylor, coordinated with Rose in writing letters to the administrators, and at one point

even offered to care for Taylor himself if the hospital would release him. The hospital administrators may have perceived Anshutz as a stand-in for Rose and Robert, which could have helped convince them that Taylor would indeed have the supervision that he needed as a condition of his release in Montana. For the isolated Taylor, having a friend and visitor —particularly one who listened patiently to his concerns—may also have been therapeutic and could have contributed to the psychological improvements his doctors were hoping to see. Whatever the case, with Rose writing regular letters to the hospital, and Anschutz providing a regular physical presence, Taylor's release and return to Montana seemed increasingly possible. There would still be a long way to go before Taylor's eventual release in 1959, but Anschutz's arrival—and his continued efforts on Taylor's behalf—seems to have been the catalyst for Taylor's return to Montana after an absence of a decade.

While fighting for Taylor's release from Central Islip, Rose remained active in her community and church. In 1925, an earthquake damaged several buildings in White Sulphur Springs, including the Presbyterian Church that Rose and her mother attended. She began attending Grace Episcopal Church, where Anshutz had served as minister from 1907 to 1911. Rose officially joined the Grace Episcopal Church as a member in 1958. That April, Rose wrote to Taylor to let him know that her work at the "hospital is going good. Good trade also I do therapy there when patients want it." She also told him, "I joined Episcopal church Jan 12, 1958, had gone there since Old Methodist Church was demolished by Quake."[46] Apparently, Rose resisted joining the Episcopalians out of loyalty to her mother, a faithful Methodist. Taylor replied, "It is alright that you joined the church. I am sure mama would not have argued with you about it, and I sure won't! . . . It was certainly not her fault that the old one grew weak enough to be cracked by any earthquake!"[47] In a postscript to a letter reporting on a visit with Taylor at Central Islip Hospital, Anschutz added his enthusiastic congratulations: "I am most happy to know that you have been Confirmed and love little Grace Church."[48]

Rose had always been a faithful churchgoer, but she became more active after joining the Episcopalian Church. In 1961, she was elected president of St. Martha's Guild, a chapter of the Episcopal Church Women.

She received correspondence from the state organization directed to the president through 1964 and helped plan the organization's annual meeting.[49] In 1962, Rose was present at an organizational meeting for the World Day of Prayer, a church-sponsored event.[50]

Rose was also an active member in the Montana branch of the American Massage Therapists Association (AMTA), which masseuses across the state had organized in response to a series of bills introduced in the Montana legislature in the late 1950s and early 1960s that aimed to regulate physical therapists. In 1959, Rose attended the national meeting of the AMTA in Long Beach, California.[51] Earlier that year, Elizabeth Hill wrote to Rose, "Glad you are enjoying the merits of your massage table, your clients will be greatly benefited with its use. Now Rose no doubt you know about the bill in the legislature against we fine people who are engaged in message therapy. . . . It passed 75–2 in the House, which is a very uncomfortable margin for us. . . . If it should go through, it would put us all out of work."[52] A letter-writing campaign helped defeat the bill in the senate, and in 1961 the organization hired an attorney to lobby on behalf of members' interests. Rose wrote to and received return letters from several members of the legislature, including Representatives Donald G. Lucas and Jack Healey. Carl Rostad, a senator representing district sixteen, which included Meagher County, wrote to Rose, "I am happy to report that I was able to kill the bill in the Senate which would have restricted your work." Rostad added a personal note: "I am enjoying the work over here very much. Helen seems to be enjoying it too."[53] The senate decision meant the threat to Rose's profession had been thwarted, which must have pleased Rose and the other massage therapists.

The same year as the AMTA's legislative victory, Taylor was granted release from Central Islip Hospital. After nearly a decade of institutionalization, he returned to Montana on a flight from New York to Billings, where Robert met him at the airport. Rose did not accomplish his release by herself, but the efforts she had made on Taylor's behalf were an essential component of his return to Montana. He subsequently lived with Rose in the Gordon family home and followed her model in making himself valuable to the community he considered home, even though he had lived there only sporadically as an adult. He performed two full concerts, one in White Sulphur Springs in 1960 and the other in Great Falls in 1961. The White Sulphur concert was "his first appearance on stage since before World War II."[54] The newspaper reported that "a program of negro spirituals, classical and secular songs was presented in a concert by Taylor Gordon, tenor, at the grade school auditorium last Saturday evening," and drew "a sizeable crowd, including a number of people from out of town . . . in spite of the below-zero weather that night."[55] The Dunbar Art and Study Club sponsored the Great Falls concert, which Elizabeth Hill organized.[56] Afterward, Taylor announced his retirement from the stage, or at least from major undertakings such as full concerts; he would still perform a song or two at special occasions.

In her devotion to her family and her community, Rose never wavered. The remaining members of the Gordon family were together again, with Rose's youngest brother finally returned home and under her care. Rose's transition from restaurant owner to massage therapist and healthcare worker was an amazing late-life transformation, but it built on skills and talents she had been developing throughout her life, including her compassion for others. Undertaken during her sixties and seventies when many people might be thinking of quiet retirement, her contributions to civic and professional organizations across Montana were remarkable. It was also during these later years of her life that Rose flourished as a writer, as the following account of Rose Gordon's literary accomplishments attests.

CHAPTER 9

A Tribute to Rose B. Gordon

I want to pay tribute to Rose B. Gordon as a writer.

Over the years that I worked on this project, I visited White Sulphur Springs several times. While there, I always made my way to the Mayn Cemetery to pay my respects to the Gordon family, and in particular to Rose and Taylor, whose graves are side by side. On each of those visits, I saw flowers, or the remnants of recently placed flowers, on Rose's gravesite. Fifty years after her death, someone remembers Rose B. Gordon and continues to pay tribute to her memory. Rose similarly paid tribute in writing to members of her community who had passed away during her lifetime.

Rose contributed letters and other items to the White Sulphur newspapers throughout her life but became a frequent contributor in the 1940s. Rose's writings—about her mother, about the grand old-timers and treasured old places of White Sulphur Springs in its pioneer heyday, as well as about her life and the lives of others—make her a literary figure worthy of consideration. Indeed, she deserves celebration as both a Western writer and African American author. Her thoughtful and historically significant newspaper writings from the 1940s through the 1960s form the core of her literary accomplishment. Rose's skill as a writer is most notable in her flexibility and willingness to adapt her writing to the outlet available to her. She used the newspaper format not only to tell the stories she wanted to tell while entertaining readers, but also as a way to present readers with stories that demanded their attention. While her memorials provided her a means of publishing her writing, especially after years of trying unsuccessfully to publish her book, they also allowed her to write about both her own life and that of her mother, as well as their shared past.

❧

Often drawing on material from "Gone are the Days," Rose's newspaper contributions fell into three categories. She often penned memorial tributes to recently deceased members of the community, which varied in length from a few lines to several columns. She also published historical reminiscences known as either "Rose Gordon's Recollections" or, during the centennial celebrations of various Montana towns in the 1960s, "Centennial Notes," both of which contained a mixture of autobiography, biography, and local history. Last, she sent in general letters to the editor, which sometimes included historical material, but could also be more directly autobiographical. Just as frequently, her letters commented on local events and activities such as weddings or offered her take on items published in the previous edition of the weekly newspaper, including commentary on current politics and social issues.

Rose's tributes were a genre well suited to her strengths as a writer, combining her interest in local history with her talent for personal narrative. Most of the tributes involve an overview of the individual's contribution to the community as well as Rose's personal memories of the deceased. A typical example is her memorial to Lavina Bandel, published in the February 15, 1950, edition of the *Meagher County News*:

> I want to pay tribute to Mrs. Lavina Bandel.
> I well remember the first time I met her. She was a charming young lady, full of life and very pleasant. She possessed stability and inner poise. Everything she did was done well. She often spoke of her childhood days, saying she was taught to be obedient, and above all to finish every duty she took part in. She married Mr. Eugene Bandel many years ago; she was a wonderful wife and real helpmate.
> I will miss her very much. She was a kind neighbor. When I was planting my front yard, she gave me lilac bushes, golden glow and many other plants. They will be living memories of her. She was a great lover of nature.[1]

Rose's memorials almost always began with some variation of the phrase "I want to pay tribute to." Although each piece in some ways resembles an obituary, key moments in the individual's public life form a much smaller part of the tribute and often serve to emphasize character traits that Rose particularly admired. She often drew attention to the person's service to others, whether family members or the entire community, highlighting little kindnesses that could be easily forgotten. Most of all, Rose celebrated the homely and the everyday through personal anecdotes that reveal the personality of the deceased, such as that "she was a great lover of nature" who also shared the natural beauty that she loved with her neighbors. Rose frequently expressed how the life of the particular individual cleared a path for others to follow. Her admiration for pioneers of all sorts, especially the "grand old timers" of the West, is clear in all her tributes.

Rose was democratic in her choice of subjects, writing memorials for both the town's prominent residents and its lesser-known citizens. In addition to acknowledging the public record of well-known citizens, she also included an anecdote from their everyday lives. In her tribute to Bide Edwards, for example, she acknowledged his public role as "county commissioner and mayor of the city for many years." Yet she placed greater emphasis on voluntary acts of kindness, however small. "Our winters were bitter cold years ago," she reminded readers, "and Mr. Edwards always did his best to see that all had coal and would leave a little extra in his wagon in case of emergency at night so people could get coal."[2] For Anna Schmid, Rose recalled, "She was always doing the nice little things that really count in life. When I operated my café on Main street, she sent flowers for my tables on big occasions."[3] In acknowledgment of another act of personal generosity, Rose remembered that Edmon Huffman helped her after she purchased a large load of wood one winter. "As I approached my home," she wrote, "I saw that the wood had been sawed. I did not know what to think as I did not ask anybody to saw it. Mr. Huffman came over and told me that he and Mr. Gushart had a quiet day off and thought they would exercise on my pile of logs." In a rare occurrence in the tributes, Rose addressed Huffman directly: "You will never know how I felt. I made a fire and then sat down and cried, for such kindness is seldom seen.

Mr. Huffman never said anything unkind about anyone. He knew the full meaning of the word neighbor."[4]

One of the earliest memorials that Rose contributed to the newspaper was occasioned by the death of Sarah Sherman in 1946. This memorial did not yet take the tribute form, and its differences from Rose's later contributions reveal a great deal about the development of her writing:

> The passing of Mrs. Sherman: The little path I used to tread across the way to see a friend; a friend who gave me all there is in life to give; love, courage and hope; this comes from the richest storeroom known to mankind and womankind alike: THE HEART. It is the spark of life; she gave of it freely to her friends.
>
> The true friends, true blue of days that are olden. In dreaming and seeming you all come to my call with joy hearts and hearts kind and tender.
>
> So a message of love that is simple and true for the best things in life with its glory and splendor are the old friends, the home friends, the real friends like you.
>
> Rose B. Gordon (Sept 6 1946)

Instead of the "I want to pay tribute" opening, Rose introduced the memorial with a statement of Mrs. Sherman's passing. Most of the article employs conventional generalities, without the specificity of place and action that make Rose's later tributes so concrete and memorable. Although Rose's later tributes were also sentimental, this early one takes a unique form, especially in the capitalization of "THE HEART," the use of rhyme, and the iambic rhythm of "the little path I used to tread across the way to see a friend." The rhyme and rhythm suggest verse rather than prose, and indeed, this tribute began as a poem handwritten on the back of a piece of paper cut from a grocery bag, its line breaks and arrangement quite different from the form of most of Rose's tributes.[5] One element, however, remains consistent throughout all of Rose's tributes: the celebration of "old friends." The theme of home is also at the center of many of Rose's tributes. In using the phrase "home friends," she deftly combined two concepts that she would consistently celebrate.

Rose's tributes to women emphasize the importance of making a home, and her personal connection to the deceased often touch on that individual's contribution to Rose's own homemaking. "When I was planting my front yard," Rose wrote of Bandel, "she gave me lilac bushes, golden glow and many other plants." In a tribute to Luella Watson, Rose drew a connection between Watson's generosity and the neighborliness that was, at the time, a characteristic of the local culture: "I had the pleasure of calling at her home several years ago and found her to be a most charming hostess. She possessed the western hospitality which is fast fading from the old west."[6] Such tributes take us to a place we seldom go in an obituary, into the intimate space of the home, a space that suddenly opens outward to represent the whole of the West, which Rose claimed cultivated a certain type of hospitality that was essential to Western identity. As is often the case in Western writing, Rose struck an elegiac tone, both because the topic was a memorial to the deceased and because, to her, that death reflected a larger sense of cultural loss. In the Watson tribute, Rose lamented the loss of hospitality, a key quality that defined the culture of her small Western town. These lamentations suggest that the passing of the individual coincided with the death of some essential quality of the West itself. For instance, she described Charles Sherman as someone who "did all in his power to help his fellow man" and "when the sun of his life went down, he took the love of the Golden West with him."[7]

That sense of individual loss representing something greater is especially apparent in her tribute to newspaperman R. N. Sutherlin. This tribute was somewhat unusual in that it was written many years after his death and appeared in a tribute dedicated not to Sutherlin but to Luella Watson. Watson was a contributor to the *Meagher County News* and other newspapers, so her death may have turned Rose's thinking toward fellow journalist Sutherlin. While Rose did not shortchange Watson in the tribute, Rose's memories of Sutherlin dominate the piece, in which she seemingly suggests that he and Watson shared a similar vision of what White Sulphur Springs could become. Those memories, in turn, become a lamentation not just for Sutherlin but for the "beautiful little town" that never came into being. In the end, Rose's tribute mourns the passing of the White Sulphur Springs of her childhood as much as it expresses the sorrow of losing both Watson and Sutherlin. It closes with a paragraph that offers a farewell to the people, the place, and the era: "Anyone who has read the history of his valley cannot but feel his deep love for his home. So Miss Luella Watson went to her rest without seeing White Sulphur Springs become the city they had dreamed of. But the deep love of the west was buried with them. They will always be remembered as the Shining stars of the west."

As a literary form, elegies follow a particular pattern, with an expression of loss followed by a consolation: although he has passed on from earth, he will live on in this poem, or, in more conventional religious terms, he has gone on to a better existence in heaven. Certainly, the closing comment that Watson and Sutherlin "will always be remembered as Shining stars of the west" suggests such a consolation and uses the conventional imagery of light and of being raised into the heavens to suggest a contrast to the darkness of death. Yet Rose's comment that "the deep love of the west was buried with them" undermines that attempt at consolation. Watson and Sutherlin may become shining stars, but their "deep love of the west" would remain entombed in the grave. The overall tone of the tribute suggests something more somber than a conventional elegy. As the "grand old timers" that Rose admired in her youth passed away, so, it seems, did their "deep love of the west" itself and the character qualities that reverence produced: a belief in the future, a desire for social improvement, and a certain kind of neighborliness that fostered inclusiveness and community.

Rose's writing demonstrates a keen awareness of place and the emotional importance of home. As did her tributes to Lavina Bandel and Luella Watson, Rose's piece about Mrs. R. G. Wight emphasized the home as both a physical shelter and a safe haven for human emotion. She knew "Lady Wight" from her babysitting days, having looked after her daughter. Rose and her mother also helped with Wight's dinner parties at various times. Rose's lengthy tribute, which looked back at the Wight family's role in the history of the community, also focused on more recent events. Following her husband's death in California, Wight returned to their home in White Sulphur Springs but decided to sell a house that she now found too empty: "Breaking up her home made her very sad. She loved everything . . . and did not wish to part with it. . . . Taylor Gordon and I helped her to pack. Every now and then she would sit down and the tears would come to her eyes and roll down her cheeks. I would cheer her up by saying, 'Lady Wight, you know we have things but for a little while on earth.' She said, 'Rose, you are good for all ills.'"[8] Even while expressing her awareness of the transient nature of life on earth, Rose paid homage to dear places as well as dear people.

This element connects Rose's writing to the African American literary tradition. In the slave narrative tradition, home and family are symbols of freedom and central topics of celebration. As author bell hooks argued, the idea of home, particularly in a society in which Black women frequently had to work outside their own homes and, instead, in the homes of white women, was an important element of Black experience:

> Since sexism delegates to females the task of creating and sustaining a home environment, it has been primarily the responsibility of black women to construct domestic households as spaces of care and nurturance in the face of the brutal harsh reality of racist oppression and sexist domination. Historically, African American people believed the construction of a homeplace, however fragile and tenuous (the slave hut, the wooden shack), had a radical political dimension. . . . One's homeplace was the one site where one could freely confront the issue of humanization, where one could resist. Black women resisted by making homes where all black people could strive to be subjects . . . where we could restore to ourselves the dignity denied us on the outside in the public world.[9]

The creation of a homeplace, hooks continued, "was about the construction of a safe place where black people could affirm one another and by so doing heal many of the wounds inflicted by racist domination. We could not learn to love or respect ourselves in the culture of white supremacy, on the outside; it was there on the inside, in that 'homeplace,' most often created and kept by black women, that we had the opportunity to grow and develop, to nurture our spirits."[10]

In Rose's stories about her mother, who supported her family and household by working for and within the families and households of white women, Rose highlighted how the process of making a home was an act of resistance against the racism that existed outside the home. Even if, as Rose asserted, she never experienced prejudice in the White Sulphur Springs of her childhood, that sense of safety testified to her mother's ability to create a homeplace that gave her children "the opportunity to grow and develop, to nurture our spirits."[11] A survivor of slavery, Anna Gordon surely had no illusions about the harsh reality of American racism. "It was so hard for Mamma to tell us that we were colored children," Rose wrote, "and that we would always have trouble because we were."[12] The conversations that she had with her children, as reported by both Taylor and Rose, demonstrate that awareness as well as Anna's desire to protect and forewarn her children.

In her essay, hooks wrote, "I had grown to womanhood hearing about black women who nurtured and cared for white families when they longed to have time and energy to give to their own." And, hooks added in a sentence that echoes the form of Rose Gordon's tributes, "I want to remember these black women today." The very act of remembrance, hooks asserted, "is a conscious gesture honoring their struggle, their effort to keep something of their own."[13] The stories that Rose told of her mother fit this description. Even though she did not emphasize the role of racist oppression in that struggle, she depicted the struggle itself, evident in the exhausting and body-damaging labor that her mother undertook to create a safe place for her children. Especially when discussing the period before the establishment of the Gordon Notion Store, Rose acknowledged the significance of her mother's efforts to care for white families in White Sulphur Springs, doing their laundry, working their parties, and expending "time and energy" to improve the lives of families that were not her own. In "My Mother Was a Slave" and various other letters and remembrances, Rose's tributes to her mother function as a conscious gesture that honors Anna Gordon's struggle to stay afloat and celebrates her ability to keep something of her own: a homeplace that nurtured the spirits of her children.[14]

In other tributes, Rose extended that act of remembrance beyond her mother to the friends and neighbors that expanded the notion of homeplace to encompass the entire White Sulphur Springs of her childhood. As hooks wrote, "Throughout our history, African Americans have recognized the subversive value of homeplace, of having access to private space where we do not directly encounter white racist aggression."[15] Rose's development as a writer, which primarily took place from the 1930s through the 1950s, happened during years when she directly encountered white racist aggression. Her re-creation of White Sulphur Springs's past might be understood as an effort to build a protective place in memory. Whether or not the reality of the town in Rose's childhood matched her nostalgic description, she created a literary version of it that served as a homeplace, one that gave her a private and public space to escape the vexations of the present.

Although Rose, like many writers of the American West, praised the beauty of the Western landscape and of the Smith River valley in particular, she emphasized people and places rather than flora, fauna, and terrain. In this way, she extended the concept of homeplace to include the man-made world of her childhood and a special group of friends, "the home friends," whose hospitality and neighborly actions were constituent elements of the White Sulphur Springs she described in her writing. In descriptions of her family home and other important buildings, she asserted a relationship to those places as a kind of friendship. What emerges in her writing is an emotional cartography of White Sulphur Springs, a mapping not just of the physical space but of her connections to that place. Within her tributes to White Sulphur citizens, we see her pay tribute to these significant places.

In a tribute to Herbert Harris, for example, Rose observed that his passing "brought back memories of the Red Brick school house which was demolished by earthquake several years ago, but nevertheless that spot is cherished by us who attended the school."[16] The tribute to Harris doubled as a memorial to the White Sulphur Springs of her childhood, as Harris's loss reminded her of other important symbols of her childhood that no longer existed. In saluting Harris, Rose also paid tribute to markers of her youth such as the Methodist church that she and the Harris family attended. Like the school building, the church had been "reduced to a few scattered bricks here and there, but its walls once echoed with song and prayer."[17] Home, for Rose, was a place of "cherished" spots: the school and the church, the house that her father bought in the mid-1880s and that she lived in until her death, the Auditorium, the Sherman Hotel, the Irwin Building, and the Old Stage Barn built by B. R. Sherman. In her later columns for the *Meagher County News*, written as some of these structures were being demolished to make way for new construction, she paid as much affectionate tribute to these pioneer buildings as she did to the long gone citizens that were so often the subjects of her writing.[18]

The tribute form, especially as Rose developed it over her life, allowed for shifts in subject matter and created opportunities for her to continue telling her own story and that of her remarkable mother. Perhaps because some of these pieces had originated in Rose's unpublished memoir, such tributes both pay homage to the person whose life has ended and offer an intimate look into Rose's own life. Many of the longer ones take several turns, beginning with a memorial to a particular individual and ending in a completely different place that pays homage to something else. For instance, Rose noted that Herbert Harris, who had been born in present-day South Dakota, "came to White Sulphur Springs, Montana when he was six months old in the days of the covered wagon." After observing Harris's success in life as a farmer and cattle rancher, the tribute shifts its attention to other members of the Harris family and to Rose's connection to them. Of Harris's sister, Lottie A. Harris, Rose wrote, "I was one of her pupils, a nervous pupil, but she was grand to us all." Harris "made us walk the chalk line and I am glad she did." This memory apparently triggered another recollection, one that tells us more about Rose herself, an occasion when Anna Gordon reinforced the teacher's firm discipline: "If we would go home and tell mamma that the teacher was cross today, mamma would say, 'Well, you were not obedient or she would not have been cross.' So we were on our own." In acknowledging Harris's influence on her life, Rose simultaneously pays homage to the values that Lottie Harris and Anna Gordon had in common. "[I] had to help mamma so much, and would get behind with my arithmetic. [Miss Harris] always helped me. My success in later years was due to her patience. One day I was really hard at work on problems and all at once I sneezed. Miss Harris said, 'Rose, you must not sneeze so loud.' I said, 'Miss Harris, I did not know it was going to be so loud.' I can still see the smile creep on her face." Miss Harris emphasized the value of hard work and demonstrated the virtue of patience, and yet her smile suggested a balancing warmth and humor that was similarly a characteristic of Rose's storytelling.

What stands out about Rose's life is her consistent and heartfelt concern for the well-being of others and her commitment to caring for them. These qualities are evident in her roles as a central figure in her family who was responsible for caring for her mother and brothers, as the "village babysitter," as a restaurant owner, as a healthcare worker and physiotherapist, and as a writer. Her memorial tributes reflect Rose's devotion to the people in her life. Marcella Sherfy, in describing how Rose blossomed in the final decades of her life, states that Rose became the community's "historian and heart."[19] In her tributes, Rose discovered the perfect conduit for joining history and heart together in a unique way. In doing so, she invented her own genre, one that blended the concept of the West as a place shaped out of human endeavor with the African American literary tradition of homeplace and identity forged in the human heart.

In addition to tributes, Rose also reported on visits she had recently made, often using such occasions to reflect on local history. "Here is a little chatter if you can use it," she began one such story, before offering that one of her "great pleasures" in life "was spending the afternoon with Miss Nellie Logan who later in life became Mrs. Isaac Stephenson." The story of the visit then turns to a family history of the Logans, specifically Nellie Stephenson's father, who came to Montana when he was stationed at Fort Logan, and beyond him to the commanding officer, Captain Gilbert. Rose also included another bit of the history of the African American West in her "chatter" by mentioning Mrs. Gilbert's maid, an otherwise unidentified Black woman who, after coming to Montana, "fell in love with a colored butler at the fort and later married him and returned to Kentucky." Her history of the people of Fort Logan as Stephenson remembered them also mentioned the story of the beloved French candy maker Dick Turbin, who broke the hearts of all the children at Fort Logan when he took a position in Helena, for "the candy man had left them."[20]

Rose maintained a sense of humor throughout her career as a writer. She recalled John Gardiner Lewis's involvement in horse trading deals: "When we children were going to school the horse buyers would be standing on the street corners. They had a habit of whittling on a piece of wood. Children in those days were not allowed to express themselves as they do now, but they could not keep us from thinking. I knew when I saw them with their heads together that someone was going to get a sway-backed horse in the deal." As Rose observed, the town's pioneers "always had a good joke and a lot of fun."[21]

In another piece, she remembered when "[o]ne of Mr. Ringling's friends brought a little monkey to the city. The children were wild about him, he was so cute." The monkey was mainly kept out of the way in the sitting room of the brick bathhouse, where Rose would sometimes give massages to patrons with arthritis or other ailments, because the town dogs were aggressively fond of it. "There was a man taking baths who really liked monkeys," Rose claimed. "He would let the little monkey sit on his shoulder and take candy from his upper coat pocket." One day, instead of candy, the monkey grabbed a bottle of Carter's Liver Pills, a laxative. When the man tried to retrieve the pills, Rose warned him "that monkey scratches were sometimes fatal." Apparently, the man's effort to retrieve the pills was unsuccessful. "I did not think the monkey would be able to get the bottle open," Rose recalled, "but he did and sat on his perch eating the sugar coated pills." The next day, the monkey "had his little hands crossed over his stomach and such a sad look on his face. I knew he was a sick monkey." After several days of slow recovery, fate intervened in the form of a stylish young woman visiting from out of town. Although Rose warned that the monkey "had been very ill and might be sick most any time," the woman refused to listen and "took the little monkey out for a walk and [insisted] he must sit on her shoulder." Without going into any unnecessary detail, Rose concluded the story by noting simply, "A tragedy took place." After that, "the monkey was not so cute" in the eyes of the stylish young woman.[22] Rose's sense of humor could also be self-deprecating, particularly when it came to her own aging. "I well remember when I was young," she wrote in one story, and then added, "It is nice to have been young once upon a time."[23] "Believe it or not," she declared in another letter, "I was young once . . ."[24]

Rose's sincere and heartfelt tributes and her reports to the paper were very popular with readers, who occasionally sent letters of appreciation. Art Watson, whose sister Luella Watson's death occasioned one of Rose's earliest tributes, wrote to the *Meagher County News* to thank Rose for her tributes to the members of his family over the years, observing, "I wonder if it isn't fitting to pay a compliment to this fine person while she is living. Just to let her know that those thoughtful expressions of sympathy and beautiful tributes to and for the deceased, have made the burdens a little easier to bear."[25] Similarly, after Rose's tribute to "Lady Wight," her daughter Florence Wight Anderson wrote to Rose to tell her, "I received the White Sulphur Springs paper today and tears poured down my face as I read your family tribute to Mother and our family."[26]

The popularity of Rose's tributes also opened a door for her to comment on political and social issues in the newspaper. After establishing her voice as a memorialist and historian, she expanded the subject matter that she covered in her letters and columns. Throughout the 1950s and 1960s, Rose commented on racial issues more frequently than she did in her earlier writing. Part of Rose's cleverness as a writer was the way she adapted even the memorial tributes to comment covertly—and sometimes overtly—on race relations in White Sulphur Springs. In this, she was encouraged by Grace Stone Coates, by then a successful and widely published author. Coates recognized the timeliness of Rose's work, telling her in 1958, "Now, while *integration* and *segregation* and the status of races are live questions, is the time to *sell* your story."[27]

When Rose addressed race in her writing, she often did so obliquely, as when she observed in her tribute to Miss Harris, "I was one of her pupils, a nervous pupil, but she was grand to us all." At first glance, this statement seemingly has nothing to do with race. But notice how Rose underscores her difference—among the pupils, she was the "nervous" one—while not revealing what might have made her uncomfortable about her situation in the school. Without stating directly that Miss Harris was notable for her equal treatment of white and Black students, she suggests as much.

The contrast that Rose draws between White Sulphur Springs's past and present is subtle in her published writing, but it becomes obvious when comparing Rose's public and private writing. In "Gone are the Days," Rose claims that she hoped to "pay tribute to those grand people of my childhood days. They did not allow prejudice to creep into the archives of their brains." She then follows that statement by suggesting her awareness of contemporary racism and expressing her own defiant attitude toward that prejudice: "Now as I sometimes see people that do not like my brown face, it does not affect me in the least." In public forums such as the newspaper, Rose adopted a strategy for addressing the prejudice in her hometown by portraying the "grand old timers" consistently, if implicitly, as a point of comparison or contrast to another group. She also expressed her attitude toward those "people that do not like my brown face" more trenchantly in manuscript form, saying bluntly, "I may make the remark that they are vulgarians."[28]

In "Gone are the Days," for example, Rose noted that the Daughters of the American Revolution refused to allow the famous Black opera singer Marian Anderson to perform a concert at Constitution Hall in Washington, D.C., in 1939. In response to that infamous moment of American prejudice, Eleanor Roosevelt intervened and made arrangements for a concert performed on the steps of the Lincoln Memorial that drew a crowd of seventy-five thousand and became one of the most famous concerts in American history. This story reminded Rose of one of her own memories involving "a certain church in my home town that I had gone to for many years, and my mother also had gone there for many years." One of the ladies at the church invited Rose to sing a spiritual for the congregation, and arrangements were made for her to do so. A few days into the preparations, the church's young minister came to her and admitted, "Some Sisters have refused to let you sing in the church." "He felt sorry for me," Rose wrote, "but I felt sorry for him, to think he was so young and had come to preach to people many years older than he was and that they had not yet learned the lessons that the man from Gallalea [sic] had taught." Rose chose to turn the other cheek, and when she discovered the identity of the "Sisters," she realized that she knew some of them "as if I had packed the sod to make them," but "in place of my feelings being hurt, I felt sorry for them." Notably, Rose prefaced this story by taking readers back to the time when her mother had attended the church: "There was a large crowd of refined and cultured people that attended the church at that time. . . . Later as the old members passed away and moved away, new ones were taking their places."[29] The implication here is that prejudice in White Sulphur Springs was a new arrival. Rose's celebration in this unpublished story of the "refined and cultured people" of an earlier time rebuked the prejudices of the "new ones" taking their places. In her published writing, the celebration of the grand old timers remains, but she strategically quieted her criticism of the later arrivals. Tellingly, the story of not being allowed to sing in the church did not make it into her newspaper writing.

Rose was not an innocent in matters of the relations between races. After traveling by train to Missoula in the early 1900s, Rose inquired at a hotel to "see if they would let a colored person have a room for the night." She quietly asked the clerk "if I might have a room, or if they catered to colored people. He said sure, you can have a room. He said you are not a bit sensitive, are you? I said, why should I be, I know this old world too well to be sensitive." After securing a room for the night, Rose commented to the clerk, "It is a terrible handicap to travel and find no place to rest and get refreshments." She reflected on what that sort of discrimination meant in the bigger picture, saying, "When you go to places where they will not feed you or let you rest, you walk about the city and on some high [place] you see the American flag flying and then you wonder what it is all about."[30] Clearly, the Rose who stepped off the train in Missoula was worldly enough to anticipate that she might encounter prejudice and racism—and genuinely appreciative when offered lodging without restriction. And, when it came to acknowledging the realities of race, Rose was, in this instant, "not a bit sensitive," even if it meant shocking a clerk unused to such directness.

In contrast to her published works, which took a more subtle approach, Rose's personal letters and other unpublished writings address candidly the prejudice that vexed her periodically throughout the twentieth century, including her experiences with the Works Progress Administration. These unpublished writings demonstrate a fiery side to Rose's personality that rarely appeared in her public writing. In an undated personal letter to a Mrs. Ashford, Rose wrote:

> I have just heard the latest gossip that Mrs. Winters is being asked to resign from her Lodge for keeping my company.
>
> Mrs. Ashford can you prove that my company is such that one would be damaged by my association?

I know my skin is black [which] I can't help, you might have been born black would that necessarily have to corrupt your character?

Mrs. Ashford I pity you as a mother would pity a child, and each night as you pray ask God to teach you to understand that each race is [His] own and that you are not to abuse and wound their feelings.

Mrs. Winters came into my life in one of the greatest sorrows that comes to a human being who loves home, the loss of my Mother, and if being kind to the sad and suffering is against the rules of your order, may God send an angel to teach them the right way.

I am sorry for Mrs. Winters. Her pleasures are limited but you know some even envy us of them. May [God] Help you and Bless you.[31]

Although clearly offended herself, Rose emphasized the offense done to Mrs. Winters. Even as big-hearted as Rose was, she was clearly willing to take to task those who deserved such a reprimand. Though angry, she still expressed Christian charity and concern. At the same time, telling someone they need this much help can hardly be considered complimentary. In the closing salutation, "May God Help you and Bless you," there is a slip of the pen, as Rose left out the word God, closing "May Help You and Bless You." That elision may suggest the frustration and anger that Rose felt, as if she could not bring herself to close the letter with a conventional statement of good wishes that might suggest a forgiveness that she was not quite ready to extend. In this letter, we see a private anger that makes clear just how carefully Rose crafted her public persona.

Rose's anger occasionally found its way into her public writing, albeit in a restrained manner. In a memorial tribute to her neighbor Fanny Gushart, Rose recalled, "One day I was having a little unpleasantness, and she said, 'Rose, you are black, but I love you.'"[32] Rose does not explain the nature of the "little unpleasantness," but Gushart's comment seems to be a response to something that Rose told her. The tribute goes on to praise Gushart for being "untainted by the foul breath of prejudice," implying that the "unpleasantness" was, in fact, racial in nature. Without directly accusing any of her neighbors of racism, Rose quietly suggested just that by emphasizing the unusual quality of another neighbor's lack of prejudice.

Rose was very much aware that her memorial tributes, her letters to the editor, and her written memories of White Sulphur Springs history constituted a public enterprise. Her writing was designed as such, and constituted a strategic entry into the public sphere of the community.[33] This tactic necessitated care in describing race relations in the town. In reading her work, we see Rose perform a balancing act between praising the Western "hospitality" of white neighbors who befriended her and patronized her restaurant and physiotherapy business, on the one hand, and protesting the incidents of inhospitable and bigoted behavior that disturbed her, on the other.

During the final years of her life, the public significance of Rose's commitment to writing local history became particularly important as towns throughout Montana celebrated their centennials during the 1960s. In 1964, both Taylor and Rose took part in the celebration of Montana's territorial centennial. A space at the annual Helena fair was reserved for each county to offer a half-hour presentation, and as part of Meagher County's contribution, Taylor sang three solos—"Wagon Wheels," "Old Man River," and "Because." Rose represented Meagher County's pioneer women. "She was given a seat in the honored guests' box. Miss Gordon wore a centennial dress and a large picture hat, which was once worn by Olive Anderson, the daughter of an early day merchant."[34]

After returning to Montana, Taylor had followed his sister's lead, contributing to the community in ways both large and small, although he gave only a few performances in the 1960s. In 1961, he sang several songs as part of Bill Schaffarizick Day, an event held to honor the loyal pharmacist's fifty years of community service in White Sulphur Springs.[35] Rose made her own contributions to the celebration and, several years later, shared her memories of Schaffarizick in one of her "Rose Gordon's Recollections" columns: "He was devoted to the noble and humane work his profession implied. He had his meals at our Café and he told me one day he wanted to be a Doctor. I replied, so did I, but things didn't work out. When he was here a short time, we would be without a doctor for two and three years at a time, he sure had the opportunity to be a doctor." The pharmacist also served at times as a small animal vet, treating the town's cats and dogs. Rose also noted in the same column, "During the flu epidemic in 1918 we had Dr. Dan McKay so Dr. William," as she referred to Schaffarizick, "had help. . . . The Epidemic was terrible. We lost many of our dear friends, so many that they were afraid to go near a patient who had the flu." Although neither Schaffarizick nor Rose achieved their ambition of becoming doctors, both found ample opportunities to help others. "Dr. William" demonstrated his courage by working with patients during the 1918 epidemic, and so did Rose, although the nearest she came to saying so was in praising Dr. McKay, who "took good care of us who nursed the ill."[36]

In 1967, when White Sulphur Springs marked its own one hundredth anniversary, Rose, who had been born in Montana while it was still a territory, was celebrated and officially recognized as a Montana pioneer. As part of a one-page spread observing the town's centennial, the *Helena Independent Record* included a lengthy article about Rose and Taylor titled "The Village Historians." The article noted that the siblings were "plain people with a keen interest in the history of White Sulphur Springs— the village historians. Ask them about the early days and they'll tell you. They've been around for a long time."[37] Just as Rose's tributes contributed to her role as the community's "heart," her "Rose's Recollections" columns and other historically oriented writing underscored her role as community historian, as did Taylor's memoir of his early life, *Born to Be*.

In anticipation of the town's centennial, residents had undertaken the restoration of B. R. Sherman's former home, locally called the Castle, which eventually housed the Castle Museum. Because of Taylor's relationship with the Shermans in his childhood and his knowledge of how the deteriorated and damaged building was supposed to look, he participated in the restoration. In addition to his assistance with the renovations, he helped raise money to support the project and gathered historic photographs of town for the Meagher County Historical Association's growing collection. He also wrote the entertaining and informative text for a forty-six-page pamphlet published by the *Meagher County News*—titled *The Man Who Built the Stone Castle*—that served as a biography of B. R. Sherman and a history of the Castle.[38] He eventually led tours of the refurbished castle, which is now a museum.[39] Taylor appeared on a local television station in Great Falls to talk about *The Man Who Built the Stone Castle*. He also sang "Because," "Old Man River," and a verse of "Camptown Races."[40]

The celebration of the town's history felt particularly necessary at a time when so much of its past seemed to be disappearing rapidly. Rose's memorial tributes appeared so frequently in part because many of the people she knew were dying or had already passed away. On July 8, 1962, Robert Gordon died at eighty-one years old, leaving Rose and Taylor as the only surviving members of the Gordon family. "Robert Gordon lived his entire life in this community," the *Meagher County News* reported. The paper also mentioned his tire shop and the twenty years he spent as "janitor at the First National bank."[41]

Letters of condolence imply that tensions had developed between the two siblings due to Robert's drinking, which Rose sometimes commented on with good humor, but could be bothersome. While Taylor was still at Central Islip, Rose wrote, "Bob is fine looking well still has his pals but he gets quite disgusted with them. They all like their afternoon tea."[42] After Robert's death, Amy Gutchel wrote to Rose, "I was sorry to hear of Bob's death. He was so happy-go-lucky and always made a person feel gayer and happier—as you always do too Rose."[43] In a more candid letter, Rose's longtime friend Olive King admitted,

> I just couldn't say I was sorry to hear of poor Bob's passing, as I know he had caused you all a great deal of worry and unhappiness, but he led his own life, and we'll never know what caused him to choose that 'sort' of one. . . . I could never understand my dear brother Roger's reason either, but never the less dear we loved them . . . and pray that they have found peace and understanding at last.[44]

Although Rose had had her conflicts with Robert, she also revealed in her letters to Taylor at Central Islip her wish to keep the family together. The fact that she and Robert were both aging added impetus to her desire to see Taylor released and returned home. Whatever familial conflicts there may have been, Rose's wish was realized when the remaining Gordon siblings were reunited in White Sulphur Springs.

In August 1968, a surprising event occurred that would have seemed too melodramatic had it been fiction. A driverless runaway truck owned by a logging company "rolled down the hill on the street and just before passing the home of Rose and Taylor Gordon, it veered and hit the east side of their home." The impact "made a shambles of the east room, ruining their piano, an antique table, sideboard, and television set. There was extensive damage to the personal property" as the truck smashed through the wall and came to a rest against the piano, "but, fortunately, there were no injuries." The driver was cited for "leaving an unattended vehicle parked in violation."[45] Rose was in the house when the truck hit, talking with her friend Wilhelmina Sharp in the kitchen. "We were both stunned," Rose wrote in a letter to the editor about the incident. "I will miss my piano," she added. "We were friends for a long time."[46] Perhaps taking her cue from the light tone of Rose's column, old friend Ruth Brewer wrote to Rose, "Heard thro the grapevine, you folks had a visitor one day when you were out. Lucky for you, they tell me, Mr. Truck bolted right into your parlor and stopped by the piano."[47]

Rose's own written reflection on the incident was a kind of memorial tribute to the damaged room and the home that had been central to her life. "My father bought this property in 1880 [in fact, 1885]," she wrote. "He paid $300 for it. It is built of native fir." A pioneer building purchased by one of White Sulphur Springs's earliest settlers, constructed from the resources the territory itself made available, the Gordon house was certainly as worthy of tribute as any of the other "grand old timers" that Rose praised. The damaged east room was a new addition to the house, but still had ties to personal and community history. It was built early in 1943 during the "hard times" of the war when many people didn't have cash to spare. "I took care of Mr. John Butler's wife, Nell Butler," Rose explained, and as pay received a load of lumber from Butler's sawmill. A man named Tex Wilson, whom Rose described as a "stranger in these parts," built the room, as he needed work to help support his ill wife.[48] Rose offered Wilson employment for a fee of twenty-five dollars. In keeping with Rose's values, she also gave the Wilsons vegetables from her garden.

The 1960s for Rose had been a time of loss, a time when old friends—people, places, and even her piano—ceased to exist except in memory.

In 1963, the Sherman Hotel shut its doors. It would be torn down a year later. "I went to the Sherman hotel October 31," Rose wrote, "to be there for the closing of the hotel at 2 A.M. November 1, 1963."[49] Workers brought down the Irwin Building, which was built before 1890 and once housed the Kumpe Drug Store, in October 1968, signaling the loss of another old friend from Rose's childhood.[50] Earlier in the year, the Old Stage Barn, originally built by B. R. Sherman, was demolished.[51] Although the Castle was restored, other buildings fell, and Rose's tributes to the people of her past often also marked the loss of these important landmarks and the times with which they were associated.

The Gordon house, too, was not just a building for Rose. In its own way, every part of the house memorialized a long history of family and community relationships. Perhaps not coincidentally, the damage done to her beloved little home preceded the failure of her own body just a few weeks later. When Rose Gordon passed away on November 19, 1968, in the Mountain View Memorial Hospital after a brief illness, White Sulphur Springs lost another old friend and a keeper of its memories. Although Rose was a member of the Grace Episcopal Church, the funeral service was held in St. Bartholomew's Catholic Church, as the larger building was needed to accommodate the throngs of mourners. The pastor from Grace Episcopal, Reverend James Anderson, led the memorial services, but her funeral was truly interdenominational, as Anderson was assisted by Reverend James Forbes of the Community Presbyterian Church and Reverend Neil Chisholm of St. Bartholomew's.

The responsibility for memorializing Rose fell on Verle L. Rade-macher, the editor of the *Meagher County News*, who wrote,

> The community is saddened by the death of Rose Gordon, a friend to all. And, as a friend to all, her community wishes to express its sentiments to her. We think that possibly, this is the best way...
>
> In this paper, Rose Gordon wrote many tributes about people of her community when they passed on. Now, who is to remember Rose? In our hearts, we all remember Rose. Her helping hands that eased an aching body, her understanding words that comforted an aching heart, her gentle

spirit that soothed a troubled soul, her humor and laugh and soft voice.[52]

Following the editorial, the newspaper printed a four-stanza poem, "Our Rose in Memory," written by several of Rose's friends:

> Dress all crisp and white as snow
> Soothing voice so soft and low;
> Gentle hands, to ease all pain
> Gentle heart, to calm all strain –
> Our Rose

Later stanzas remembered and praised Rose's years at the restaurant, her performances on stage at the auditorium, and "above all in our memory," her singing. "When the worldly gave way to ethereal tone / 'Swing Low Sweet Chariot' comes to 'Carry Her Home.'"[53]

The next week's edition of the paper carried a full page of memorial tributes, including a letter of thanks to the editor from Taylor as well as messages from Isobel Choquette, Olive King, Julia Klaue and family, Art Watson, and Mildred Robinson. Later, Grayce Brewer Allen wrote, "We all feel sad about the passing of Rose Gordon. It will be hard to think of White Sulphur Springs without her. Rose was always like a tower of strength and always seemed to be like one of God's ministering angels."[54] The Meagher County Historical Association passed a resolution at its November 1968 meeting:

> BE IT RESOLVED: The Meagher County Historical Asso-
> ciation, as well as the community has lost, with the death of
> Rose Gordon, a faithful member and personality who gave
> distinction to our group.
>   Rose, a lifelong resident of this community, had a remark-
> able memory of people and events. This was an invaluable
> contribution. Rose also had a priceless gift: To her people
> were never dull. Life was never hum-drum. People who
> seemed ordinary to the unendowed, were to Rose colorful
> personalities who moved in majestic progression across her
> memories. They were raised in stature, in perspective, lit by
> the glow of her compassion, affection, wisdom and quiet

acceptance of life. To Rose, almost everyone was great, good and unforgettable. And now we, in turn, resolve that Rose was indeed a great lady, a good lady, and truly unforgettable.[55]

In a letter of condolence to Taylor, Francis and Lacy Kern of Bozeman remembered that Rose "gave of herself with great healing qualities for both body and soul. We saw her many times at the blood letting sessions in WSS when she dispensed sandwiches and drinks to the blood donors." The letter concluded, "When Bill Schafferzick [*sic*] died, I thought the community lost its most colorful character, and now that Rose has gone, it appears to us that it is a loss of the most loveable character."[56] Elizabeth Campbell of San Francisco also wrote to Taylor to share her deep admiration for Rose. "In her last letter to me, Rose had expressed deep thanks to her Lord for having been permitted to still help people at her advanced age. She seems to have felt that He had generously granted her many more years than she herself would dare to ask for. This makes me aware that she must have died with a sense of deep fulfillment which happens rarely to people." She ended the message by noting, "I shall never feel that Rose has quite left us. . . . So generous was her heart, and so considerate her soul, that this generosity and this consideration must still have a place with us in our hearts."[57]

Emmanuel Taylor Gordon, the last living member of the remarkable Gordon family of White Sulphur Springs, Montana, followed his sister in death less than three years later. He died at Mountain View Hospital on May 5, 1971, and James Anderson officiated his May 11 funeral.[58] "He was preceded in death," the *Meagher County News* noted, "by his sister Rose, and three brothers, Robert, George and Francis. There are no survivors."[59]

In one of the final letters Rose wrote to the *Meagher County News* before her death, she commented explicitly on what she called the "Battle of the Pigment," a battle that had been brought to the foreground in the 1960s by the civil rights movement and the April 4, 1968, assassination of Dr. Martin Luther King.

> On a beautiful summer day when you take a ride and gaze
> upon the beautiful hills, valleys and running streams and all
> the different colors of nature, it is difficult to think the Great

Creator made this all for people of one color. . . . It is our
different colors that makes this world such a wonderful place
in which to live. If everything was one color we would soon
go mad. . . . It is a great adventure to be born with dark skin.
While traveling about, you meet many people who do not
like the idea. This is what puts you to the test.[60]

"Never once when I was a child," Rose had stated in "Gone are the
Days," "was I treated as if I were any color except white."[61] In "Battle of
the Pigment," Rose alternately implies that she had been aware of race
and racial prejudice from the very beginning of her life: "It is a great
adventure to be born with dark skin." Perhaps the difference in these two
statements, one written in the 1940s and the other in the 1960s, suggests
how Rose's way of seeing herself evolved. Like the Montanans whose lives
she memorialized, Rose, too, had been a pioneer. Her "dark skin" did not
preclude—and may have added to—her living a life that was as much of
a "great adventure" as that of any of the other "grand old timers." Rose
received dozens of letters commenting on and praising her "Battle of the
Pigment" column, which was, in many ways, her culminating philosophical statement.

In the decade of Montana's centennial celebration, Rose used her
writing to remind her fellow citizens of the continuing African American
presence in the state and in her hometown. In writing about White
Sulphur's past, she offered the community a service it clearly wanted. In
telling her own—and her mother's—story of making a home in Montana,
she made herself part of the larger story of the settling of the American
West. Through giving of herself, Rose made a home in the hearts of her
neighbors, who honored her life of paying tribute to others with an out-
pouring of tributes of their own when she passed away just months after
publishing this letter advocating her view that "it is our different colors
that makes this world such a wonderful place in which to live." Being Black
may have indeed "put her to the test" at times, but in writing about the
past of which she was an integral part, she asserted her right to belong and
her right to call Montana "home."

A Selection of Newspaper Writings by Rose B. Gordon

My Mother Was a Slave
Meagher County News 25 May 1955
Dear Editor:

I am giving you the story of my mother's life and of her struggle to raise her family of five children. In her heart was a song. She had a clear soprano voice.

My mother was a slave. She was bought by the wealthy Poindexter family. They were distillers and race horse people. She told me of her childhood with them. She said they were kind to her. She took care of the little children and went everywhere with them. They took her to New Orleans to see the Mardi Gras; also took her to see P. T. Barnum's great hippodrome which she never forgot. They took her to see Blind Tom the great musician. These pleasures were the things that were to somewhat drown out the horrors of slavery which she said the half was never told.

Her mother and father and sister were sold to different owners. She never saw them again.

In the evening when we had finished our work which was always late I would sit down on a little stool by her side. She would tell me about slavery. I was young and her stories filled me with misery and made me very sad to think life had to be that way. Some of the rich people bought whole families and let them work on the plantations. She well remembered auction day when slaves were sold to different owners. She saw families bidding farewell to father, mother, sister and brother never to see them again. They had hard masters and this must be forgotten for there was toil and labor ahead. They had only God to look to. Mother was truly a Christian. All through her life her God was first. With all these sad memories mamma loved Kentucky, the blue grass and all its scenic beauty. The slaves were the making of the south but had no pay. They could not entertain the thought of seeing their loved ones. The only hope they had was being bought by some owner who had bought some of their relatives.

Mamma said the south was very angry when Abraham Lincoln came out and declared his opinion about slavery as they were a commercial asset in the making of the south. The colored mammies were a great help to the slaves. They took care of the lady of the house and through the doctor gained information to help the slaves who were ill. Some owners would seek medical aid for the slaves. Others would not. Mamma said they had so much pork to eat they became sick from eating it. They were very fond of chicken as it was a change from pork. They had very little beef.

During the war it was Mamma's duty to keep the fine race horses hid in the hills so the soldiers who were marching through the country would not take them. Many of the slaves guarded the property of their masters.

Mamma told me of her experience of having a number of Northern soldiers riding up to their plantation. They had been separated from their unit. They were looking for food. They dismounted from their horses and came to the house. The people were all frightened as they did not know what the northern soldier was like. The captain said to mamma who had cooked there for many years, "My men are hungry and we want something to eat." They gave them food which consisted of corn bread, pork and vegetables. They were very grateful but insisted on having some food to take with them. Mamma said, "We have no food, hardly enough for ourselves." The captain said, "You look well fed." Mamma said, "Tom and I are just old and fat." They searched all their buildings but found no food. The food was kept in caves and buried in the ground in boxes.

When Sherman made his march to the sea, the south really suffered widespread destruction.

Mamma said the faithful old slaves stayed by the masters and helped them get back on their feet. Mamma said many owners left their plantations to their slaves. In a land seared by death, battle and poverty, yellow fever and smallpox, the Negro race had to fight something as bad as slavery: prejudice. Mamma said the rich southern people were always the friend to the Negro and helped them raise money for schools to educate the Negro. It was so hard for Mamma to tell us that we were colored children and that we would always have trouble because we were.

But thank God, the grand old timers never let us know we were black and they were southern people, eastern people and western people and by the time we grew up we had it all figured out. We would say to ourselves, they just don't know the world is made up all races, colors and creeds.

When Mamma was very young she married John Francis Gordon. They went to Cairo, Illinois to live. They lived there some time, where my brother Robert James Gordon was born. Papa, like other men, had the urge to go west. In 1881 Papa started west leaving mother in Cairo till such time as he could send for her. Mamma said she was not well at the time. She had child bed fever after her baby was born. It affected her heart and she had to take medicine all the time. The doctors became alarmed over the many cases of child bed fever and found out the germ was being carried by one nurse from one patient to the other under her fingernails. Great care was taken after that in cases of childbirth.

Father came to Montana and was located at Barker, then a thriving mining camp. After working for a while he sent for Mamma. The day came when Mamma must leave her beautiful Kentucky home.

In the year of 1881 a brown-skinned colored woman who bore the name of Mrs. Annie Gordon stood at the boat landing at Cairo, Illinois, where the Ohio flows into the might Mississippi. Tears rolled down her cheeks and were falling on her baby boy whom she held in her arms. Her friends had gathered to bid her farewell. Her baggage and trunks had been loaded on the river steamer called the Katie. She sailed up the Mississippi river to Saint Louis and from there she began her journey up the Missouri river. She was on her way to Fort Benton to join her husband. She was three months coming up the river. She told me she was glad it took a long time to come up the river as it gave her time to think things over.

One day she was weeping and thought she could not stand the ordeal, when a large brown skinned woman appeared on the scene and said, "Child, what are you crying about?" Between sobs mamma tried to tell her what it was all about. The stewardess said, "Laws a massy, child, you are going to a tough country and you must nerve up." Mamma dried her tears and watched the large brown skinned woman walk away, who filled her position so well on the boat and was well liked by the passengers. Mamma said she felt it her duty to at least try to make the best of it. The stewardess let her wait on the table while coming up the river. Meeting the passengers helped her to take her mind off the thoughts of leaving Kentucky.

The Katie stopped at a boat landing. There was a large band of Indians all dressed in gay regalia making a lot of noise. Some of them came down to the boat landing. Mamma was frightened and said, "I am glad I don't live in this part of the country. I would surely be afraid of the Indians." The stewardess said, "Laws a massy, child, you are going where there are lots of those folks, and there are some fine folks among them." These words gave Mamma courage.

Mamma often told me that the stewardess was responsible for her being able to brave the great difficulties that confronted her in the wild west. In the winter evenings she would tell me all about the "Katie." It carried with it such beautiful linen and silverware all marked "The Katie" and had a fine captain. All the passengers were going to Fort Benton. The Katie made just one trip up the river. After returning it caught fire and was burned. On the dock Mamma often spoke of the Robert E. Lee. While coming up the river there was large herd of buffalo drinking. They watched as they slowly wandered across the prairie.

Mamma finally reached the end of her journey at Fort Benton. There she met Pappa. He was very glad to see her. Next morning they took the stage to Barker, which was a mining camp. There were no well marked highways as there are today. The stage coaches just followed the trails over the plains. Storms and blizzards came up quickly. And one of those storms made its appearance at that time while they were on the way from Fort Benton to Barker. The stage driver was an old timer with horses but the storm was so severe the horses would not face it so they went round in a circle till they were lost and had to camp all night on the prairie. Mamma took her turn watching for Indians while some of the passengers slept. Next morning the storm cleared away and they were on their way to Barker. Pappa was employed as a cook for the mining company. Their headquarters were in Chicago. Pappa had a neat little cabin for Mamma to live in, but when she reached there she thought it was the end of the earth. Everywhere she looked she saw Indians.

Next day Pappa had come home and they were having lunch. Someone knocked at the door. Pappa went to the door. It was an Indian woman. She came in and Pappa said, "See my squaw."

The Indian woman said something. Mamma did not know what it was. Mamma gave her some coffee and cake and she was very much pleased and carried the news to all the Indian women in the camp. She had many tea parties after that. Mamma did not like the idea of Pappa calling her a squaw, so she asked him why he did it. He told her he had to use language the Indians would understand. Mamma said the Indian women were splendid midwives. Mamma loved to recall the days of the mining town, Barker. People were so friendly. Mr. Conrad had a store there at that time. I was born in this mining camp and claim the distinction of being the first white child born there. All the rest of the babies were Indian babies. I was delivered by an Indian woman. Barker was in Meagher county at that time.

It was a thriving silver mine. It was discovered by Joseph Meek, a Civil War veteran who lived in White Sulphur Springs in a little house north of town on a hill top for many years. Mrs. Meek was a nurse and nursed for many families in time. Mr. Meek is buried in Mayn cemetery. Mrs. Meek is buried in Helena, where she went to live after her husband's death. They were great friends of our family. We loved to hear Mr. Meek tell Civil War stories. The mining camp at Barker played out as all mining camps did in Montana. Pappa then moved to White Sulphur Springs where he was employed as a cook in the Higgins house. He bought a small cottage and this with some improvements has been our home for many years.

After working here for some time he was offered more money to work in Castle, then a thriving camp with a population of three thousand people. We were always glad when Pappa came home. I still remember the good food he used to cook for Mamma and everybody that came along.

Pappa worked in Castle for two years. He came home for a rest but he did not rest long. Judge Gaddis of Fort Logan and some of the big ranchers wanted him to cook for them on the roundup. He did. They took their cattle over land to Livingstone in those days to ship. He returned home and decided to go to Alaska, to the gold rush country. I was twelve years old when he left home. We never saw him again.

There was a railroad wreck in Canada. Many were killed. We wrote the police in Canada and a man of his description was among the dead. Mother was heartbroken. She was then a widow and had to face the world alone with five children to support. She took in washing and ironing and worked for the wealthy people of the town. Washing and ironing were done by main strength and awkwardness in those days. It was the wash board and irons heated on the top of the range; plenty of ruffles, frills, fine linens and what have you. The water was bought by the barrel at twenty-five cents a barrel. Jake Zehnter was the water man. He was a fine person. He also had his trials. The village boys would fill his well up with rocks and delay his work. Mamma would always say, I hope my boys were not in on it. We were glad when they put in the water works. We then had to haul water from the fire hall in express wagons using five gallon coal oil cans. My brother had a lot of fine pals who always helped haul water and also helped saw the wood. Every fall Mamma would have a yard full of wood bought from the farmers of the valley.

I recall one day a man drove up to the house with a load of wood and started to unload it. Mamma went outside and told the man he had made a mistake. She had not ordered any wood. The man kept unloading. Mamma said, "Listen, mister. I have no money to pay for that wood." He said, "You don't have to pay for it. Mr. Sherman sent it to you." Dear Mamma came in the house, sat down and cried. Mr. Sherman let the boys have a cow to milk so we had all the milk and cream we wanted. Mr. Sherman was so good to people who had large families to support. When the boys started to school there was more trouble for Mamma. The boys always had big battles after school. This worried Mamma. She had enough to endure without school fights. All the boys who went to school in those days had to show their fighting ability. They had some great battles but their friends were legion. Whenever the boys came home telling what the teacher did, Mamma said, "You must be in the wrong or the teacher would not scold you." So the boys had to face the music.

Nearly everybody in town had their own cow. You had to keep your cow in the barn or in a pasture. Some of the cows would get out and cause trouble so it was a twenty dollar fine if your cow got out. Bob was milking Max Waterman's cow. It got out and the marshal wanted Mamma to pay the fine. Mamma went to the city hall and pleaded her own case and won out on the cow deal.

Mamma's church was her refuge. She never missed church on Sunday. The brick Methodist church was dismantled many years ago. She was a faithful church worker. Reverend Hoskins baptized all the Gordon kids. We all attended Sunday school. It was a grand sight to see all the families going to church, merchants and all.

Mamma helped at all the parties for the wealthy people's weddings and all kinds of parties. When I was old enough to set tables I would go with her and help. The wealthy people all kept help, but large parties were given and Mamma and I helped. Miss Mamie Guiltman was a real society woman. She was from Boston. Every year she went to Boston and brought back the latest in serving. "What a headache." There were so many forks and spoons on the table you did not know which one to pick up first. Some of the guests would come out in the kitchen and ask Mamma what to do. Mamma said, just watch the host or hostess and take your time. I shall never forget the time when we first used finger bowls. There was no chance for Mamma and me to miss. We were trained by Miss Guiltman. We sure felt sorry for the guests. This grand affair was at the home of Mrs. R. G. Wight. I took in the finger bowls at the proper time. A gentleman who shall be nameless drank out of the bowl. I felt sorry for him. I brought in two more bowls and put a clover leaf in each one so they would know, not for drinking.

The style and linens, silverware, Haviland china, and cut class dishes— all this meant work, especially when you were shining up for a party. People wore full dress at dinner parties and dances. Mamma carried on this hard work for years. She developed rheumatism from cold and exposure. She became quite lame in her feet. Walking to and from work was hard for her. I was glad when I grew old enough to help her at parties. She became so lame for a while she could not go out to parties but did her laundry at home.

She spent lots of money for liniment to rub her feet with. I read an advertisement in the San Francisco Examiner of a sure cure for rheumatism.

It was put up by a doctor Schlocum. At that time he was specializing in tuberculosis. It was ten dollars a bottle. Mamma saved the money. We sent for it. It helped her so much she was able to do party work again. George Gordon and John Francis were getting old enough to help with the work. On cold winter nights they would go and get Mamma and haul her home on the large sled. They hauled water. One day a woman came and asked Mamma if she would like to put her children to work in other people's homes. Mamma said, "Only over my dead body. They are too young." It was her prayer, "God let me live to raise my children." We all had a chance; if we did not take, it was not her fault.

I must not forget to tell you about the day the Gordon kids were looking for excitement. Pappa had one of those old muzzle loading shotguns and we were wondering how it would be to fire one of those old guns. Pappa always kept it hanging up on the wall so we got a chair and stood on it and got the gun off the wall, took it out behind the house, placed it on a large log. We all sat down. Bob had his hand on the trigger. We sat down and held on to each other. In case the gun kicked one could brace the other. Bob pulled the trigger. The muzzle loader exploded. There were pickaninnies rolling in all directions.

The explosion raised the town. The marshal came to see what had happened at the Gordon house. The marshal was James Brewer. He gave us a ginning up. It was a tragedy when Mamma came home. Her heart was broken. She said what am I going to do? I can't leave the children home alone and I must work. I said, Mamma I will never do anything again. I never did. I grew up right now. No more pranks. I realized I must make the children be good.

They still had battles but no more shooting.

On the north side of the house was the tenderloin district. There were all kinds of women; some handsome and others not so handsome. I must say they treated us children with the greatest of respect. They never smoked in our presence, or used bad language. They would dress like queens and look like pictures just ready to step into the frame. There was one I remember. They called her Dolly. She was the most beautiful woman I ever saw, slender figure, good manners, a wealth of chestnut hair.

Mamma raised Plymouth Rock chickens. The ladies come to buy eggs and chickens. Mamma always sent me out of the room when they came. They always had troubles to tell. One day a handsome blonde came with a hat in her hand. She was crying. She had sent the hat to her mother and her mother sent it back. It had a bird of paradise on it. It was very expensive. Her mother wanted something plain and did not want her daughter to spend her money that way. She wanted Mamma's opinion on the matter. Mamma told her to send her mother the money and let her do with it as she pleased.

I soon found out by their visits that all that glittered was not gold. They were always trying to hide things from the folks at home. I well remember one called Morphine Ollie. Tall, dark complexioned, rugged features, always begging for money to buy morphine. One day she came to our house to buy eggs. It was summer. She had on short sleeves. There was not a spot on her arms that had not been pierced by a hypodermic needle. I was young and asked her how she hurt her arms. She began to cry and told me that she was a fiend. She said to me, don't ever be a fiend. I told her I would not spoil my arms like that. She was married later and became a Christian Scientist and lived on the west coast. Many of those women married farmers and became fine wives.

As I look back over those days and compare them with the present day it is appalling. One of the ladies was taken before the judge and fined 15 dollars for appearing in men's attire. Now they wear shorts and get under the wire nicely. Those people moved along till time in its flight saw fit to remove them. Those people were great spenders and merchants missed their trade. They were not a moral asset but commercial asset, and that has been the main thing since I have inhabited this "pig iron world." Even in this day and age they look you up in Bradstreet and if you don't have the rating it is too bad for you.

I was glad when I grew old enough to take care of children. I brought the money home to Mamma. It was a great help to her. I got a dollar a night for babysitting. I went to homes where they had such wonderful books. I would read and they always left fruit and food for me to eat.

Mamma cooked the first meal served in the auditorium. The opening was grand. Five hundred people were served. As I gaze on the ruins I see the grand people who spent happy hours there.

On June 7, 1924, God saw fit to take mother to her rest. Her last words were, "My Lord, it is all over now." She lived her life for others, caring for the sick and giving comfort to troubled minds. People from all walks of life followed her to her last resting place.

Rose Gordon Recalls Story of Wight Family

Meagher County News 29 April 1949

The death of Mrs. R. G. Wight as reported in this paper last week recalls a name which appears often in the chronicle of the Smith river valley. The Wight family lived in White Sulphur Springs and Mr. Wight was one of the promoters of mining in the Neihart area.

Your editor has asked Rose Gordon to write a short account of her recollections of these people. Her writing follows:

It was with deep regret that I read of the death of Lady Wight at Orlando, Florida. It brought back many beautiful memories of the Wight family. I was just old enough to be what they now call a baby sitter. But to me the baby sitting sounds mechanical, for I loved all the children that I cared for. The Wight family was a loving family. The home was so full of harmony. Mrs. Florence Anderson of Tallahassee, Florida, and Dr. Charles Wight of Riverside, California, were twins. They surely kept things busy. There was never a dull moment, and on down the years I saw them grow up to be two brilliant children. Mr. Frank Wight lives in Portland, Oregon. I just remember him. He was an older brother. Mr. and Mrs. R. G. Wight built a fine home on Murray hill, and raised their family there. Lady Wight gave many fine dinners and parties. My dear mother and I always assisted the maid with the parties. Lady Wight was a wonderful hostess. I recall one fine dinner at the Wight home. The finger bowls were being used and one of the guests drank out of the finger bowl. It was unnoticed by the hostess.

Mr. R. G. was one of the early day surveyors in Montana. Mr. R. G. Wight and Mr. A. M. Henry owned and operated the Florence mine at Neihart, out of which they gathered a great deal of wealth. Mr. Wight was a fine husband, father, and citizen. Mr. Wight had a horse and spring wagon which was used so much in those days. One day he was taking a group of children out for a ride. The horse started to run away. I said, "Oh, Mr.

Wight, what is the matter with your horses?" "Oh, just keep still," he said, "There are too many pickininnies in the wagon." I still laugh about that. We had so much fun.

Mr. R. G. Wight spent the last years of his life in Pasadena, California, leaving Lady Wight a widow. She returned to White Sulphur Springs and remained here for some time. Realizing she could not live alone in her large home, she decided to sell it. Breaking up her home made her very sad. She loved everything about her [home] and did not wish to part with it. She had so many beautiful and expensive things which meant so much to her. Taylor Gordon and I helped her to pack. Every now and then she would sit down and tears would come to her eyes and roll down her cheeks. I would cheer her up by saying, "Lady Wight, you know we have things but for a little while on earth."

She said, "Rose, you are good for all ills."

Lady Wight, like myself, loved Montana, its beautiful sunsets, its valleys and running streams. She loved to fish and had many pictures of the beautiful scenery of Montana.

After selling her home she made a trip to Vermont and spent some time there, later moving to Florida and living with her daughter, Mrs. Anderson.

Lady Wight was the highest type of womanhood. She defended everything that was upright and honorable, and was a real Christian at heart, a good wife, mother and homemaker, and a noble friend. I can only write the words of the poet:

> Green be the turf above you,
> Friend of my better days:
> None knew you but to love you,
> None named you but to praise.

Rose Gordon Writes

Meagher County News 23 November 1949

I had the pleasure of attending the wedding of Miss Mable Ringling and Mr. Russell A. Anderson of Great Falls. I watched the bride grow up in Smith river valley. She was always very sweet. I recall one day she came home from school very early. I said to her, "Mable dear, why are you out so soon?" She replied, "I will tell you why, Rose, because I get so tired of sitting in school." She was just six years old.

The wedding was beautiful. It was a candlelight service and as I looked at the burning candles, their lights reflected many memories of the past to me. Mable Ringling's grandfather, Powell Black, came to Montana many years ago. He was a brilliant young attorney from Kentucky and was known as a great orator and had the greatest power over a jury than any other attorney in this part of the country. He was elected to the legislature as representative from White Sulphur Springs, Meagher County. He possessed a great personality and was very much admired by all classes. I well remember the night there was a large reception held at the Higgins house, now known as the Sherman hotel, in honor of Mr. Powell Black. I was a little girl, just old enough to help mamma a little. I looked into the dining room and saw a beautiful woman sitting by Mr. Powell Black. I said, "Who is that beautiful woman with Mr. Black?" Mamma replied, "That is his bride, just from Kentucky."

After the banquet was over, Mr. Black introduced his bride to mamma. When she found out that mother was from Kentucky, a mist of tears filled her beautiful eyes—she felt as if she had found a friend. Mamma and Mrs. Black remained friends till she was called to a Better World. Mrs. Black was kind and loving and I never heard her say anything unkind about anyone. A few years later, Mr. Black bought a house just one block south of our home. There was where they lived the remaining part of their lives. They had two lovely daughters who were much admired, Miss Aubrey and Miss Olga Black. When they were little children, I took care of them while their parents attended social affairs. I watched them grow up to be fine young ladies.

In later years, Mr. Richard Ringling came to the valley and he was the son of Alfred Ringling, one of the Ringling Brothers of the Greatest Show on Earth. He engaged in farming and stock raising and bought and built up one of the largest ranches in the valley and built one of the largest dairy barns between White Sulphur Springs and St. Paul, Minnesota. He built up one of the finest herds of Holstein cattle in the state, and one time he milked over a hundred head of cows and built the Springs creamery. It was noted for its Castle Mountain Gold Butter. The creamery was operated by Mr. Harley Long of Bozeman.

Mr. Ringling spent a great deal of time here, when not away attending to other business. He had not been here very long until he met the charming Miss Aubrey Black. It was not long until they were wedded. I was operating a café at that time and had the pleasure of cooking their wedding breakfast. Mr. Richard Ringling was a grand person, was liked by all who knew him; no one was too poor or no one too rich. He was kind to all. Three lovely children were born to them. Mr. Paul Ringling has always made his home here with the exception of the time spent with the circus and in college and the United States army overseas. He is now married and engaged in ranching in Smith river valley. Mrs. Jane Ringling Lowry lives in Great Falls, Mrs. Mable Ringling Anderson in Great Falls.

During the reign of Richard Ringling in White Sulphur Springs, dear old Sam Snyder was assessor of Meagher County when it included about seven counties, the way they are divided now. He covered the whole country in a spring wagon and a team of horses and always had a brown jug and his dog in the wagon. In later years the little brown jug became his master. One day he came to my store and café. I said "Good morning, Mr. Snyder. How are you?" He said, "I had my feelings hurt this morning. A man told me I was too poor to own a dog. I told him I had just as much right to own a dog as Rose Gordon and Richard Ringling." He certainly placed me in a high bracket with a millionaire. Mr. Richard loved the west and wanted to be buried here.

Mrs. Aubrey Ringling Haley has always been very kind to the poor but she did not mention it. Many children would have gone without milk if she had not been so kind. The mothers did not fail to speak of it. The great depression was a hard blow. It was through the kindness of Mrs. Aubrey Ringling that I had the pleasure of seeing the Greatest Show on Earth. Behind the tent it was just one happy family, mothers doing fancy work, children playing—so much harmony. I sincerely hope the bride and groom will be very happy and live a long and successful life.

Tribute to Cyrus Allen

Meagher County News 10 December 1952

I wish to pay tribute to Cyrus Allen. I deeply regret his passing. For three years he had been looking forward to our class reunion but it happened that some one or the other could not get here. We all liked Cyrus so much. Some times in chemistry class we would be having a terrible time with our experiments, but Cyrus was always calm and would say we will come out all right. We always did. He always had a kind word for everybody. No one was all bad with Cyrus; he always saw the good in everyone. He was a gentleman always, never said unkind things about anyone. I recall when Mr. Lenning named me as valedictorian of the class. Cyrus came to me and said, "Rose, I am so glad for you, for you have had to work so hard to get your education." I will never forget his kindness. He was so tolerant. I can say the same of the entire class. Cyrus will be missed by his many friends for he knew how to be a friend.

Story of Millie Ringold,
Pioneer of Yogo Sapphire Mine

Meagher County News 11 January 1958

I have read two or three articles about the sapphire mines of Yogo. I had the pleasure of knowing [Millie] Ringold, pioneer of the sapphire mines. She came to Montana from the south with a wealthy southern family. The people she came with did not like the west. They returned to the south leaving Millie Ringold here. She filed on this land as a homestead and raised turkeys and chickens and was a nurse for all the people in the neighborhood. One day when she was dressing turkeys for sale she found a sapphire in the craw of the turkey. This created quite a bit of excitement. She then tried to sell the mine, but at that time men had a lust for gold. She came to White Sulphur Springs on the stage coach and asked where she could stop. They told her to go to Mrs. Gordon's house. She was here a week.

I was just a child old enough to go to school. She went to the merchants of the town at that time. But she could not get them interested in the gems. She was a very interesting person. She was very musical. She played odd instruments, hand saws, mouth harps and dish pans. We couldn't get home from school soon enough to visit Millie.

I have the photograph of Millie Ringold given to my late brother George Gordon. It was by T. B. Story of Bozeman. Stewart and Nelson Story had a store in that part of the country at that time about 1880. The picture bears the autograph.

Millie passed away without realizing anything out of the mine. I was in Lewistown in 1910 and the beautiful sapphires were being sold on the street.

I liked the deep blue coloring and bought some of them. While Millie received no money from her mine, her love of the west made up for it all. She spoke of the golden sunsets, the vast prairies and the mountain scenery. Within her lived a love of the West that no gems could replace.

The Sherman Hotel
Meagher County News 6 November 1963

I went to the Sherman hotel October 31 to be there for the closing of the hotel at 2 a.m. November 1, 1963. The hotel was built by Jonas Higgins projecting into the street to spite Dr. William Parberry who owned the Parberry addition. Jonas Higgins owned much of the land north and east and south of the hotel. The hotel was built in 1884.

The hotel not only stood as a memento of the wild and wooly west, but an age of culture which existed here at one time. There were many distinguished guests registered at the hotel, from many foreign countries. They came to bathe in the spring water and gaze upon the beauty of the Smith river valley. The hotel at that time was a place where grand parties were held. Ladies and gentlemen in full dress attended gala events there, held in the spacious dining room. The cooks were the finest. Many banquets and wedding parties were held there.

The large parlor was used for weddings and many activities. Mrs. W. D. Edwards and her two sisters had their pictures taken in the parlor when they graduated from the eighth grade.

During the reign of Frank Phelps at the hotel it was still flourishing. In those days gambling was wide open, and the town was a lively place.

Cowboys would ride in from Rock creek, ride into the saloons on horseback and order a drink. "It was wild."

Mr. Phelps was a man well liked. He conducted a fine hotel. On one occasion Sam Snyder, our assessor, went to the hotel with his favorite dog "Nosey" and asked for a bed. There was a celebration in town and Mr. Phelps was deep in rum. Mr. Snyder asked for a room. He too was celebrating. Sam said, may I take my dog Nosey to the room? Mr. Phelps said, no dog. Sam said, don't you think Nosey is the more respectable of the two of us? Sam won out.

There are many things to be said about the hotel. It would take much time.

The late Percy Miller was the last one to own the hotel. He was well liked. His wife Mary E. Miller was operating the hotel at the closing.

We enjoyed a pleasant evening. To me it was like losing an old friend.

I know the old must make way for the new. I feel myself fortunate to be able to attend the closing night of the Sherman. Mr. Sherman bought the hotel many years ago. He was a cattle raiser and rancher of the early days. My father was the first cook at the hotel. My late brother Robert worked there many years.

When Calamity Jane Came to Town
Meagher County News 5 February 1964

The Sherman hotel and the Auditorium had a great deal to do with making our small town a pleasant place in which to live.

Many talented people came to the Auditorium, fine singers, violinists and stage players. This is to say nothing of the grand balls and parties given there.

All these people found rooms, and were served the best of foods at the Sherman hotel.

Pat Twohey was the last to have the dining room at the hotel. They made a specialty of Sunday dinners. Their homemade ice cream was a great hit. Mr. and Mrs. Twohey remodeled the hotel, bought new furniture and other fixtures. The first furniture was brought up the river in the steamboat days. It featured red velvet carpets and furniture upholstered in red velvet. It was beautiful. The hotel was kept very clean.

Many fine parties were served in the dining room when the Twohey's operated the hotel.

Claude Kiff was one of the fine musicians at that time. He played the saxophone and clarinet. Wilma MacLean played the piano and Glen Roscoe the guitar. The Twohey family were a musical family; most all of them played some musical instrument, if only the mouth harp.

The Auditorium stood sentinel on the hill just above the home of Mrs. Art Solberg, the spot where the home of Albert Johnson now stands. R. N. Sutherlin called it the Temple of Fun. Mr. Sutherlin, with other men of the valley, helped build this fine building. They were on circuit with the Sutton Opera House of Butte. We had the pleasure of seeing and hearing many fine artists, singers and musicians, and the famous Fisk Jubilee Singers.

I must tell you about the thrill we children had the day they told us that Calamity Jane was coming in on the six-horse stage coach. She was a legend to us. The day came and we saw her. She was a rugged looking woman and weather beaten. When she smiled at us you could see so much kindness in her face. She wore dark clothes and a black cap that came down to her neck. It was very cold. We went to bed that night very happy. We had had the pleasure of seeing "Calamity Jane." We saw many other western characters in Montana, including Charles M. Russell.

Robert Sutherlin, editor of the Rocky Mountain Husbandman, worked hard to keep the hotel filled with noted people. Once a year we had the Harvest Festival. People came from miles around to attend the event. A display of vegetables, wheat and rye was held in the Auditorium. It was a grand display and ended with a "Grand Ball."

One year they asked the Home Talent Folks if they would like to give a play at the festival. We all said yes, so they turned it over to us. We were in practice for six weeks—what a deal! My late brother George was director and sang tenor. We had a cast of 13 people, a grand bunch to work with. Our play was a success. It was a black-face minstrel. Blackie LaRue was one of the stars of the play. We had a fine collection of voices. We took in $300 which was divided among the cast. They gave us the hall for free.

About three months later a man came from Kansas City to book us for the road. We decided to stay "where bacon and eggs were easy to get." Thomas Meixsell was the last one to have the Auditorium. His New Year

Ball was some event. He always had Momma to cook the midnight supper. On the stage you could seat 100 people. Tom had dishes and all equipment for the affair. Just as the clock struck 12 Tom would stand on the stage and fire a number of real bullets into the attic of the stage which was never quite finished. He really shot the old year out and the new year in. "Those were the days." Tom had a great outlook on life. He loved the west and had many friends. He passed away at the Sherman hotel at the age of 92 years.

Tribute to Gertrude Backus
Meagher County News 18 January 1967

I wish to pay tribute to Gertrude Backus, who was born in White Sulphur Springs.

She was always such a lady and from childhood was loved by all who knew her. As a young girl she was very talented. She played the piano and had a beautiful singing voice. She played the organ at the Episcopal church for many years. Down the years she did not forget the Little Church. Her parents donated the organ to the church many years ago.

Mr. and Mrs. Charles Mayn were her parents, pioneers of the valley. Mrs. Mayn was one of the leading merchants for years. Her brother, Harold Mayn, preceded her in death. Her memory will always be cherished by all who knew her as a lady who loved her friends.

We will miss her so much.

Battle of the Pigment
Meagher County News 9 May 1968

The daily papers are filled with news, seems like, it is hard for some folks to make up their minds about the colors. On a beautiful summer day when you take a ride and gaze upon the beautiful hills, valleys, and running streams and all the different colors of nature, it is difficult to think the Great Creator made this all for people of one color. This life is too short to waste it on such thoughts, for the power of thought is the greatest power there is. It will destroy you or make you. It is our different colors that makes this world such a wonderful place in which to live. If everything was one color we would soon go mad. I hope that God will set all men free to all the thoughts of every race, color and creed to float down their memory untainted by the foul breath of prejudice.

It is a great adventure to be born with dark skin. While traveling about, you meet many people who do not like the idea. This is what puts you to the test and if you do not have a Christian background, you may become bitter. When you know that Christ had to bear his cross and you must also bear your cross it is very easy. We come into this veil of tears to suffer and we must learn to unite through our tears—makes no difference what the color of the skin. Dr. Martin Luther King carried his cross. I will let God be his judge.

Our colored soldiers have shown the highest courage and have won unstinted praises for their bravery, loyalty and fidelity. They have indeed been baptized into full citizenship by their bloodshed in the defense of their country and have earned the protection of that honorable emblem, the stars and stripes.

Rose B. Gordon

Bibliographic Essay

African American Women in the American West

"Since the 1970s," Herbert G. Ruffin II writes, "the history of the African American West has evolved into an exciting branch of scholarship."[1] *A Black Woman's West: The Life of Rose B. Gordon* is part of this ongoing, evolving, and exciting branch of scholarship taking place across a variety of disciplines and fields, including history, literature, and biography, the three areas that this book addresses most explicitly. In this bibliographic essay, I aim to place *A Black Woman's West* in the context of the evolving study of African American experience in the American West, drawing connections between Rose Gordon's story and other histories of African American women, and of Western women more generally. By doing so, I also want to acknowledge some of the histories and biographical studies that have been important philosophical and methodological influences on *A Black Woman's West*. The study of the African American West is an area of research that continues to have significant absences, some of which, I hope, my study of Rose Gordon's life has addressed.

Important early studies of the African American West include Kenneth Wiggins Porter's *The Negro on the American Frontier* (1971), Sherman W. Savage's *Blacks in the West* (1976), and Nell Irvin Painter's *Exodusters: Black Migration to Kansas after Reconstruction* (1977).[2] The essential book in the field is Quintard Taylor's *In Search of the Racial Frontier: African*

Americans in the American West, 1528–1990 (1998), which provides a comprehensive account of African American migration and community building in every western state and is essential for any study of the Black West.[3] *African American Women Confront the West: 1600–2000* (2008), an anthology of criticism edited by Quintard Taylor and Shirley Ann Wilson Moore, provides a comprehensive overview of African American women's experience in the region.[4] This collection makes clear that since the first European explorers entered what we now know as the American West, Black women, "whether they resided in populous urban areas or in small, agrarian communities," were deeply immersed "in the political and social currents affecting all black people and, by the twentieth century, all westerners."[5]

In the twenty-first century, scholarly interest in the African American West has increased—particularly in literary and cultural studies, though there is still much to do in these areas. Some of the more recent examples of notable studies include Blake Allmendinger's *Imagining the African American West* (2005), my own *Hoo-Doo Cowboys and Bronze Buckaroos: Conceptions of the African American West* (2014), Emily Lutenski's *West of Harlem: African American Writers and the Borderlands* (2015), Eric Gardner's *Unexpected Places: Relocating Nineteenth-Century African American Literature* (2009) and *Jennie Carter: A Black Journalist of the Early West* (2007), Daniel Widener's *Black Arts West: Culture and Struggle in Postwar Los Angeles*(2010), and Kellie Jones's *South of Pico: African American Artists in Los Angeles in the 1960s and 1970s* (2017).[6]

Urban life in the twentieth and twenty-first centuries has become "the largest and most dynamic area of study" regarding Black people in the West according to Ruffin.[7] The various listings in Ruffin's bibliographic essay reflect that emphasis, as do the individual chapter selections for *Freedom's Racial Frontier*. Although some essays in *Freedom's Racial Frontier* focus on places such as Hawaii and Washington, the African American experience in Texas and California receives the most emphasis. Less populous areas such as the Great Plains states and the Intermountain West outside of Denver, however, are underrepresented. As a coeditor of "New Directions in Black Western Studies," a special issue of *American Studies Journal* in 2019, I discovered a similar lack of balance regarding the urban and rural African American West, as all the submissions we received addressed the African American experience in California and Texas, with the vast majority of contributions focusing on California.[8] As editors, we wished to include a wider geographical range of articles about the African American West, but the issue ended up accurately reflecting the current state of the field—which, as Quintard Taylor noted in 1998, still reveals significant gaps and absences.

In addition to the urban/rural imbalance, one of the other areas of sparse knowledge is the history of African American women in the West. Glenda Riley comments that Black women have "suffered near-invisibility in western history" in part because many "archivists neglected to collect these women's source materials," and therefore "most historians disregarded their stories."[9] That neglect is even more pronounced with Black women who lived ordinary lives in the West, and whose lives are potentially more revelatory of the experiences of African American women in general than are the lives of the few better known figures, such as that of nineteenth-century San Francisco entrepreneur Mary Ellen Pleasant.[10]

In *Remembering Lucile* (2018), a biography of Lucile Berkeley Buchanan Jones, author Polly E. Burgros McLean describes the first Black woman to graduate from Colorado State University and the University of Colorado: "One of the challenges of writing about a non-celebrity is that you do not have one main repository of the person's papers."[11] The story of Lucile Jones, the child of former slaves who after the Civil War migrated from Kentucky to the emerging city of Denver in search of a life of freedom and possibility in the American West, is a fascinating one that in tracing the arc of a family's movement from slavery to emancipation and migration west parallels that of the Gordons. There are, no doubt, other such stories waiting to be told, but there have been—and continue to be—obstacles in the way of telling those stories, including a lack of source materials and a prevailing interest in celebrity lives over ordinary ones.

McLean's book is part of an ongoing scholarly effort to construct a more accurate history of the American West, one that is inclusive of the wide variety of individuals who are part of that history. Emphasizing the biographies of famous figures has distorted the region's history by prizing the "heroic model of western history in which the American West bred remarkable individuals," mostly white male individuals "who lived and died larger than life." For that reason, Dee Garceau-Hagen writes in *Portraits of Women in the American West* (2005), Western women's historians have regarded biography with suspicion as a genre prone to historical distortion: "If historical significance were defined only in terms of exceptional women whose deeds merited biographical study, then the lives of ordinary women would go unexamined. Much of western women's history, then, has cast a wider net, exploring patterns in the lives of women grouped by cultural identity, region, or era, to create a gendered analysis of the American West."[12]

As McLean's *Remembering Lucile* demonstrates, and as the biographical portraits in *Portraits of Women in the American West* similarly suggest, an approach to Western biography that looks at the lives of individual women does not have to repeat the "heroic model of western history" in order to tell a good story and illuminate elements of the region's history that remain under-examined. A Western history attentive to the lives of individual women, according to Garceau-Hagen, "allows subtleties of attitude, relationship, and choice to emerge."[13] Of the biographical sketches included in the *Portraits of Women in the American West* collection, Garceau-Hagen notes that each one "reveals dynamics of social change, enacted in daily choices, in shifts of perception, in moments of dislocation or resolution. When an individual woman disrupted, challenged, or redefined gender norms or racial codes, we see the consequences with a human face. When a community reinforced racial-ethnic categories of exclusion or affirmed a gender hierarchy, its effects on an individual woman come into bold relief." Collectively, the essays "explore how individual women in the American West negotiated their place in a landscape of shifting power and privilege."[14] Rose Gordon's story contributes to this developing portrait of Western women's lives by exploring how Rose herself and other members of her family, especially her mother, engaged in a negotiation of a complex racial landscape, one that changed dramatically over time as the Black community in White Sulphur Springs dwindled.

Like *Remembering Lucille*, Ethelene Whitmire's biography of Regina Anderson Andrews traces the ordinary life of a Black woman, in this case a librarian who became a key figure in the Harlem Renaissance. Whitmire notes, "While this biography tells the story of one woman's life, it is illustrative of other New Negro women who belonged to what W. E. B. Du Bois called the "Talented Tenth"—the small minority of upper-class, educated African Americans whom he believed could uplift the masses out of poverty"[15] Andrews entered an emerging professional field in 1920 when she joined the Chicago Public Library as a library assistant. Two years later, when she moved to the Harlem branch of the New York Public Library, there were only 15,297 librarians employed in the United States. Of them, only forty-seven were African American women and twenty-two African American men.[16] Andrews was among a "small number of first-generation African American female librarians who forged a career in a sometimes unwelcoming profession." As a result, Whitmire argues, her biography of Andrews "increases our understanding of the personal and professional lives of these women and the strategies employed to counter the obstacles they faced."[17] Although not a story of the African American West, Whitmire's book again demonstrates the value of examining the "ordinary" African American life.

Excluded from most professional and subprofessional employment by virtue of race, African American women were not among Du Bois's "Talented Tenth." The story of Rose Gordon's life increases our understanding of the lives of "ordinary" African American women more generally, making us aware of "the strategies employed to counter the obstacles they faced" in a prejudiced society that excluded them from full economic and political participation. As *A Black Woman's West* demonstrates, the Gordon family employed a variety of strategies to not only survive but thrive. Although the lives of Rose B. Gordon and Regina Anderson Andrews could not be more different in many ways, Whitmire's biography suggests several ways that their stories might be compared.

A Black Woman's West also joins a small set of biographical writing about African American women who lived in Montana. Notably, the Montana Historical Society published a collection of one hundred bibliographical essays on Montana women as part of the state's celebration of woman's suffrage in Montana. Originally published online in 2014 as installments of the Montana Women's History Matters project, the essays were compiled into a book, *Beyond Schoolmarms and Madams: Montana*

Women's Stories, and published in 2016. Chapters featuring African American women include those on Mary Fields, who worked as a laborer at St. Mary's Mission for over a decade before becoming the first female postal carrier in Montana; Great Falls activist and longtime librarian Alma Smith Jacobs; homesteaders Annie Morgan and Bertie Brown; pioneer businesswoman Sarah Gammon Bickford; war nurse Octavia Bridgewater; restaurateur and physiotherapist Rose Gordon; and the Montana Federation of Colored Women's Clubs. *Beyond Schoolmarms* also includes a significant number of essays on American Indian women who, like African Americans, are largely overlooked by historians and biographers alike and for the same reasons.

Recent book-length publications on Black Montana women include biographies of Mary Fields and Sarah Bickford. In *Deliverance: Mary Fields, First African American Woman Star Route Mail Carrier in the United States* (2016), Miantae Metcalf McConnell combines historical research with a fictional retelling of Fields's life history, offering both a factual account and adventurous storytelling.[18] McConnell describes how Fields, a Black woman who moved to Montana in 1885 and lived mostly in the Cascade area until her death in 1914, managed a successful existence in a largely white community. After working as a laborer for over a decade for the St. Peter's Mission—a boarding school for Indigenous and Métis students—Fields became "the first known African American woman star route mail carrier in the United States."[19] Despite Fields's general acceptance within the community and her unique occupation as a female rural mail carrier, McConnell notes the absence of any mention of Fields in the newspapers: "During a twenty-nine year span of active enterprise and cooperative ventures in the Birdtail [area], there was no mention of Mary in any newspaper account until 1910, when an anecdotal tribute surfaced."[20] Mary Fields's life in Cascade should have been considered newsworthy, and yet McConnell lists multiple events directly involving Fields that went unreported, including when her house—located near the *Cascade Courier* office—burned down. Fields was very much a part of Cascade's public sphere, but her rare appearance in the local press is indicative of how African Americans were overlooked in the documentation of the community.[21]

Published just a few years after McConnell's account of Mary Fields's life, Laura J. Arata's *Race and the Wild West: Sarah Bickford, the Montana Vigilantes, and the Tourism of Decline: 1870–1930* (2020) tells the story of a woman born into slavery in Tennessee who traveled to Montana as a teenager after the Civil War and settled in the mining town of Virginia City where she married twice, raised a family, and became a successful business owner.[22] "As an African American proprietor of a business in a mostly white community," Arata observes of Bickford, "she was remarkable." Bickford owned and operated Virginia City's water company. Her office was located in the "Hangman's Building," the site of an infamous extralegal hanging executed by the "Montana Vigilantes," and she chose to preserve and promote the building's history. That Bickford "was a black female public utilities owner who promoted tourism at the site of a lynching" was "strange, if not incongruous." Considering Bickford's unusual role as a Black Montana businesswoman during Montana's territorial period, "it defied logic," says Arata, that Bickford "had managed to go nearly unnoticed in scholarship on the West for this many decades after her death."[23]

Many such logic-defying absences, unfortunately, remain to be corrected. In 2005, Montana's Historic Preservation Office initiated the African American Heritage Resources Project to better understand the experiences of Blacks in Montana by documenting historically significant sites and investigating archival records related to the state's African Americans. "These resources provide documentation on the myriad ways that Montana's African American community contributed to the region's development within the context of national issues and historical themes, enabling the public to engage with Black historical experiences in Montana," says Community Preservation Coordinator Kate Hampton, who oversees the project.[24] At present, the project is working on a documentary to publicize Montana's Black history, much of which has remained understudied and forgotten until now.

A Black Woman's West lifts up Rose Gordon's voice so that she will be remembered into and beyond the twenty-first century. One of the major influences and inspirations for this book is Eric Gardner's *Jennie Carter*, an edited volume of Carter's contributions to two African American newspapers—the San Francisco *Elevator* and the *Christian Recorder*—in the late nineteenth century. The book also includes a long biographical introduction to Carter and her work. Writing under the pen names "Ann J. Trask" and "Semper Fidelis" ("Always Faithful"), and eventually sometimes under her own name, Carter wrote "pithy essays and narratives" and commented on "California and national politics, race and racism, women's rights and suffrage, temperance, morality, education, and a host of other issues."[25] Carter's writing, Gardner argues, "must be seen as one of the most significant contributions to African American women's writing during the Reconstruction and to black writing in the West." Despite the significance of Carter's work, it took the publication of this book to make a collection of her work available for the first time.[26]

"We should have found Jennie Carter long ago," Gardner writes. Arriving more than a century after it should have, *Jennie Carter* "reminds us that black voices may often have circulated in what, for many generations, was dismissed as ephemera."[27] That dismissal reflects a "confluence of different kinds of neglect" in literary studies, the neglect of publishing venues such as newspapers generally and African American newspapers, as well as "the neglect of shorter forms of literature like letters (in favor of books), the neglect of the literature of the Reconstruction, and the sense that early black literature and the literature of the West cannot be synonymous."[28] Gardner closes his introduction with a reminder and call that I wish to borrow: "Our loss and the gradual, partial regaining of her memory are in some ways emblematic of the fact that research means searching again and again. Only as we continue such recovery work will we be 'always faithful' to the memory of Jennie Carter and countless other voices in the black West that we have misheard, heard only quietly, or not heard at all."[29]

Rose Gordon's is one of those voices that we need to hear—and not a century from now, but while a handful of those who knew her or knew of her are still alive to recall how she was an integral part of White Sulphur Springs, Montana. Her community heard her voice very clearly during her lifetime, and *A Black Woman's West* provides an opportunity for it to be heard once again and more widely, not forgotten. That this Black woman found a means of expression in the local newspaper of a mostly white small Western town should remind us that hearing the unheard voices requires listening and relistening. It also sometimes requires us to set aside our assumptions and to listen for voices even when we expect to hear only silence. I suspect that Rose Gordon was not the only African American living in the West who found a means of expression in an unexpected place, and my hope is that ongoing attentive acts of listening will enable us to hear those voices as well.

Notes

Introduction

1. Taylor Gordon, *Born to Be* (New York: Covici-Friede Publishers, 1929; first repr., Seattle: Univ. of Washington Press, 1976; second repr., Lincoln: Univ. of Nebraska Press, 1995). Subsequent citations from 1995 reprint.
2. In July 1968, Montana author Ivan Doig interviewed Taylor and Rose Gordon for a manuscript he hoped would be published in *Montana The Magazine of Western History*. While the article was not published, Doig recognized the value of the Gordon family's writings. After Taylor's death in 1971, Doig worked with librarian John Coleman to have the Gordon family papers donated to the Montana Historical Society. Doig's recorded interviews with Taylor and Rose Gordon are located at the Ivan Doig Archive at Montana State University-Bozeman.
3. Historians note that most Black women in western cities in the early 1900s worked in domestic service: "As late as 1930 the proportion of black women in [the occupational category of 'domestic service'] ranged from a low of 83 percent in Seattle to a high of 93 percent in Dallas." Shirley Ann Wilson Moore and Quintard Taylor, "The West of African American Women, 1600–2000," in *African American Women Confront the West, 1600–2000*, eds. Quintard Taylor and Shirley Ann Wilson Moore (Norman: Univ. of Oklahoma Press, 2003), 12.
4. Rose Gordon, "My Mother Was a Slave," *Meagher County News*, May 25, 1955.
5. Quintard Taylor, *In Search of the Racial Frontier: African Americans in the American West, 1528–1990* (New York: W.W. Norton & Co., 1998), 23.
6. Glenda Riley, "African American Women in Western History: Past and Prospect," in Taylor and Moore, *African American Women Confront the West*, 22–27.
7. Rose Gordon, "Gone are the Days," MC 150 (7:4–1), fldr 2, bx 11, Emmanuel Taylor Gordon Family Papers, Montana Historical Society (MHS), Helena (hereafter Gordon Family Papers).
8. *Meagher Republican*, Nov. 25, 1904.
9. *Meagher County News*, Nov. 21, 1968.
10. For more on Taylor Gordon's life and career, see Michael K. Johnson, *Can't Stand Still: Taylor Gordon and the Harlem Renaissance* (Jackson: Univ. Press of Mississippi, 2019).

Chapter 1

1. Rose Gordon, "My Mother Was a Slave." Rose refers to her mother as "Annie" in "My Mother Was a Slave," but all other documents I encountered use the name "Anna," so I use that name throughout.
2. *Rocky Mountain Husbandman*, Aug. 25, 1892.
3. The Poindexter "plantation" was likely the farm owned by Zach and Matilda Poindexter, located in Clark County, Kentucky. Thanks to Nancy O'Malley, William S. Webb Museum of Anthropology, University of Kentucky, for sharing her research on this topic.
4. Rose Gordon, "My Mother Was a Slave."
5. Taylor Gordon, *Born to Be*, 5.

6. U.S. Census 1870; U.S. Census 1880. Thanks to Nancy O'Malley for tracking down this information.

7. U.S. Census 1880.

8. Rose Gordon, "My Mother Was a Slave."

9. Ibid.

10. Ibid.

11. Joseph Kinsey Howard, *Montana: High, Wide, and Handsome* (1943; repr., Lincoln: Univ. of Nebraska Press, 2003), 43.

12. Howard, *Montana*, 143.

13. Barbara Carol Behan, "Forgotten Heritage: African Americans in the Montana Territory, 1864–1889," *Journal of African American History* 91:2 (Winter 2006): 23–40, quotes from pages 23–24, 24, 29. Taylor, *In Search of the Racial Frontier*, 104, 135.

14. Rose Gordon, "My Mother Was a Slave."

15. The Little Belt Mountains comprise part of the traditional Blackfeet (Amskapi Piikani) homeland and was used by Blackfeet, Crow (Apsáalooke), Gros Ventre (A'aninin), and other tribes. By 1881, when the Gordons arrived, the Blackfeet were largely confined to treaty lands farther north, although they still hunted in central Montana Territory until the demise of the bison in 1882. The region was integral to the fur trade, which drew Chippewa, Cree, Assiniboine, and Métis laborers, as well as the Indigenous wives of white traders. Many of these people settled in central Montana communities like Lewistown (founded in the 1870s by Métis families), Fort Benton, and elsewhere, as they had no reservation of their own in Montana. It is likely that the "Indian" midwife who became friends with Anna Gordon was a Métis woman.

16. Rose Gordon, "My Mother Was a Slave."

17. Rose Gordon, "My Mother Was a Slave." Joe Meek's name is spelled variously as Meaks, Meeks, and Meek.

18. Taylor Gordon, *Born to Be*, 4.

19. In 1890, White Sulphur Springs had 640 residents. Census Bureau, Twelfth Census of the United States, "Population of Montana by Counties and Minor Civil Divisions," *Census Bulletin No. 33*, Jan. 17, 1901.

20. *Rocky Mountain Husbandman*, Feb. 14, 1892. The springs were well known by the area's Indigenous peoples. Brewer's so-called discovery came about after he encountered a group of Flathead Indians who helpfully suggested that he would find a better camping spot at a nearby hot springs.

21. *Rocky Mountain Husbandman*, Feb. 16, 1899.

22. During World War II, Rose wrote a letter to the *Meagher County News* observing how much she missed her hometown. She closed the letter: "Well dear people take care of your selves and don't drink too much coffee and use too much sugar. A man from Minneapolis is telling the people that you had better buy your whiskey, that is if you drink it, for it might play out. We have good water in White Sulphur Springs and don't need it." No one seems to have claimed, as in the old joke, that White Sulphur Springs was so healthy that they had to shoot someone to start a cemetery, but Rose was a firm believer in the healing power of the springs' mineral water. *Meagher County News*, Nov. 18, 1942.

23. Meagher County, named for territorial secretary Thomas Meagher, was founded in 1867. In 1865, Blackfeet representatives signed a treaty with American authorities to sell their lands south of the Missouri River—today's central Montana—to the United States. Congress failed to ratify the treaty, but white settlers moved into the area nonetheless, displacing Indigenous owners. In time, the United States forced the Blackfeet to relinquish the area, which comprises some two thousand square miles of land. See Amelia Hagen-Dillon, "Evolution of Indian Territories in Montana," *Native News 2018*, https://nativenews.jour. umt.edu/2018/history/.

24. Lee Rostad, "White Sulphur Springs: In the Smith River Valley," *Montana Magazine* (Nov./ Dec. 2003).

25. Taylor Gordon, *Born to Be*, 10.
26. The Virginia-born (1830) James Scott Brewer "had traveled west in 1855 as far as St. Joseph, Missouri, where he had established a livery business. Six years later he had moved farther west, to Denver and then to Nevada and finally in 1864 to Virginia City, Montana Territory." After Brewer "sold the springs to Dr. William Parberry in June 1877," he remained in the area and "continued his various entrepreneurial adventures," including operating a livery stable, "in and around the Smith River area" until his death in 1914. Marilyn McMillan, "'An Eldorado of Ease and Elegance': Taking the Waters at White Sulphur Springs, 1866–1904," *Montana The Magazine of Western History* 35:2 (Spring 1985): 36–49, 39–40.
27. Dr. William Parberry had come to Montana Territory to seek "his fortune in the gold fields," but wisely continued practicing medicine as his primary livelihood (McMillan, "Eldorado of Ease and Elegance," 40). Born in Kentucky in 1833, Parberry came to Montana Territory, as did many of White Sulphur Springs's citizens, by way of Missouri. That the town was founded by a physician, combined with Parberry's own enthusiasm for the springs as a treatment for rheumatism, contributed to its appeal as a destination for those seeking the "medicinal possibilities of hot springs." McMillan, "Eldorado of Ease and Elegance," 40, 42.
28. Taylor Gordon, *The Man Who Built the Stone Castle* (White Sulphur Springs, MT: *Meagher County News*, 1967), 12
29. *Meagher County News*, Feb. 5, 1964.
30. Ibid.
31. Anti-Chinese sentiment was so strong throughout Montana that "few of the Chinese remained long in Montana. By 1900, most of them had returned to China or had moved to the Pacific Coast." Michael P. Malone, Richard B. Roeder, and William L. Lang, *Montana: A History of Two Centuries*, rev. ed. (1976; Univ. of Washington Press, 1991), 85. An extensive discussion of the Chinese presence in Montana and the American West is beyond the scope of this project. For more discussion of the topic, see Laura Arata, "Beyond the 'Mongolian Muddle': Reconsidering Virginia City, Montana's China War of 1881," *Montana: The Magazine of Western History* 62:2 (Spring 2012): 23–35; Liping Zhu, *Chinaman's Chance: The Chinese on the Rocky Mountain Mining Frontier* (Niwot: Univ. Press of Colorado, 1997).
32. See Malone, Roeder, and Lang, *Montana*, 114–44.
33. Taylor Gordon, *Born to Be*, 3.
34. Taylor Gordon, *Born to Be*, 4.
35. Rose Gordon, "My Mother Was a Slave."
36. Rose Gordon, "Gone are the Days."
37. Rose Gordon, "Gone are the Days," 11.
38. *Rocky Mountain Husbandman*, Feb. 24, 1887.
39. *Rocky Mountain Husbandman*, Mar. 25, 1886.
40. *Rocky Mountain Husbandman*, Feb. 24, 1887.
41. *Rocky Mountain Husbandman*, Jan. 1, 1885.
42. Deed and Warranty, fldr 12, bx 14, Gordon Family Papers.
43. Taylor Gordon, *Born to Be*, 6–7.
44. Taylor Gordon, *Born to Be*, 3.
45. Frank Grant, "Rocky Mountain Husbandman: Embattled Voice of the Montana Farmer," *Montana The Magazine of Western History* 24:2 (Spring 1974): 34–43, 34.
46. Theresa Buckingham, "Centennial Notes," *Meagher County News*, Feb. 23, 1967. For more on R. N. Sutherlin and the importance of his newspaper to Montana's agricultural sector, see Frank Reginald Grant, "Robert N. Sutherlin| prophet for the people; a study of the editor of the *Rocky Mountain Husbandman*, 1875–1926," (master's thesis, Univ. of Montana, 1971), https://scholarworks.umt.edu/etd/3456.
47. Grant, "Rocky Mountain Husbandman," 36.
48. Grant, "Rocky Mountain Husbandman," 42.
49. Grant, "Rocky Mountain Husbandman," 43.

50. Grant, "Rocky Mountain Husbandman," 34.
51. The feud between the two newspapers exploded after Waterman revived the *Meagher Republican* in 1902. At this point, the editors truly became rivals, not only in terms of the rival political parties their newspapers represent but also in terms of competing for printing contracts with the Meagher County Board of Commissioners, on which, much to the displeasure of *Rocky Mountain Husbandman* editor R. N. Sutherlin, *Meagher Republican* editor Max Waterman held a seat. The issue that dominated the pages of the papers involved a proposal supported by Sutherlin for a free county high school in White Sulphur Springs. Waterman adamantly opposed the school and even published an "anonymous" pamphlet attacking the proposal. Sutherlin's commentary on his rival editor's actions is exemplary in its colorful name-calling: "Waterman, the 'dictator,' of Meagher County, has not the manhood to publish his attack on the high school over his own signature, but sends it out a waif with no one to father it" (*Rocky Mountain Husbandman*, Aug. 21, 1902). "We recommend to the back-biting, mud-slinging bulldozer of our town [aka, Max Waterman] that he read the article on our fifth page, which will on sight recommend itself as befitting his case" (*Rocky Mountain Husbandman*, Oct. 30, 1902). "Max is merely a grafter and a humbug, a fakir and a montebank, and the people of Meagher county know it" (*Rocky Mountain Husbandman*, Oct. 30, 1902).
52. *Meagher Republican*, Jan. 1, 1904.
53. *Rocky Mountain Husbandman*, Aug. 25, 1892.
54. *Rocky Mountain Husbandman*, Jan. 14, 1892.
55. *Meagher County News*, Jul. 29, 1967.
56. *Rocky Mountain Husbandman*, May 5, 1892.
57. *Rocky Mountain Husbandman*, Jul. 21, 1892.
58. *Meagher County News*, Nov. 6, 1963.
59. *Meagher County News*, May 17, 1944.

Chapter 2

1. Rose Gordon, "Gone are the Days," 15.
2. Taylor Gordon, *Born to Be*, 233.
3. Taylor Gordon, *Born to Be*, 76.
4. William Loren Katz, *The Black West: A Documentary and Pictorial History of the African American Role in the Westward Expansion of the United States*, rev. ed. (1971; New York: Touchstone, 1996), 183.
5. Scott Meredith, "Identifying African American Resources Project," *Montana The Magazine of Western History* 57:1 (Spring 2007): 61–66, 61.
6. Meredith, "Identifying African American Resources Project," 61. The majority of the African American population in 1870 was in Helena (43 percent), but groups of African Americans could be found in Virginia City (10.4 percent), Fort Benton (8.9 percent), and Bozeman (7.8 percent). In terms of professions, occupations listed in the census include "servants and domestics (23 percent), laborers (19 percent), barbers (17 percent), cooks (14 percent), and farm or ranch workers (4 percent)," as well as several miners. Meredith, "Identifying African American Resources Project," 61, 61–63.
7. Taylor, *In Search of the Racial Frontier*, 135.
8. Behan, "Forgotten Heritage," 21.
9. Behan, "Forgotten Heritage," 33.
10. Meredith, "Identifying African American Resources Project," 63.
11. William L. Lang, "Helena, Montana's Black Community, 1900–1912," in *African Americans on the Western Frontier*, eds. Monroe Lee Billington and Roger D. Hardaway (Niwot: Univ. Press of Colorado, 1998), 200.
12. Lang, "Helena, Montana's Black Community," 213.
13. U.S. Census, 1880, 1900, 1910, 1950.

14. *Indianapolis Freeman*, Sep. 13, 1890.
15. Behan, "Forgotten Heritage," 30.
16. *Indianapolis Freeman*, Nov. 21, 1891.
17. *Indianapolis Freeman*, Aug. 31, 1895.
18. *Indianapolis Freeman*, Apr. 22, 1893.
19. Malone, Roeder, and Lang, *Montana*, 84.
20. J. W. Smurr, "Jim Crow Out West," in *Historical Essays on Montana and the West*, eds. J. W. Smurr and K. Ross Toole (Helena: Western Press, 1957), 160.
21. Behan, "Forgotten Heritage," 24.
22. *Rocky Mountain Husbandman*, Feb. 18, 1886. Of Millie Ringold, the *Rocky Mountain Husbandman* observed that the "bonanza queen" was also "a citizen of White Sulphur Springs, and is earning a livelihood by washing" although "she spends the summer in the mountains and handles the pick and shovel with as much vigor and dexterity as a man."
23. The 1880 U.S. Census records Millie Ringold [Ringgold] as living in Belt City, Montana. The same census lists her age as thirty-seven and her place and date of birth as Maryland in 1843. She is listed as a head of household with the occupation of keeping a hotel. The 1900 census places her in Barker, Montana, and lists her occupation as prospector.
24. *Meagher County News*, Feb. 22, 1950.
25. *Meagher County News*, Jan. 11, 1950.
26. *Meagher County News*, Feb. 22, 1950.
27. The 1880 U.S. Census records thirty-seven-year-old Joseph Meek, a shoemaker, as living in Belt City, Meagher County, Montana. Meek was a neighbor of Millie Ringold at the time, and lived in the same household as Solomon Chone, a German immigrant and merchant. At the time, he was married to Laura Meek, with whom he appears on the 1870 census for Kansas City. Joseph is listed as single in the 1880 census, and the 1900 census records Joseph Meek as being married for thirty-three years to Sarah A. Meek. By 1900, Joseph and Sarah Meek lived in White Sulphur Springs.
28. Luis F. Emilio, *A Brave Black Regiment: The History of the 54th Massachusetts, 1863–65* (1891; repr., New York: Da Capo Press 1995), 362. Joseph W. Meeks is listed as a member of Company E in the extensive roster of the Fifty-Fourth Massachusetts Infantry.
29. Rose Gordon, "My Mother Was a Slave."
30. Rose Gordon, "Gone are the Days," 6.
31. Information on Charles M. Meek from Ken Robison, "Soldiers, Miners, Police, Businessmen—Blacks Arrived Early," *Great Falls Tribune*, Feb. 5, 2007.
32. *The Colored Citizen* was something of a special case, as the newspaper was financially supported in part (and temporarily) by white patrons who wanted "to encourage black voters to support Helena as the permanent capital," although J. P. Ball maintained his editorial independence from his patrons. Behan, "Forgotten Heritage," 34.
33. Taylor, *In Search of the Racial Frontier*, 211.
34. *Indianapolis Freeman*, Nov. 5, 1892.
35. *Indianapolis Freeman*, Apr. 5, 1913. Ironically, Washington's praise of Helena's Black community came as that community was beginning a precipitous decline.
36. Lang, "Helena, Montana's Black Community," 201–2. African Americans in Helena lived "in nearly every residential section but the wealthiest of the city," a pattern that appears to have been repeated in Meagher County as well. This is not to say that the state was "immune to the racial prejudice that swept the nation during the Jim Crow era," Lang acknowledges, but he notes that "distinctions should be made between the racial prejudice there and that which raged elsewhere."
37. Laura Joanne Arata, "Race and the Wild West: Sarah Bickford and the Construction of Historical Memory in Virginia City, Montana, 1870–1930" (PhD diss., Washington State University, 2014), 94. Arata's dissertation has since been revised and published as a book. See Laura J. Arata, *Race and the Wild West: Sarah Bickford, the Montana Vigilantes, and the Tourism of Decline: 1870–1930* (Norman: Univ. of Oklahoma Press, 2020).

38. Arata, "Race and the Wild West," 130–40.
39. Arata, "Race and the Wild West," 33.
40. Arata, "Race and the Wild West," 150. Arata identifies the race of many of the African American individuals mentioned in the *Madisonian* (the Virginia City newspaper) by census records.
41. Arata, "Race and the Wild West," 150.
42. Irvin Smith's first name is spelled at various times as Irvin, Irwin, or Irving.
43. Gayle K. Berardi and Thomas W. Segady, "The Development of African American Newspapers in the American West, 1880–1914," in Billington and Hardaway, *African Americans on the Western Frontier*, 225.
44. Berardi and Segady, "Development of African American Newspapers," 226.
45. Malone, Roeder, and Lang, *Montana*, 199.
46. *Rocky Mountain Husbandman*, Oct. 29, 1891.
47. Taylor Gordon, *Born to Be*, 6.
48. *Rocky Mountain Husbandman*, May 23, 1895.
49. For example, the *Rocky Mountain Husbandman* reports that "N. B. Smith and Joe Meek made a trip to the summit of the castles last week to inspect the Abednego lead found by Mr. Meek last year. After a thorough examination Mr. Smith concluded to go in with the veteran prospector for the development of this lead." *Rocky Mountain Husbandman*, Jul. 23, 1888.
50. In a deed recorded on April 13, 1881, Smith purchased a parcel of land in White Sulphur Springs on Hampton Street, just north of Main Street, from William Parberry and Matilda Parberry for one hundred dollars, which was likely the location of his first smithy. Deed, Meagher County Courthouse.
51. *Meagher County News*, Jun. 1, 1967.
52. *Meagher County News*, Jan. 27, 1894. A local news item describes Smith telling a Civil War story of "turning files and rasps into daggers to cut up the 'blue-bellied yankees'" on the order of his master.
53. *Rocky Mountain Husbandman*, Oct. 21, 1897.
54. As was the case with Ben Stone, the only reference I've found to African American resident Lee Thornton is the notice of his death: "Lee Thornton, (colored) son of Mrs. Rose, of this place, died Tuesday morning." *Rocky Mountain Husbandman*, Dec. 26, 1889.
55. Following the death of Robert Thompson, the *Husbandman* printed the following item: "Robert Thompson, (colored) a well-respected citizen of this place, died Saturday last from a severe attack of pneumonia. Deceased was a great favorite among the colored people and had many friends among the whites. He was a native of Canada and his parents, of whom he was the only child, reside in Pennsylvania. Rev. Stickelman preached the funeral discourse Sunday afternoon and the band played the funeral march as the cortege moved to the cemetery. Deceased being a member of the colored band the military band turned out to pay its last tribute to his memory" (*Rocky Mountain Husbandman*, Oct. 31, 1889). The general respect paid to Thompson is indicated as well by the presence of "Rev. Stickelman" (or, as his name was usually printed, Stickleman), the pastor of the Methodist Episcopal Church, the first church established in White Sulphur Springs, which the Gordons attended. Although the church had a predominantly white congregation, Stickleman's presence officiating at Thompson's funeral suggests that the M. E. Church provided a home for the town's African American congregants.
56. *Rocky Mountain Husbandman*, Dec. 13, 1888.
57. Rose Gordon, "Gone are the Days," 14.
58. *Meagher Republican*, Feb. 12, 1904. The only existing census report that includes Caesar Fields is from 1900. According to the *Meagher Republican* report on his death at age seventy-five, Fields had lived in White Sulphur for twenty-two years, which would have placed his arrival in 1882. The 1900 census records Fields's age as fifty-four, which is probably inaccurate, as both Rose Gordon's writing and items in the newspapers suggest

that he was a much older man. The 1900 census also records that Fields was at one point married, although his wife is listed as deceased. Suffering from chronic rheumatism, Fields was admitted to the county Poor House in the 1890s. The Poor House Record indicates his date of arrival in Meagher County was in December 1880. Poor House Record, Meagher County Courthouse.

59. Both the *Husbandman* and the *Meagher County News* frequently refer to women by their husbands' names (e.g., Mrs. Irvin Smith), a normal practice at the time. More unusual, perhaps, is their tendency to refer to African American women by reference to race only and not by name (and this practice may be reserved for unmarried women). For example, the *Husbandman* reported in 1885, "Three colored women were fined $10 each and costs for a breach of the peace recently" (*Rocky Mountain Husbandman*, Oct. 1, 1885). Five years later, the *Meagher County News* reported, "The colored woman who was sent to the insane asylum from White Sulphur last July was declared sane and released this week" (*Meagher County News*, Aug. 23, 1890).

60. *Meagher Republican*, Jun. 11, 1915. As this news item reported, "Eli Shelby, colored, of Great Falls, is visiting in this city at the Gordon home."

61. Robert Langhorne was prominent in both the colored band and in several minstrel entertainments produced between 1892 and 1893 in White Sulphur Springs. Robert Langhorne appears in the 1900 U.S. Census as living in Libby, Flathead County, Montana, age forty-one, born in Kentucky in August 1858. His wife is listed as deceased. It is possible that his wife was alive when Langhorne lived in White Sulphur, although her presence is not recorded.

62. *Meagher County News*, Mar. 4, 1892.

63. John Wilson is listed in the 1900 U.S. Census as living in White Sulphur Springs. His age in 1900 is listed as sixty-three, his birthplace as Virginia in March 1837, his occupation as "day laborer," and his marital status as "widowed."

64. *Rocky Mountain Husbandman*, Oct. 4, 1888.

65. *Rocky Mountain Husbandman*, Oct. 25, 1888.

66. Meredith, "Identifying African American Resources Project," 65–66.

67. *Rocky Mountain Husbandman*, Oct. 25, 1888.

68. *Meagher County News*, Feb. 18, 1893.

69. *Meagher County News*, Jan. 11, 1950.

70. *Rocky Mountain Husbandman*, Sep. 5, 1889.

71. *Meagher County News*, Oct. 15, 1892.

72. *Meagher County News*, Feb. 26, 1892.

73. *Meagher County News*, Apr. 8, 1892.

74. Performers were usually arranged on the stage in a horseshoe-shaped formation, with the open end of the horseshow facing the audience. The "end men" were positioned at the ends of the horseshoe, making them the performers closest to the audience.

75. *Meagher County News*, Apr. 8, 1892.

76. *Rocky Mountain Husbandman*, Apr. 21, 1892.

77. Ibid.

78. Ibid.

79. *Rocky Mountain Husbandman*, Dec. 13, 1888.

80. Billy Emerson, 1846–1902, organized and performed with Emerson, Allen and Manning Minstrels. According to the obituary published in the *New York Times*, his first stage appearance was in 1857 as a member of Sweeny's minstrels, and "during the latter part of his career he is said to have received the highest salary ever paid to an individual performer in minstrelsy." *New York Times*, Feb. 24, 1902.

81. *Rocky Mountain Husbandman*, Jan. 8, 1885.

82. African Americans in White Sulphur also participated in other types of performances, including recitations and staged debates, which may have helped alleviate some of the stereotypes associated with minstrelsy. Having African Americans on stage in various

venues performing multiple roles may have helped undermine minstrelsy's claim to authenticity by providing multiple examples of "authentic" Black performance. An African American performer who could flawlessly recite a speech from Shakespeare as well as speak in the fractured dialect associated with minstrelsy would at least call into question the widely held assumption that such dialect was not a put-on but a natural and realistic representation of Black speech.

83. *Meagher County News*, Sep. 30, 1964.
84. *Meagher County News*, Oct. 18, 1950.
85. *Rocky Mountain Husbandman*, Apr. 21, 1892.
86. In the acknowledgments to Ivan Doig's *Prairie Nocturne*, a novel in which one of the main characters ("Monty") is inspired by Taylor Gordon's life and career, Doig remembers interviewing Rose and Taylor in 1968, when Rose recounted "their habitual pause just out of hearing before joining in on the otherwise all-white gatherings in town, to remark wryly to one another: 'Well, the two colored persons are here.'" The "habitual" comment suggests that even in the friendliest of gatherings, awareness of race was always present. Ivan Doig, *Prairie Nocturne* (New York: Scribner, 2003), 369.

Chapter 3

1. W. E. B. Du Bois, review of *Born to Be*, in *Crisis* 37 (Apr. 1930): 129.
2. Taylor Gordon, *Born to Be*, 62.
3. Ibid.
4. Rose Gordon, "My Mother Was a Slave."
5. Ibid.
6. Ibid.
7. Taylor Gordon, *Born to Be*, 3.
8. Rose Gordon, "My Mother Was a Slave."
9. Du Bois, review of *Born to Be*, 129.
10. Anna Gordon to John Francis Gordon, Jul. 22, 1889, fldr 3, bx 14, Gordon Family Papers.
11. Anna Gordon to John Francis Gordon, Sep. 15, 1889, fldr 3, bx 14, Gordon Family Papers.
12. *Rocky Mountain Husbandman*, Sep. 5, 1889.
13. "An Act to provide for a system of common schools," Jan. 12, 1872, Laws, Memorials, and Resolutions of the Territory of Montana (7th sess.) (Deer Lodge: "New North West," 1872).
14. Smurr, "Jim Crow Out West," 179.
15. Robert Hemenway, "Introduction," in Taylor Gordon, *Born to Be*, ix–xliv, xxvi–xxvii.
16. Lang, "Helena, Montana's Black Community," 201. For an extensive overview of segregated education in Montana, see Smurr, "Jim Crow Out West," 172–83. In Fort Benton, in 1881, "the local board granted permission for a colored boy to attend the public school," which resulted in a dozen or so whites withdrawing their children from the school. Although the territorial superintendent and the attorney general concurred that "under the statute Negroes could not be admitted into the public schools," they were "apparently . . . ignored," as "the progress of the Negro children in the school was being described some weeks later" in the local newspaper. In Helena, a separate school operated during 1875, and "the result was very expensive to taxpayers, an average of $50 per colored student to $10 for the whites." Segregation in Helena ended in 1882 when overcrowding caused the school board to authorize transferring white children into the underpopulated school reserved for Black children. The issue went to election, and voters ended segregation by a vote of 195 to 115 (a small turnout, but "larger than any school vote previously held in the district"). Above quotes (listed in order) from Smurr, "Jim Crow Out West," 176, 177, 172, 183.
17. *Rocky Mountain Husbandman*, Mar. 8, 1883. Although the school segregation statute was not officially repealed until 1895, as J. W. Smurr explains, "The old system evaporated rapidly after 1883 and was repealed in fact if not in law." Smurr, "Jim Crow Out West," 185.

18. *Meagher County News*, Oct. 27, 1954.
19. Smurr, "Jim Crow Out West," 179.
20. Smurr, "Jim Crow Out West," 201.
21. Although this is only anecdotal evidence gleaned from my conversations with people in White Sulphur Springs, according to unofficial community history, the town complied with the state statute on segregation only when state officials inspected the schools. That is, if there was going to be an inspection, they would have the African American students attend in the afternoon and the white students attend in the morning. But on a usual day, all the students would be in the same classroom. Again, I've not seen documentary evidence of this practice, but it seems a logical and practical way of "complying" with territorial law while at the same time evading the inconveniences, expenses, and unequal treatment it caused.
22. *Rocky Mountain Husbandman*, Jun. 21, 1894. Rosa was Rose Gordon's birth name. She began going by Rose at some point during childhood.
23. *Rocky Mountain Husbandman*, Dec. 24 and Dec. 31, 1896.
24. Rose Gordon, "My Mother Was a Slave."
25. *Rocky Mountain Husbandman*, Dec. 26, 1895.
26. *Rocky Mountain Husbandman*, Feb. 20, 1896.
27. *Rocky Mountain Husbandman*, Jun. 2, 1898.
28. *Rocky Mountain Husbandman*, Jun. 22, 1899.
29. *Rocky Mountain Husbandman*, Mar. 24, 1898, Apr. 7, 1898.
30. *Rocky Mountain Husbandman*, Apr. 14, 1898.
31. *Rocky Mountain Husbandman*, Jun. 2, 1898, Jul. 7, 1898.
32. *Rocky Mountain Husbandman*, Jan. 12, 1899.
33. *Rocky Mountain Husbandman*, Jan. 26, 1899, Feb. 2, 1899, Feb. 23, 1899, Mar. 2, 1899.
34. *Rocky Mountain Husbandman*, Mar. 2, 1899, Mar. 27, 1899.
35. *Rocky Mountain Husbandman*, Mar. 30, 1899.
36. *Rocky Mountain Husbandman*, May 1, 1902.
37. *Rocky Mountain Husbandman*, Mar. 30, 1899.
38. Rose Gordon, "My Mother Was a Slave."
39. Rose Gordon, "Gone are the Days," 6.
40. Rose Gordon, "My Mother Was a Slave."
41. Clyde Reichelt, "Singer Returns to White Sulphur Springs Home," *Great Falls Tribune*, May 8, 1960.
42. *Meagher County News*, Mar. 13, 1957.
43. Howard, *Montana*, 50.
44. *Meagher County News*, Nov. 6, 1963.
45. Taylor Gordon, *Born to Be*, 11.
46. Taylor Gordon, *Born to Be*, 21.
47. *Rocky Mountain Husbandman*, Dec. 28, 1899.
48. Rose Gordon, "My Mother Was a Slave."
49. *Meagher Republican*, Dec. 30, 1904.
50. *Meagher County News*, Feb. 5, 1965.
51. Rose Gordon, "Rose Gordon's Recollections," *Meagher County News*, Jul. 20, 1967. Richard Ringling was the son of Alfred T. Ringling, one of the Ringling Brothers of circus fame, and nephew of John Ringling, who was involved in a land development company in White Sulphur Springs and Meagher County in the early 1900s. Richard moved to White Sulphur Springs in 1917 and raised cattle and sheep. He also operated a creamery, which produced and distributed Castle Mountain Gold Butter. The Gordons were friendly with Richard, and Rose and Anna used Castle Mountain Gold Butter in their restaurant. When Richard married Aubrey Black (daughter of one of the town's early residents), Rose hosted them at her café for their wedding breakfast. Rose Gordon, "Rose Gordon Writes," *Meagher County News*, Nov. 23, 1949.

52. *Meagher Republican*, Feb. 17, 1905.
53. Rose Gordon, "Gone are the Days" draft, unnumbered page, fldr 15, bx 11, Gordon Family Papers.
54. Rose Gordon, "My Mother Was a Slave."
55. Glenda Riley, "American Daughters: Black Women in the West," in Billington and Hardaway, *African Americans on the Western Frontier*, 169.
56. Riley, "American Daughters," 170.
57. Rose Gordon, "My Mother Was a Slave."
58. Taylor Gordon, *Born to Be*, 14.
59. Ibid.
60. Rose Gordon, "My Mother Was a Slave."
61. Ibid.
62. *Rocky Mountain Husbandman*, Feb. 23, 1899.
63. *Meagher Republican*, Jun. 13, 1924.

Chapter 4

1. Booker T. Washington, *Up from Slavery* (1901; repr., Oxford Univ. Press, 1995), 128.
2. Rose Gordon, "My Mother Was a Slave."
3. Washington, *Up from Slavery*, 128–29.
4. Ibid.
5. W. E. B. Du Bois, *The Souls of Black Folk* (1903; repr., New York: Penguin, 1989), 50.
6. With the exception of the Gordon family and the Meeks, every African American individual listed in the 1900 census as living in White Sulphur Springs was gone by the time of the 1910 census.
7. As the 1870 census suggests, African Americans in Montana predominantly worked as laborers (19 percent), as domestics (23 percent), and in service occupations such as barbers (17 percent) and cooks (14 percent). Meredith, "Identifying African American Resources Project," 61–63.
8. Psyche A. Williams-Forson, *Building Houses Out of Chicken Wings: Black Women, Food, and Power* (Chapel Hill: Univ. of North Carolina Press, 2006), 7.
9. Williams-Forson, *Building Houses Out of Chicken Wings*, 35.
10. Washington, *Up from Slavery*, 91.
11. Ida B. Wells-Barnett, *Southern Horrors and Other Writings: The Anti-lynching Campaign of Ida B. Wells, 1892–1900*, ed. Jacqueline Jones Royster (Boston: Bedford, 1997).
12. Clifford Edward Watkins, *Showman: The Life and Music of Perry George Lowery* (Jackson: Univ. Press of Mississippi, 2003), 9
13. Grayce Brewer Allen to Taylor Gordon, published in the *Meagher County News*, Jul. 29, 1959.
14. *Rocky Mountain Husbandman*, Feb. 14, 1892.
15. At some point in her life, Grace became Grayce. Her name is spelled both ways in print, with Grayce being used more consistently later in her life.
16. For a collection of programs and flyers related to the careers of Grayce Brewer and Ruth Marea Brewer, see fldr 2, bx 15, Gordon Family Papers.
17. Articles about Kathryn Janie Sutherlin appeared periodically in the *Meagher County News*. Sutherlin returned to White Sulphur Springs to offer her hometown a concert in 1924, much as Taylor would years later. *Meagher County News*, Sep. 19, 1924.
18. *Rocky Mountain Husbandman*, Mar. 28, 1903.
19. A later news item about the concert described a remarkable display of skill from the two children: "The entertainment given by Misses Ruth and Grace Brewer at the Auditorium Saturday evening proved all that was claimed for it. . . . Little Grace with great emphasis and positive decision called each note as it was sounded and gave the variety of chords both major and minor, and then wrote a couple of pieces on the blackboard by sound as they were played on the piano with her back to the instrument. The sound tests were given

under blindfold. Little Ruth is also a born artist, and is as graceful on the stage as an actress of mature years and performs her part well. She sings and dances and is clever in every role." *Rocky Mountain Husbandman*, Jun. 4, 1903.

20. *Fergus County Democrat*, Aug. 20, 1914.
21. *Meagher County News*, Feb. 18, 1893.
22. *Rocky Mountain Husbandman*, Jun. 24, 1897.
23. *Rocky Mountain Husbandman*, Mar. 25, 1897.
24. The popularity of white Americans acting out caricatures of non-whites was not limited to minstrel shows. During this same era, whites play-acted stereotypes of American Indians as well. For more, see Philip Deloria, *Playing Indian* (Yale Univ. Press, 1996), or Clyde Ellis and Mabel F. Knight, "'More Real than the Indians Themselves': The Early Years of the Indian Lore Movement in the United States." *Montana The Magazine of Western History* 58:3 (Autumn 2008): 3–94, http://www.jstor.org/stable/25485733.
25. *Rocky Mountain Husbandman*, Jun. 29, 1899.
26. *Rocky Mountain Husbandman*, Jul. 6, 1899.
27. *Meagher County News*, Feb. 5, 1964.
28. *Rocky Mountain Husbandman*, May 17, 1900, Feb. 2, 1899.
29. Taylor Gordon, *Born to Be*, 7.
30. *Rocky Mountain Husbandman*, May 29, 1902.
31. *Meagher Republican*, Jul. 8, 1904.
32. *Meagher Republican*, Sep. 30, 1904.
33. *Meager County News*, Jan. 16, 1969.
34. Taylor Gordon, *Born to Be*, 31.
35. *Meagher Republican*, May 1, 1908.
36. *Meagher Republican*, May 8, 1908.
37. *Meagher Republican*, Jun. 17, 1904.
38. R. T. O'Neill to Rose Gordon, Aug. 1, 1968, fldr 1, bx 9, Gordon Family Papers; Laura Carrier French to Taylor Gordon, Nov. 25, 1968, fldr 21, bx 1, Gordon Family Papers.
39. *Meagher County News*, Jan. 16, 1969.
40. Rose Gordon, "Gone are the Days," 37.
41. Du Bois, *Souls of Black Folk*, 5. Du Bois refers to this phenomenon as "double-consciousness": "this sense of always looking at one's self through the eyes of others. . . . One ever feels his two-ness,—an American, a Negro; two souls, two thoughts, two unreconciled strivings; two warring ideals in one dark body."
42. Washington, *Up from Slavery*, 124, 123.
43. Rose Gordon, "Gone are the Days," 36–37.
44. Washington, *Up from Slavery*, 127.
45. Rose Gordon, "Gone are the Days," 37.
46. *Meagher Republican*, Jan. 1, 1904.
47. *Meagher Republican*, Jun. 17, 1904.
48. Rose Gordon paraphrases here a section from a December 18, 1903, speech on "The Negro Problem" by South Carolina governor Charles Brantley Aycock. "Charles Brantley Aycock," Wikipedia, https://en.wikipedia.org/wiki/Charles_Brantley_Aycock, accessed Dec. 11, 2021.
49. *Meagher Republican*, Jun. 17, 1904.
50. Ibid.
51. *Rocky Mountain Husbandman*, Aug. 4, 1904.
52. *Meagher County News*, Jan. 16, 1969. The 1910 U.S. Census records indicate that Rose had moved back to White Sulphur Springs and was residing again with the rest of the Gordon family by 1910.
53. Rose Gordon, "Gone are the Days," 62.
54. Rose Gordon, "Gone are the Days," 43.
55. *Meagher County News*, Apr. 20, 1949.

56. Lee Rostad, *Grace Stone Coates: Her Life in Letters* (Helena: Riverbend Publishing, 2004), 17–21.
57. Rose Gordon, "Gone are the Days," 43.
58. Grace Stone Coates to Rose B. Gordon, Dec. 16, 1958, fldr 5, bx 8, Gordon Family Papers.

Chapter 5

1. Rose Gordon, "Gone are the Days," 42.
2. Gene Plowden, *Those Amazing Ringlings and Their Circus* (Caldwell, ID: Claxton Printers, 1967), 101–2.
3. Henry Ringling North, *The Circus Kings: Our Ringling Family Story* (New York: Doubleday, 1960), 138. One such missing link was a fifty-five-mile connection between Hannibal, Missouri, and Bowling Green, Ohio, "which Uncle John proudly named the St. Louis and Hannibal, though it went nowhere near the Missouri metropolis."
4. North, *Circus Kings*, 139.
5. *Meagher Republican*, Sep. 2, 1910.
6. *Rocky Mountain Husbandman*, Jan. 3, 1907.
7. *Meagher Republican*, Sep. 2, 1910.
8. *Rocky Mountain Husbandman*, Apr. 28, 1910.
9. *Rocky Mountain Husbandman*, Jun. 28, 1910.
10. *Rocky Mountain Husbandman*, Jul. 7, 1910.
11. *Rocky Mountain Husbandman*, Nov. 10, 1910.
12. *Meagher Republican*, Nov. 18, 1910. Sutherlin was also invited to speak on the occasion, and the *Republican* couldn't resist taking a good-natured dig at its old rival's speech, observing that the editor of Montana's agricultural newspaper "ventured a few prophecies as to the adaptability of our soil to fruit-raising."
13. *Meagher Republican*, Nov. 18, 1910.
14. Ibid.
15. Ibid.
16. *Meagher County News*, Mar. 13, 1957. Fred Ward, who took over editorship of the newspaper in the 1950s, likely wrote this editorial.
17. *Meagher County News*, Nov. 19, 1947.
18. The newspaper he started in 1875 had a good long life, extending beyond the death of its founder in 1926. As Grant writes, "[T]he paper survived its founder-editor by some sixteen years, continuing publication until 1942, and continued to maintain the editorial tone Robert Sutherlin had set sixty-seven years before." Grant, "Rocky Mountain Husbandman," 35.
19. *Meagher County News*, Nov. 19, 1947.
20. Marilyn McMillan, "'An Eldorado of Ease and Elegance': Taking the Waters at White Sulphur Springs, 1866–1904," *Montana The Magazine of Western History* 35:2 (Spring 1985): 48–49. Optimism about the future of White Sulphur Springs in the 1900s, evident in various investors arriving in the area and seeking to develop land in and around town, did not play out "despite the high hopes of its citizens."
21. County Commission Minutes, Meagher County Courthouse Records.
22. A notice in the *Husbandman* informed readers: "John Wilson (colored) died at the county home Tuesday after a brief illness. Mr. Wilson was born in slavery and raised by the father of J. W. Henton, he and Mr. Henton having been boys together and corresponded regularly. Deceased was faithful, honest, and performed his part in life as best he could." *Rocky Mountain Husbandman*, Apr. 25, 1901.
23. *Meagher Republican*, Feb. 12, 1904.
24. *Meagher Republican*, Dec. 6, 1907.
25. Ibid.
26. I am indebted to Jodie Foley at the Montana Historical Society for locating the information on Irwin Smith in the Warm Springs records.

27. Charlie Vernon, a twenty-nine-year-old single Black male who resided in the household of Frank Miller, a thirty-four-year-old white German man, was gone by 1910. So too were the following single Black women: Mabel Wilson (age twenty-one) and her roommate Violet Morris (age twenty); Hanna Smith (age thirty-five), listed as a "restaurant keeper" in White Sulphur Springs in 1900; and Stellah Robinson (age twenty-four), who boarded with Belle Price).

28. According to the Montana Office of Vital Statistics, Joseph Meek died on August 27, 1912. On the 1910 census, the agent used the abbreviation "Mu" under the race category, an indication of "mulatto," which was no longer a category used by the census at that time. Because of this, the Meeks do not seem to have been counted in the larger statistical totals of Montana's Black population in 1910. The 1910 census also notes that Sarah Meek gave birth to one child, who was no longer living at the time of the census. Although Sarah Meek's first name is nearly illegible in the document, this is clearly the same Joseph W. Meek, whose occupation is listed here as prospector.

29. Lang, "Helena, Montana's Black Community," 213.

30. Taylor, *In Search of the Racial Frontier*, 222.

31. Taylor, *In Search of the Racial Frontier*, 223.

32. Taylor Gordon, *Born to Be*, 54.

33. *Meagher Republican*, May 8, 1908. A 1902 report listed Robert Gordon among the bachelors in a match game at the bowling alley between the married and the single men. *Meagher Republican*, Dec. 19, 1902.

34. *Meagher Republican*, May 20, 1904.

35. Taylor Gordon, *Born to Be*, 7.

36. Lang, "Helena, Montana's Black Community," 212. Although interracial relationships may have been looked down upon, they nonetheless existed in Montana. As Laura Arata documents in her biography of Sarah Bickford, her "two marriages to white men" in Virginia City, Montana, seem to have been regarded as unremarkable, and certainly did not prevent her from being "integrated" in and "respected" by the members of the community. Arata, "Race and the Wild West, 6. For discussion of other examples of documented mixed marriages in nineteenth-century Montana, see Arata, "Race and the Wild West," 182–86.

37. Quoted in Lang, "Helena, Montana's Black Community," 212. The *Montana Plaindealer* was started by Bass in 1906 and published weekly through 1911.

38. *Montana Plaindealer*, Jul. 29, 1910.

39. *Montana Plaindealer*, Sep. 30, 1910.

40. The statute was repealed in 1953, when both Robert and Rose had reached their seventies.

41. Rose Gordon, "Gone are the Days," 99.

42. Robert Gordon to Rose Gordon, Sep. 7, 1907, fldr 1, bx 7, Gordon Family Papers.

43. Rose Gordon, "Gone are the Days," 45.

44. Mabel Hoffman to Rose Gordon, Nov. 7, 1907; Hoffman to Gordon, Dec. 30, 1907, fldr 1, bx 7, Gordon Family Papers.

45. Rose Gordon, "Gone are the Days," 45.

46. Rose Gordon, "Gone are the Days," title page.

Chapter 6

1. *Meagher Republican*, Oct. 26, 1911.

2. *Meagher County Republican*, Dec. 13, 1912.

3. Marcella Sherfy, "Rose Beatris Gordon," in *African American National Biography*, vol. 3, eds. Henry Louis Gates Jr. and Evelyn Brooks Higginbotham (Oxford: Oxford Univ. Press, 2008), 556.

4. Sherfy, "Rose Beatris Gordon," 556.

5. John Rosamond Johnson would eventually become Taylor's performing partner in the 1920s, playing piano accompaniment as Taylor sang songs from Johnson's own two-volume

book of arrangements of traditional spirituals, *The Books of American Negro Spirituals*. From 1898 to 1911, Rosamond with his brother James Weldon Johnson and collaborator Bob Cole wrote hundreds of songs for Broadway shows. Rosamond also performed a popular vaudeville act with Bob Cole from 1903 to 1911. As a pianist, performer, and composer, Rosamond Johnson enjoyed a long career that kept him on stage through the 1940s. *The Books of American Negro Spirituals* (1925, 1926; repr., New York: Da Capo Press, 1969).

6. *Meagher Republican*, Nov. 8, 1907. According to census records, John Phillip Anshutz was born July 4, 1879, in Cincinnati, Ohio, and died June 23, 1966. He served in the U.S. Army during World War I, his term of service beginning on May 29, 1918.

7. The *Meagher Republican* reprinted the following laudatory notice from the *Judith Gap Journal*: "Rev. J. Phillip Anshutz, rector of Judith Gap's flock of Episcopalians, held services in Hays' restaurant Wednesday evening, at which the Journal force attended in a body. It was a cold stormy evening, one that would take a sledge hammer attraction to draw one from his comfortable fire to face the fierce elements that were waging unrelenting war upon mankind, but the writer would go farther and through worse weather to hear this brilliant young minister. The fact that he could move a printer at all is the highest compliment to his strong personality and brilliant attainments that can be paid him. He will hold services again on Thursday, Jan. 21, and everybody should turn out to hear him. Rev. Anshutz is certainly worth while." *Meagher Republican*, Jan. 15, 1909.

8. *Meagher Republican*, Sep. 18, 1908.

9. *Meagher Republican*, Jul. 3, 1908, Apr. 23, 1909.

10. *Meagher Republican*, Sep. 2, 1910.

11. *Meagher Republican*, Dec. 23, 1910.

12. *Meagher County News*, May 31, 1950.

13. Rose B. Gordon, "When Calamity Jane Came to Town," *Meagher County News*, Feb. 5, 1964.

14. *Meagher Republican*, Aug. 18, 1911.

15. *Meagher Republican*, Jan. 13, 1913.

16. *Meagher Republican*, Mar. 7, 1913.

17. *Meagher Republican*, May 18, 1914.

18. "Rose Gordon's Recollections," *Meagher County News*, Jul. 20, 1967.

19. Rose Gordon, "Gone are the Days," 75.

20. *Meagher County News*, May 17, 1944

21. Rose Gordon, "Gone are the Days," 73.

22. Rose Gordon, "Gone are the Days," 77–78.

23. Rose Gordon, "Martinsdale" (unpublished sketch), fldr 5, bx 11, Gordon Family Papers.

24. Rose Gordon, "Gone are the Days," 63.

25. At the time of the incident, Earl Fretwell was a resident of Oklahoma. However, despite the fact that his Montana experience included being hit with a gun, shoved from a moving train, and shot, he ultimately made his home in White Sulphur Springs. He initially worked for "Jack Soden, contractor for the White Sulphur Springs-Martindale road," subsequently served in World War I, and returned to White Sulphur Springs, where he operated a grocery business. Rose was a patron of Fretwell Grocery and became friends with the owner. Although she likely didn't know Fretwell at the time of the incident, her later friendship with one of the central victims in that incident adds another layer of complexity to understanding how she might have thought about the events around the execution of Hall, Gibson, and Fahley. *Meagher County: An Early-Day Pictorial History, 1867–1967.* (White Sulphur Springs, MT: *Meagher County News*, 1968). 52.

26. *Meagher Republican*, Feb. 16, 1917.

27. Ibid.

28. "A Woman Wrestles with a Disturbing Family Memento," National Public Radio, Jul. 2, 2014, https://www.npr.org/2014/07/02/327245430/a-woman-wrestles-with-a-disturbing-family-memento.

29. *Meagher Republican*, Feb. 16, 1917.

30. "A Woman Wrestles with a Disturbing Family Memento."
31. Ibid.
32. *Meagher County News*, Feb. 6, 1963. Another witness to the execution, Walter A. Donaldson, wrote to the *Meagher County News* (Feb. 24, 1963) to give his account. As might be expected after nearly fifty years, both accounts differed in multiple ways from the 1917 reportage in the *Republican* (and from each other). Oddly, both Donaldson and Holmes remembered there being only a few spectators witnessing the execution.
33. *Meagher Republican*, Apr. 27, 1917.
34. *Meagher Republican*, May 3, 1918.
35. *Meagher Republican*, Nov. 14, 1919.
36. *Meagher Republican*, Apr. 23, 1920.
37. *Meagher Republican*, Feb. 10, 1922.
38. *Meagher Republican*, Jan. 2, 1925.
39. Robert Gordon also served the community in other ways. For instance, he was called to jury duty when the county court was in session in the winter of 1920. *Meagher Republican*, Feb. 6, 1920.
40. *Meagher Republican*, Aug. 6, 1915.
41. *Meagher Republican*, Jul. 14, 1916.
42. *Meagher Republican*, Sep. 8, 1916.
43. *Meagher Republican*, Jun. 22, 1917.
44. Reid Badger, *A Life in Ragtime: A Biography of James Reese Europe* (Oxford: Oxford Univ. Press, 1995), 78–92. In 1914, the Castles hired Europe's orchestra to perform for a dance demonstration at the Palace Theatre and at Hammerstein's Victoria Theatre in New York City. The American Federation of Musicians union local objected, "fearing that black orchestras might come to dominate the theaters as they had done in cabarets." As a result, Europe's orchestra accompanied the Castles seated on the stage, which technically honored the union's demand that the African American musicians "did not play in the pit" (Badger, *Life in Ragtime*, 89). In the orchestra pit or on the stage, however, the barrier had been broken, and New York theaters increasingly opened up to African American musicians.
45. *Meagher Republican*, Sep. 15, 1922.
46. Taylor Gordon, *Born to Be*, 171.
47. Rose Gordon, "Gone are the Days," 121.
48. *Meagher Republican*, Jun. 13, 1924.
49. *Meagher Republican*, Jun. 13 and Jun. 29, 1924.
50. *Meagher Republican*, Dec. 4, 1925.
51. *Meagher Republican*, Sep. 18, 1925.
52. *Meagher Republican*, Jun. 14, 1926.

Chapter 7

1. *Meagher Republican*, Apr. 8, 1927.
2. *Meagher Republican*, Mar. 25, 1927.
3. *Meagher Republican*, Apr. 15, 1927.
4. *Meagher Republican*, Apr. 22, 1927.
5. "Sing Negro Spirituals," *New York Times*, Feb. 17, 1927.
6. Although African American choirs had toured Europe since the late nineteenth century, Taylor Gordon was the first solo vocalist to give concerts devoted to African American spirituals. Johnson, *Can't Stand Still*, 149–50.
7. *Meagher Republican*, Dec. 31, 1926.
8. *Meagher Republican*, Dec. 23, 1927.
9. *Meagher Republican*, Sep. 20, 1929.
10. During the 1920s, the Ku Klux Klan organized throughout Montana, peaking at just over five thousand members statewide by the end of the decade. Kayla Blackman, "Montana

Women of the Ku Klux Klan," in *Beyond Schoolmarms and Madams: Montana Women's Stories*, ed. Martha Kohl (Helena: Montana Historical Society Press, 2016), 210–13. For more on the KKK in Montana, see Christine K. Erickson, "'Come Join the K.K.K. in the Old Town Tonight': The Ku Klux Klan in Harlowton, Montana, during the 1920s," *Montana The Magazine of Western History* 64:3 (Autumn 2014): 49–92. www.jstor.org/stable/24420011.

11. Robert Hemenway notes that Taylor's book sold well enough to go through two printings. Hemenway, "Introduction to the 1975 Edition," in Gordon, *Born to Be*, xxi.
12. *Meagher Republican*, Feb. 23, 1929.
13. *Meagher Republican*, Jan. 25, 1929.
14. Receipt, Feb. 6, 1929, fldr 9, bx 9, Gordon Family Papers.
15. *Meagher Republican*, Feb. 8, 1929.
16. *Meagher Republican*, May 3, 1929.
17. *Meagher Republican*, Aug. 9, 1929.
18. *Meagher Republican*, Nov. 1, 1929.
19. *Meagher Republican*, Jun. 27, 1930.
20. *Meagher Republican*, Jul. 3, 1931.
21. *Meagher Republican*, Nov. 6, 1931.
22. Amelia Ostby to Rose Gordon, Aug. 1932, fldr 5, bx 7, Gordon Family Papers.
23. *Meagher Republican*, Aug. 2, 1933.
24. Legal documents, fldr 4, bx 11, Gordon Family Papers.
25. Sherfy, "Rose Beatris Gordon," 557.
26. *Meagher Republican*, Jul. 19, 1929.
27. Virginia Wolfe to Rose Gordon, Sep. 24, 1934, fldr 5, bx 7, Gordon Family Papers.
28. *Meagher County News*, Jul. 3, 1935. In 1934, Fred Ward, the editor who oversaw most of Rose's newspaper contributions, took over the *Meagher Republican* as editor and publisher. On July 4 of that year, the paper returned to its original name: the *Meagher County News*.
29. *Meagher County News*, Jul. 10, 1935.
30. *Meagher County News*, Jul. 24 and Sep. 18, 1935.
31. *Meagher County News*, Oct. 2, 1935.
32. *Meagher County News*, Sep. 25, 1935.
33. *Meagher County News*, Oct. 16, 1935.
34. Taylor Gordon to Carl Van Vechten, Oct. 30, 1935, bx G, Van Vechten Correspondence, James Weldon Johnson Collection, Beinecke Library, Yale University, New Haven, CT.
35. Taylor Gordon, "Born to Be Sequel" (unpublished manuscript dated Dec. 23, 1970), insert page 86, fldr 3–5, bx 5, Gordon Family Papers.
36. *Meagher County News*, May 20, 1936.
37. Taylor Gordon to Elizabeth Webb Hill, Mar. 4, 1958, fldr 17, bx 2, Gordon Family Papers.
38. Grayce Brewer Allen to Rose Gordon, Nov. 1, 1939, fldr 5, bx 7, Gordon Family Papers.
39. Grayce Brewer Allen to Rose Gordon, Apr. 16, 1940, fldr 7, bx 7, Gordon Family Papers.
40. Caxton Printers to Rose Gordon, Apr. 1934, fldr 5, bx 7, Gordon Family Papers.
41. Sherfy, "Rose Beatris Gordon," 557.
42. Caxton Printers to Rose Gordon, undated, fldr 9, bx 7, Gordon Family Papers.
43. Caxton Printers to Rose Gordon, Nov. 3, 1959, fldr 7, bx 8, Gordon Family Papers.
44. WPA Form 402, Notice to Report to Work on Project, fldr 4, bx 11, Gordon Family Papers.
45. Rose Gordon to Jessie Moore, Aug. 21, 1940, fldr 4, bx 9, Gordon Family Papers.
46. Ibid.
47. Ibid.
48. Rose Gordon to Roy E. Ayers, Sep. 10, 1940, fldr 4, bx 9, Gordon Family Papers.
49. Taylor, *In Search of the Racial Frontier*, 227–29.
50. *Meagher County News*, Apr. 9 and Apr. 16, 1941.
51. *Meagher County News*, Apr. 21, 1943.
52. *Meagher County News*, Nov. 18, 1942.
53. *Meagher County News*, May 27, 1942.

54. *Meagher County News*, Jun. 23, 1943.

55. *Meagher County News*, Aug. 27, 1943.

56. Ledger, Rose's Café accounts, 1916–1930, 1942–1944, fldr 12, bx 9, Gordon Family Papers.

57. *Meagher County News*, Jun. 7, 1944.

58. *Meagher County News*, Oct. 25, 1944.

59. Rose Gordon Appointment Book, fldr 2, bx 10, Gordon Family Papers.

60. Rose Gordon Therapy Treatment Accounts, fldr 3, bx 10, Gordon Family Papers.

61. Della M. Stephens to Rose Gordon, Aug. 6, 1956, fldr 1, bx 8, Gordon Family Papers; Della M. Stephens to Rose Gordon, Aug. 11, 1957, fldr 3, bx 8, Gordon Family Papers.

62. Creditor's Claim No. 436, Oct. 23, 1952, fldr 6, bx 9, Gordon Family Papers; Notice of Rejection of Claim, Dec. 18, 1952, fldr 6, bx 9, Gordon Family Papers.

63. Joseph T. Wilson to Rose Gordon, May 18, 1953, fldr 13, bx 7, Gordon Family Papers.

64. John Francis Gordon to Robert Gordon, Oct. 21, 1947, fldr 4, bx 14, Gordon Family Papers.

65. John Francis Gordon to Robert Gordon, Jan. 22, 1948, fldr 4, bx 14, Gordon Family Papers.

66. George Gordon to Rose Gordon, Jul. 31, 1939, fldr 5, bx 7, Gordon Family Papers.

67. *Meagher County News*, Jun. 25, 1947.

68. Ibid.

69. Ibid.

70. See Johnson, *Can't Stand Still*, especially pages 207–26.

71. George Gordon to Bob Gordon, Sep. 2, 1947, fldr 4, bx 14, Gordon Family Papers.

72. John H. Travis to Rose B. Gordon, Sep. 18, 1947, fldr 9, bx 7, Gordon Family Papers.

73. Taylor Gordon, "Born to Be Sequel."

74. *Bozeman Courier*, Oct. 22, 1948.

75. *Meagher County News*, Oct. 27, 1948.

76. Rose Gordon to John Francis "Sam" Gordon, undated, fldr 1, bx 14, Gordon Family Papers.

77. *Antler*, Mar. 1947, fldr 16, bx 14, Gordon Family Papers.

78. Art Duntsch to George Gordon, Jan. 10, 1948, fldr 1, bx 14, Gordon Family Papers.

79. *Bozeman Courier*, Oct. 22, 1948.

80. *Meagher County News*, Jan. 3, 1945.

81. Unknown to George Gordon, undated, fldr 1, bx 14, Gordon Family Papers.

82. Beatrice Simms to Rose Gordon, Oct. 12, 1967, fldr 16, bx 8, Gordon Family Papers.

83. Elizabeth Hill to George Gordon, Oct. 14, 1948, fldr 1, bx 14; Butte Branch of the NAACP to George Gordon, undated, fldr 17, bx 14, Gordon Family Papers.

84. *Meagher County News*, Nov. 12, 1952.

85. Rose Gordon to Taylor Gordon, Nov. 13, 1948, fldr 5, bx 1, Gordon Family Papers.

Chapter 8

1. For a history of Montanans winter vacationing in California, see Nancy Cooper, "'Ho for the City of Angels and Sunny Skies': The Union Pacific's Midwinter Excursions to California," *Montana The Magazine of Western History* 67:4 (Winter 2017): 3–90, www.jstor.org/stable/45200724.

2. *Meagher County News*, Jan. 2, 1952.

3. Ibid.

4. Ibid.

5. *Meagher County News*, Jan. 16, 1952.

6. Robert Gordon to Rose Gordon, Feb. 24, 1952, bx 7, fldr 12, Gordon Family Papers.

7. Rose Gordon to John Francis Gordon, Mar. 7, 1952, bx 14, fldr 2, Gordon Family Papers.

8. *Meagher County News*, Mar. 5, 1952.

9. *Meagher County News*, Apr. 13, 1955, Oct. 14, 1959.

10. Sherfy, "Rose Beatris Gordon," 557.

11. Ibid.

12. Rose Gordon to Dr. Myron Tripp, undated, MC 281, fldr 4, bx 2, Montana Federation of Colored Women's Clubs Records, MHS (hereafter MFCWC Records).

13. Riley, "American Daughters," 174.
14. B. M. Griff, "State Historian for Montana Federation of Negro Women's Clubs: 1922 Report," fldr 14, bx 1, MFCWC Records.
15. Peggy Riley, "Women of the Great Falls African Methodist Episcopal Church, 1870–1910," in Taylor and Moore, *African American Women Confront the West*, 124.
16. Riley, "Women of the Great Falls African Methodist Episcopal Church," 127. African American women's clubs, as Riley observes, "were grounded in middle-class values, particularly education, material progress, and the importance of home and women's moral influence in it," similar to white women's clubs. The national association's motto, "lifting as we climb," Riley adds, "reflects the commitment of black club women to improve the welfare of all black people, regardless of class, region, or educational level."
17. Griff, "State Historian for Montana Federation of Negro Women's Clubs, 1922 Report."
18. For a good overview of the Federation's political activity, see Annie Hanshew, "'Lifting as We Climb': The Activism of the Montana Federation of Colored Women's Clubs," *Women's History Matters*, Jul. 1, 2014, http://montanawomenshistory.org/lifting-as-we-climb-the-activism-of-the-montana-federation-of-colored-womens-clubs.
19. Katherine Smith and Marguerite Clark to Mattie Anderson, Apr. 27, 1926, fldr 14, bx 1, MFCWC Records.
20. Ellen Baumler, "Contributions of a Mother and Daughter," *Women's History Matters*, Jul. 24, 2014, http://montanawomenshistory.org/contributions-of-a-mother-and-daughter/#more-1468.
21. [untitled], fldr 14, bx 1, MFCWC Records.
22. Baumler, "Contributions of a Mother and Daughter."
23. Undated newspaper clipping, fldr 11, bx 2, MFCWC Records.
24. Ellen Baumler, "Helena Remembers Octavia Bridgewater," *Helena Independent Record*, Mar. 3, 2013.
25. *Meagher County News*, Oct. 29, 1952.
26. *Meagher County News*, May 20, 1964.
27. Mrs. Chris (Frances) Peterson obituary, unidentified clipping, 1965, fldr 4, bx 17, Gordon Family Papers.
28. Webb is likely her father's last name. At some point, her mother married Chris Peterson, whom Hill refers to in letters as "Chris" while referring to her mother as "mom."
29. Lulu B. McCabe to Rose Gordon, Jul. 25, 1947, fldr 9, bx 7, Gordon Family Papers.
30. Eva E. Robinson to Rose Gordon, Sep. 24, 1947, fldr 9, bx 7, Gordon Family Papers.
31. *Meagher County News*, May 14, 1947.
32. *Meagher County News*, Jun. 2, 1948.
33. Sherfy, "Rose Beatris Gordon," 557.
34. "Annonomus" to Rose Gordon, Mar. 15, 1951, fldr 11, bx 7, Gordon Family Papers.
35. Sherfy, "Rose Beatris Gordon," 557.
36. *Meagher County News*, Apr. 11, 1951.
37. Minutes, Annual State Convention, Jul. 16, 1951, fldr 4, bx 1, MFCWC Records.
38. *Meagher County News*, Jul. 3, 1957.
39. Rose Gordon to Taylor Gordon, Sep. 29, 1958, fldr 11, bx 1, Gordon Family Papers.
40. Robert Gordon to Rose Gordon, Feb. 24, 1952, fldr 12, bx 7, Gordon Family Papers.
41. Taylor Gordon to Robert Gordon, Jul. 23, 1953, fldr 4, bx 14, Gordon Family Papers.
42. Robert Gordon to Taylor Gordon, Aug. 16, 1955, fldr 8, bx 1, Gordon Family Papers.
43. Taylor Gordon to Rose Gordon, Oct. 9, 1956, fldr 2, bx 8, Gordon Family Papers.
44. J. Phillip Anshutz to Rose Gordon, Mar. 23, 1957, fldr 3, bx 8, Gordon Family Papers.
45. J. Phillip Anschutz to Rose Gordon, Mar. 28, 1957, fldr 3, bx 8, Gordon Family Papers.
46. Rose Gordon to Taylor Gordon, Apr. 6, 1958, fldr 11, bx 1, Gordon Family Papers.
47. Taylor Gordon to Rose Gordon, Apr. 18, 1958, fldr 6, bx 8, Gordon Family Papers.
48. J. Phillip Anshutz to Rose Gordon, Feb. 1, 1958, fldr 5, bx 8, Gordon Family Papers.
49. Various correspondence, fldr 9, bx 8, Gordon Family Papers.
50. *Meagher County News*, Mar. 7, 1962.

51. Program, 14th American Massage and Therapy Association, 1959, Long Beach, CA, fldr 12, bx 11, Gordon Family Papers.

52. Elizabeth Hill to Rose Gordon, Feb. 15, 1959, fldr 7, bx 8, Gordon Family Papers.

53. Donald G. Lucas to Rose Gordon, Jan. 27, 1961; Jack Healy to Rose Gordon, Feb. 15, 1961; Carl Rostad to Rose Gordon, Jan. 28, 1961, fldr 10, bx 8, Gordon Family Papers.

54. Clyde Reichelt, "Singer Returns to White Sulphur Springs Home," *Great Falls Tribune*, May 8, 1960.

55. *Meagher County News*, Mar. 2, 1960.

56. "Tenor Sings Tonight at College," *Great Falls Tribune*, Feb. 24, 1961.

Chapter 9

1. *Meagher County News*, Feb. 15, 1950.

2. *Meagher County News*, Jan. 20, 1965.

3. *Meagher County News*, May 27, 1953.

4. *Meagher County News*, Apr. 23, 1952.

5. The poem originally appeared as follows: "The little path I used to trod across the way to see a friend. A / friend, a friend that gave me every /thing there is in life, to give, love, courage / and hope. This comes from the richest store room / known to mankind a woman kind alike the Heart, it is / the spark of life. She gave of it freely to her / friends." Handwritten manuscript, undated, fldr 7, bx 11, Gordon Family Papers.

6. *Meagher County News*, Nov. 19, 1947. The tribute to Luella Watson, who had died the previous week in a car accident, is the first letter from Rose that follows the "I want to pay tribute" form. Watson owned a ranch with her brother Art and contributed letters, columns, and news items to the *Meagher County News* and other newspapers. Both Luella and Art Watson were friends and correspondents of the Gordons. Art Watson's book, *Devil Man with a Gun*, is an entertaining personal account of his family's ranching history in the early days of Martinsdale. Art H. Watson, *Devil Man with a Gun* (White Sulphur Springs: Meagher County News, 1967).

7. *Meagher County News*, Feb. 12, 1958.

8. *Meagher County News*, Apr. 20, 1949.

9. bell hooks, *Yearning: Race, Gender, and Cultural Politics* (Boston: South End Press, 1990), 42.

10. Ibid.

11. Ibid.

12. Rose Gordon, "My Mother Was a Slave."

13. hooks, *Yearning*, 43.

14. Rose Gordon, "My Mother Was a Slave."

15. hooks, *Yearning*, 47.

16. *Meagher County News*, Jan. 25, 1950.

17. Ibid.

18. *Meagher County News*, Nov. 6, 1963.

19. Sherfy, "Rose Beatris Gordon," 557.

20. *Meagher County News*, Jun. 6, 1956.

21. *Meagher County News*, Jan. 6, 1954.

22. *Meagher County News*, Nov. 8, 1950.

23. *Meagher County News*, Jan. 14, 1953.

24. *Meagher County News*, Nov. 22, 1944.

25. *Meagher County News*, Mar. 3, 1965.

26. Florence Wight Anderson to Rose Gordon, Apr. 26, 1949, fldr 10, bx 7, Gordon Family Papers.

27. Grace Stone Coates to Rose B. Gordon, Dec. 16, 1958, fldr 5, bx 8, Gordon Family Papers.

28. Rose Gordon, "Gone are the Days," 15.

29. Rose Gordon, "Gone are the Days," 120.
30. Rose Gordon, "Gone are the Days," 121.
31. Rose Gordon to Mrs. Ashford, undated, fldr 5, bx 9, Gordon Family Papers.
32. Letter published in *Meagher County News*, undated clipping, Rose Gordon scrapbook, fldr 7, bx 13, Gordon Family Papers.
33. *Rocky Mountain Husbandman*, Apr. 21, 1892.
34. *Meagher County News*, Jul. 29, 1964.
35. *Meagher County News*, Jun. 14, 1961.
36. *Meagher County News*, Aug. 24, 1967.
37. Mike Voeller, "The Village Historians," *Helena Independent Record*, May 21, 1967.
38. Taylor Gordon, *The Man Who Built the Stone Castle*. The pamphlet is still available from the Meagher County Historical Association.
39. *Meagher County News*, Jun. 2, 1966.
40. *Meagher County News*, Oct. 26, 1967. Taylor appeared on the *Today in Montana* show, hosted by Norma Ashby, on local station KRTV.
41. *Meagher County News*, Jul. 11, 1962.
42. Rose Gordon to Taylor Gordon, Sep. 29, 1958, fldr 11, bx 1, Gordon Family Papers.
43. Amy Gutchel to Rose Gordon, Mar. 1963, fldr 11, bx 8, Gordon Family Papers.
44. Olive King to Rose Gordon, Sep. 11, 1962, fldr 11, bx 8, Gordon Family Papers.
45. *Meagher County News*, Aug. 29, 1968.
46. *Meagher County News*, Sep. 5, 1968.
47. Ruth Brewer to Rose Gordon, Sep. 15, 1968, fldr 13, bx 2, Gordon Family Papers.
48. *Meagher County News*, Sep. 5, 1968.
49. *Meagher County News*, Nov. 6, 1963.
50. *Meagher County News*, Oct. 17, 1968.
51. *Meagher County News*, Apr. 25, 1968.
52. *Meagher County News*, Nov. 21, 1968.
53. Ibid.
54. *Meagher County News*, Jan. 16, 1969.
55. *Meagher County News*, Nov. 28, 1968.
56. Francis and Lacy Kern to Taylor Gordon, Nov. 23, 1968, fldr 21, bx 1, Gordon Family Papers.
57. Elizabeth Campbell to Taylor Gordon, Jan. 6, 1969, fldr 22, bx 1, Gordon Family Papers.
58. *Helena Independent Record*, May 9, 1971.
59. *Meagher County News*, May 13, 1971.
60. *Meagher County News*, May 9, 1968.
61. Rose Gordon, "Gone are the Days," 15.

Appendix B

1. Herbert G. Ruffin II, "Bibliographic Essay: The Twentieth- and Twenty-First-Century West," in *Freedom's Racial Frontier: African Americans in the Twentieth-Century West*, eds. Herbert G. Ruffin II and Dwayne A. Mack (Norman: Univ. of Oklahoma Press, 2018), 363–85. For an extensive overview of the hundreds of articles and books dedicated to the study of the African American West that have appeared over the last half century, there are few better sources than Ruffin's bibliographic essay in this critical anthology.
2. Kenneth Wiggins Porter, *The Negro on the American Frontier* (North Stratford, NH: Ayer, 1971); Sherman W. Savage, *Blacks in the West* (Westport, CT: Greenwood Press, 1976); Nell Irvin Painter, *Exodusters: Black Migration to Kansas after Reconstruction* (New York: Knopf, 1977).
3. Quintard Taylor, *In Search of the Racial Frontier: African Americans in the American West, 1528–1990* (New York: W.W. Norton & Co. Inc., 1998)
4. Shirley Anne Wilson Moore and Quintard Taylor, *African American Women Confront the West, 1600–2000* (Norman: Univ. of Oklahoma Press, 2008).

5. Moore and Taylor, "The West of African American Women," 16.
6. Blake Allmendinger, *Imagining the African American West* (Lincoln: Univ. of Nebraska Press, 2005); Michael K. Johnson, *Hoo-Doo Cowboys and Bronze Buckaroos: Conceptions of the African American West* (Jackson: Univ. Press of Mississippi, 2014); Emily Lutenski, *West of Harlem: African American Writers and the Borderlands* (Lawrence: Univ. of Kansas Press, 2015); Eric Gardner, *Unexpected Places: Relocating Nineteenth-Century African American Literature* (Jackson: Univ. Press of Mississippi, 2009); Eric Gardner, *Jennie Carter: A Black Journalist of the Early West* (Jackson: Univ. Press of Mississippi, 2007); Daniel Widener, *Black Arts West: Culture and Struggle in Postwar Los Angeles* (Durham, NC: Duke Univ. Press, 2010); Kellie Jones, *South of Pico: African American Artists in Los Angeles in the 1960s and 1970s* (Durham, NC: Duke Univ. Press, 2017).
7. Ruffin, "Bibliographic Essay," 363.
8. "New Directions in Black Western Studies," eds. Kalenda Eaton, Michael Johnson, and Jeannette Jones, special issue of *American Studies Journal* 58:3 (Fall 2019).
9. Riley, "African American Women in Western History," 22.
10. See, for example, Lynn M. Hudson, "Mining a Mythic Past: The History of Mary Ellen Pleasant," in Taylor and Moore, *African American Women Confront the West*, 56–70.
11. Polly E. Burgros McLean, *Remembering Lucile: A Virginia Family's Rise from Slavery and a Legacy Forged a Mile High* (Boulder: Univ. Press of Colorado, 2018), xxi.
12. Dee Garceau-Hagen, introduction to *Portraits of Women in the American West*, ed. Dee Garceau-Hagan (New York: Routledge, 2005), 1–19.
13. Garceau-Hagen, introduction, 2.
14. Ibid.
15. Ethelene Whitmire, *Regina Anderson Andrews: Harlem Renaissance Librarian* (Urbana: Univ. of Illinois Press, 2015), 2.
16. Whitmire, *Regina Anderson Andrews*, 3–4.
17. Whitmire, *Regina Anderson Andrews*, 13.
18. Miantae Metcalf McConnell, *Deliverance: Mary Fields, First African American Woman Star Route Mail Carrier in the United States* (Columbia Falls, MT: Huzzah Press, 2016).
19. Miantae Metcalf McConnell, "Mary Fields's Road to Freedom," in *Black Cowboys in the American West*, eds. Bruce A. Glasrud and Michael N. Searles (Norman: Univ. of Oklahoma Press, 2016), 157.
20. McConnell, "Mary Fields's Road to Freedom," 162. McConnell refers to the Birdtail region as encompassing the mail route from Cascade to St. Peter's Mission, saying the mission was "located on the west side of the Continental Divide in a region called Birdtail, named after a monolithic stone sculpture geologically carved into the shape of tail feathers." McConnell, 152.
21. McConnell, "Mary Fields's Road to Freedom," 162.
22. Laura J. Arata, *Race and the Wild West: Sarah Bickford, Montana Vigilantes, and the Tourism of Decline, 1870–1930* (Norman: Univ. of Oklahoma Press, 2020). I draw on Arata's dissertation work, "Race and the Wild West," which became the basis for her recently published book, at various places here.
23. Arata, *Race and the Wild West*, xiii.
24. Kate Hampton, "Montana's African American Heritage Resources Project," *Montana The Magazine of Western History* (online special edition), Summer 2020, https://mhs.mt.gov/pubs/magazine/DigitalIssueSum2020/MMWHDigitalSum2020_Hampton.pdf.
25. Gardner, *Jennie Carter*, vii.
26. Gardner, *Jennie Carter*, viii.
27. Gardner, *Jennie Carter*, xxxi.
28. Gardner, *Jennie Carter*, xxviii.
29. Gardner, *Jennie Carter*, xxxi.

Index

MICHAEL K. JOHNSON is professor of American literature at the University of Maine at Farmington. His previous works include *Black Masculinity and the Frontier Myth in American Literature*, *Hoo-Doo Cowboys and Bronze Buckaroos: Conceptions of the African American West*, and *Can't Stand Still: Taylor Gordon and the Harlem Renaissance*.